S
F
HQ1061.F63   gerontology.

S0-BFE-014

3 2911 00003681 4

FOUNDATIONS OF PRACTICAL GERONTOLOGY

Edited by

Rosamonde Ramsay Boyd
Charles G. Oakes

UNIVERSITY OF SOUTH CAROLINA PRESS
Columbia, South Carolina

Copyright © 1969 by the
University of South Carolina Press

First Printing, August 1969

Second Printing, May 1972

Published in Columbia, S.C., by the
University of South Carolina Press

International Standard Book Number: 0–87249–154–4

Library of Congress Catalog Card Number: 71–79128

Suggested Library of Congress classification furnished by
McKissick Memorial Library of the University of South Carolina:
HQ1061.F

Manufactured in the United States of America

The illustrations on the cover are taken from photo-
graphs supplied by the Administration on Aging,
Department of Health, Education, and Welfare, and
by two projects (Spartanburg Senior Center and
Senior Citizens Craft-Mobile) of the South Carolina
Interagency Council on Aging, funded under Title
III of the Older Americans Act.

HQ
1061
F63
C,3

TO JESSE AND CAROLYN

Pal My 73

FOREWORD

The dust has settled. The battles over the aging have been won, and lost. The politician quoted as saying, "There is plenty of glory for all of us in aging," has his reward. The American Medical Association has scar tissue where once were wounds. The skirmishers of the White House Conference on the Aging have found other causes, but the aged are still with us. The time and setting are ripe for a clear-headed examination of the status, the wishes, the psychic and material requirements of the increasing numbers of aging in our society. This volume is a rational step toward greater understanding.

Simultaneous equations have threatened and rewarded millions of aspiring mathematicians over the years. This collection of papers may be unique in its simultaneity. Data, observations, experience, and policy implications found here share a common, contemporary time frame. This is a rare quality, and a crucial one. Observations and discovered relationships in the physical sciences may be timeless, but much that is important in human behavior is time-bound. The failure to recognize this fact has led to endless confusion, and no little silliness. One of the early textbooks in gerontology was perforce founded on a temporal miscellany of data, in which facts a generation or two apart were treated as simultaneous. More recently, the Gallup and Harris political polls disagreed because, Gallup and Harris assured us, the data were gathered two days apart!

These readings share another quality. Among other things, courage is the willingness to confuse with the facts those whose minds are made up. The consistent strain toward substituting "something of value" for the outworn stereotypes of the aging, dating from Shakespeare's Ages of Man, removes the corpus of this work far beyond the polemic. The Copernican students of the aged have already suggested that the earth is not flat, but the Columbians represented here still sail uncharted seas.

We are, nonetheless, faced with difficulties. How can we determine the credibility of generalizations, however great the care with which they are reached? How much confidence can we place in today's findings for futuristic projections? A first answer is inevitably faith, and, strangely, faith in the conservative nature of man in his environment. Powerful though this faith be, and useful, it may be based on sand. The foundations of faith may be strengthened, while faith itself is merely buttressed.

When we read reports on the aged, we need not question honesty when we question generalization. Rather, we must evaluate the sources of the information on which generalization rests. How many aged respondents have been involved? Were they chosen accidentally, or because they were convenient or captive, like college students? If they were not systematically chosen, representing the total population, we cannot know how much confidence is warranted. But even with systematic selection, *ten* subjects produce an error for generalization of about 33 percent, *above* or *below* the true characteristics of the reference group.

What we are told about the aged may be entirely accurate, though projections are not dependable. The facts may, first of all, be time-bound. Fads, styles, personal preferences, even physical symptoms may be as temporary as other status symbols. Equally important, and especially in the United States, the facts may be place-bound. Our great regions maintain both differences and similarities with considerable stability. Are the aged in Idaho deprived because they do not have any grits?

Regrettably, there is one more caution. This is to call attention to the "improbability principle," which I have discussed at length in another publication. Fortunately, it is not used in the present volume, but it may be easily identified. It is simply making the exception the rule—to support a value position. In the field of gerontology, it appears when a destitute old lady is discovered and all old ladies become destitute (*because* she is improbable.) Equally, when Mrs. Joseph Kennedy is discovered, and all old ladies become wealthy. The improbability principle leads *away* from truth and understanding. Faith in the probable remains.

The aged, as individuals and as category, are Gestalten. For understanding, they are analyzed into several aspects which may or may not ever be put back together. Our authors appropriately emphasize biological, medical, sociomedical, psychological, psychiatric, familial, social, employment, and economic facets of the sometimes flawed diamonds under the glass. Recreation, the religious setting, sources of support for and helping techniques for the aged are thoughtfully treated. These matters have a major importance.

It seems possible that we are, in effect, preparing for permanent "custodial" care of those who are "too many of the wrong kind of people" for our several institutional structures. Any dramatic change in population characteristics places great stress on societal structure, whether it produces too many or too few of *the right kinds* of people. Age-grading is older than civilization and must, in the long run, reflect the characteristics of the population. The historic and prehistoric solutions of infanticide and parricide are not available; such are our values. I share these values!

The Western tradition includes age-grading throughout the "expected" life span, and even beyond in some traditions. We have not yet discovered what to do with those who do not die. The aged, as several of our authors point out, do not fit the stereotypes. Our institutional inertia is such that we expel them from the structure rather than modify the structure itself.

Some halting steps have been taken. Since our social system has been "designed" for early death, we have realistically extended the range of age grades in some specifics. In a cultural context which fosters upward mobility, we have millions waiting for death—someone else's. So we have added grades to the civil service and military distributions. In business we have multiplied vice-presidents. Colleges and universities have followed the pattern. We find widespread *super* grades, and generals of the Army with *five* stars.

This incongruity of aging population and social structure

is not the most exciting of research areas. It does, however, offer promise of long-term gains in integrating the aged back into society. The life-span continues to increase, largely because attention *is being given* to health—at all ages. To what end?

Since the readers of these pages are vicariously sharing the two institutes to which they were presented, I invite you to share this homily.

> *You are not here . . . to meet present or prospective* personal *needs. I believe that you share in some way my own experience of some years ago. As I sat in Church on Sunday morning, my mind wandered from the sermon to the pew in which I was sitting. Suddenly I was aware that an earlier generation had built the church, placed the pew— had given me a setting, with comfort, to which I had not contributed. Figuratively, I was still sitting in the lap of an older generation.*
>
> *You are here, I believe, at least partly out of gratitude. This I applaud. Your motivation cannot be improved.*
>
> *Now we face together the consequent problem. Without discrimination, we may substitute discomfort for comfort, uncertainty for certainty, and the unfamiliar for the hearth of home. If we do not recognize the abilities of the aged, their capabilities for independence and their determination to maintain it, we either treat these adults like children or insist they should be "our kind" of adults.*
>
> *As we seek solutions to problems, let us not force our solutions on all. Not all have problems. Let us serve those who are truly helpless, but with respect and tolerance. And let us cheer, not molest, those of advanced years who are really models of adjustment and mature happiness.*

James W. Wiggins

Spartanburg, South Carolina
February 1969

PREFACE

Foundations of Practical Gerontology is a collection of papers
drawing on several disciplines. It is offered as a resource for
short-term programs of instruction for specialists of varied
backgrounds, for advanced undergraduate or graduate seminars in gerontology, and for interested citizens who seek to
improve their knowledge and understanding of the field of
aging.

The papers first appeared in the published proceedings of
two institutes held at Converse College in the spring and
summer of 1967. The institutes were supported by Title III
funds of the Administration on Aging, the Department of
Health, Education, and Welfare, administered by the South
Carolina Interagency Council on Aging, and Title I funds
of the Higher Education Act, administered by the College of
General Studies, Office of the State Coordinator, the University of South Carolina.

Chapters one through sixteen are divided into five groupings. Each section is introduced in a general statement, giving
perspective to the points of view it represents. The Conclusion summarizes the preceding chapters and suggests avenues
for future inquiry.

Because the problems of the elderly are thought by some
to be sufficiently far-ranging to warrant their being a *social*
problem, the sociological papers comprise the first section.
It is important to mention initially the prevailing images of
the aged. In both their valid and invalid senses, images influence our interpretations of the biological, psychological, and
economic factors specific to the aging process which are discussed in Parts II through IV. In the final analysis, our
concern for the elderly requires that we examine each issue
within the context portrayed collectively by all the chapters.
In Part V some specific programs and strategies for action
are discussed.

For the professional and others who wish to pursue a particular topic further, each chapter ends with a list of selected references.

Two main considerations have guided the authors' presentations. First, they use a minimum of technical terms, but where exceptions occur definitions are given as footnotes. Second, there is an awareness of the enduring advantages of *joint* efforts of interested and informed laymen and professionals in the local community. This is true whether the financial support for community programs is derived locally or from state or federal sources. Each author, therefore, has sought to translate his technical knowledge of gerontology into terms that serve as the bases for developing projects that utilize the human and material resources found practically everywhere.

The emphasis on the vitality of lay and professional effort at the local level does not, however, exclude the important state and federal resources that aid in implementing programs conceived by community leaders. In the Appendixes such resources are described, and program developers are urged to study these closely for their potential in leading to sources of financial assistance, or as guides to those in government who can be called upon for consultative services.

The titles of the proceedings of the aforementioned institutes are given here to assist the reader further in appreciating the theme or spirit of the papers. "Our Elderly Americans: Challenge and Response" and "Older Americans: Social Participants" connote several ideas, the most important to us being that old age, while no respecter of persons, does *not* necessarily exclude those in the later years from continuing participation as citizens.

Several authors emphasize that only a minority of the aged, perhaps not more than five percent, are institutionalized and thus excluded from the mainstream of life. If and when they exist, then, the problems of the majority seemingly result from inevitable factors *presently* associated with becoming old. The solutions to these problems may be simple if the talents of all citizens are mobilized, and this is the challenge which confronts us today. As the challenge is adequately met, we will discover that what may today be defined as a social problem, or what may presently be considered inevitable consequences of becoming old, may tomorrow be merely the easily circumvented contingencies of a normal phase in the life cycle.

Rosamonde Ramsay Boyd
Charles G. Oakes

CONTENTS

Contents

PART I

THE SOCIOLOGY OF AGING

PART I

THE SOCIOLOGY OF AGING

Since Social Gerontology, the science of aging in society, is a new and developing discipline, the sociologists are bringing their research skills to bear in studying the aged and in seeking to formulate theories as predictive foundations for programs to meet the needs of the elderly in our culture. Previously, "the man on the street" and even the professional person have too readily applied a generalized stereotype to include all older persons in a composite picture which has obliterated individual differences. This is both unscientific and unfair, since the elderly represent as wide a range of personality types and of social behavior as any other category of our population.

In this section sociologists have exposed and refuted some of the most widely diffused stereotypes. George Maddox questions a general characterization of persons 65 and above, although he recognizes that some traits *are* applicable to many older persons. He points out the roles arising from class and sex differences. These he applies to the elderly in their varied

2

reactions to retirement, in their relationships with their children, and in their philosophies of "life satisfaction." He emphasizes that problems of aging are a continuation of those of earlier periods, though they are "intensified" at the later date, and that solutions and adjustments in age are conditioned by previous life experience.

Ruth Albrecht continues the theme of stereotypes, questioning the arbitrary age of 65 as the magical demarcation between middle and old age, and cites examples of differential aging in the United States and around the world. Social roles and norms for the aged may also become stereotyped. The former need clarification relative to circumstances and the variations accounting for individual and social differences. The illusion that our aged are mostly institutionalized is refuted: "4.3 per cent of the older women and 3.5 per cent of the older men" are in any kind of institution. Elsewhere, Adriaan Verwoerdt supports this. Miss Albrecht further develops the types of families in which elderly men and women live, and makes a distinction between the grandparent roles of the "white collar" and "working class" categories. Rosamonde Boyd elaborates on this by differentiating between the grandparent and great-grandparent roles as the individual advances through the life cycle.

The elimination of obsolescent stereotypes is a challenging aspect of the articles included in this section since they are repeated in every one of the chapters. But removal of outworn composite pictures, important as this may be, creates a vacuum unless the public is offered and accepts a more valid picture of the aging, three possibilities of which are presented by E. Grant Youmans. First is the Cumming and Henry emphasis on disengagement from activity as age advances. Second is the subculture theory presented originally by the late Arnold Rose. This maximizes the congenial and common interests of older persons. The third combines the more pessimistic disengagement with the more optimistic subculture approach in what is termed by Leonard Cain the "life-course" theory. Here aging is seen as a normal process in which each period of life evolves into the next. Hence, one's past experiences and cultural patterns continue to influence adjustments in each phase of the life course, although each phase offers new challenges and possesses its own "core set of values."

Since there is a core set of values for each phase in the life cycle, the possibilities exist for either disengagement or involvement in a subculture of one's peers, but a combination of these two views is an alternative to polarities. In any event, there is a need to reorganize the roles once played, as is pointed out in Mrs. Boyd's analysis of the four-generational family.

1

GROWING OLD:
GETTING BEYOND THE STEREOTYPES
George L. Maddox

INTRODUCTION

In a society which values youthfulness and productivity, older people have the capacity simultaneously to fascinate, to trouble, and to embarrass. Older people are a commentary on what it means to be finite. Older people live on a frontier which every man sooner or later must explore. They remind us that in the normal course of life bodies change, physical prowess and capacity diminish, families dissolve, social contacts alter, and the world of work must sooner or later be left behind. Every young person at one time or another observes older people who evoke feelings such as, "I hope at his age I am as much in control of my situation as he seems to be," or, "I hope I die before that happens to me." The occasions for such positive or negative reactions are increasing as the sheer number and social visibility of the elderly in society are increasing. By the end of this century, approximately 11 percent of our population, or an estimated 28 million people, will be at least 65 years old. And if the increasing number of elderly people alone fails to get our attention,

George L. Maddox is professor of sociology, Department of Sociology and Anthropology, Duke University, Durham, North Carolina. Partial support from the Center for the Study of Aging and Human Development for the preparation of this paper is acknowledged. The Center is supported by grants from the National Institute of Child Health and Development (HD-668 and HD-164).

continuing public debate on various aspects of medicare, social security payments, and housing for older citizens will certainly increase their social visibility in the years ahead. We can depend on it; the elderly will continue to be visible reminders of human troubles.

The troubles about which the elderly will remind us are both personal and social. The old will continue to remind us that, under the best of circumstances, the probability of personal troubles involving health and income in the later years of life is high. In the elderly, everyone encounters a prophecy about himself. But perhaps of greater consequence, the fate of the old is a commentary on the way in which our society deals with human beings at the end of the life cycle. Much that we see is hopeful. Our society has a humanitarian tradition, as our social welfare legislation illustrates. In spite of this, the economic plight of many elderly people reminds us that our system of providing adequate income over a lifetime remains imperfect. Half of our older citizens, for example, have an annual income of less than $3,000. And the sense of isolation and rejection experienced by many is a commentary on how inadequately our social experience prepares us for the enforced leisure of the later years, and how poorly we provide social opportunities for older people to use those skills which they have.

In fact, the social visibility of many troubled older people is a source of considerable embarrassment. For never in history has a nation accumulated more things, assembled more information, or achieved more control over so many aspects of the environment as we have. It is, therefore, something of a scandal that the social problems of the aged persist. It is also something of a scandal that, among professional as well as lay people, we have as little authoritative information as we do about what it means to grow old. Stereotypes of the elderly and of the aging process, which reflect reality more or less accurately, abound.

There is nothing inherently wrong with stereotypes; we depend on them. Human beings understandably attempt to reduce complex experiences to simple categories as a defense against being undone by the complexities of the events which swirl around them. Our stereotypes of how men as distinct from women are likely to behave in given situations can be reasonably accurate; and, to the extent that they are accurate, they can be useful. Similarly, our shared ideas about how doctors and patients, parents and children, priests and parishioners, and other social categories usually react in situations of everyday life reflect a shared wisdom which helps simplify getting on with the complex business of living. But stereotypes can be rigidly and slavishly applied, even when they are accurate. And worse, stereotypes can be partially or even totally inaccurate. It is appropriate, therefore, to review and assess some of the common stereotypes one encounters which presume to characterize the elderly and what it means to grow old. In some instances we may find it necessary and desirable to get behind and to go beyond the stereotypes.

BEYOND THE STEREOTYPES

WHO ARE THE ELDERLY? While there is some wisdom in the observation that a person is as old or as young as he feels, our social security legislation, our retirement policies, and our statistics on morbidity and mortality suggest another way of determining who is old. There is obviously some merit in thinking of persons who are 60, 62, or 65 as older, and our stereotypes about what life is like for people 65 years of age and older are at least partially accurate. But the value of a stereotype, which is to simplify our characterization of complex situations, is also its greatest weakness, which is oversimplification. Thus references to *the elderly* correctly suggest that older people, as a result of aging, probably have many similar characteristics and experiences. However, it does not follow that significant differences are absent among the elderly. It does not follow that the behavior of elderly people is the inevitable expression of intrinsic processes within them; people of the same age simply are not all the same. Observed differences among them reflect their biographies and the opportunities and limitations in the social environment in which they live.

In fact, for purposes of argument, the proposition is advanced that differences among the elderly are as striking and significant as the similarities among them. If we were discussing *the adult*, rather than *the elderly*, we would probably be just a bit uneasy if our characterization of *the adult* failed to take into consideration whether we had in mind adults who are 35 years old or 50 years old. We would also be uneasy if our characterization failed to take note of socio-economic differences which are proxy indicators of differences in values, personal and social resources, and preferred styles of life.

We ought to be equally uneasy when we fail to distinguish between older people who are 65 and those who are 80. We ought to be uneasy when we fail to distinguish between older people whose experience classifies them as middle class and those whose experience is summarized by the label working class or lower class. We ought to keep such distinctions in mind when we talk about *the elderly*. But we do not always do so. The result is often a caricature of the elderly and the aging process; and such caricatures lead both professionals and laymen to misunderstand particular elderly individuals if not most elderly individuals. Moreover, stereotypes are a poor basis for social planning. Let me illustrate my point with some observations about two important aspects of growing old: retirement from work and the relationship of parents to their children. The first issue is of special importance for older men, the second for older women. In the next decade we will become increasingly aware that women also retire from work, although one rarely sees any discussion in the current professional literature on the female retiree; for our purposes here, however, concentration on retirement among males, for whom work is the central life task, will be sufficient. Similarly, while both men and women may be concerned about changes in family structure and relationships between generations, family matters are the focal concern of women.

RETIREMENT. In our cultural tradition work has been the central life task for men. A man's job has been his price tag and calling card, the regulator of his social life, and his opportunity for integration in communal life. To the extent that we accept this characterization of work, we are probably prepared to believe that retirement from work precipitates a crisis. This stereotype is not all wrong, but it is misleading. First, even a moment's reflection would make us wonder about those individuals who have spent a lifetime at routine jobs economically, socially, and psychologically unrewarding. Would not such individuals welcome relief from work, especially if an adequate retirement income were available? The answer is yes. Many blue collar workers who anticipate adequate retirement benefits not only look forward to retirement, they also, in increasing numbers, retire early when permitted to do so. White-collar workers, especially those who find some fulfillment in their work, are more likely than blue collar workers to be attached to their work. But even for the white collar worker, it is not clear that retirement precipitates a crisis that is severe or is sustained for any length of time.

Clearly, retirement is not inevitably a major problem of crisis proportions for the American male. But we do know something about the conditions under which a retirement crisis is likely. What we know can be summarized in part by the observation that individuals who have problems with work have problems in retirement. The problems which people have with work are varied. For some, the problems are economic. Their incomes are inadequate even while they are working; their retirement income is impossible. For others, the problems may be personal and social even when there is the prospect of adequate retirement income. An individual who despises his job may nonetheless discover that he depended on that job to regulate his daily life or that his new leisure brings conflict with his wife. Or, an individual who is attached to his job may discover that his attachment is compulsive and a defense against his perceived inadequacy to adapt to and to exploit the leisure which retirement offers.

In sum, it is nonsense to talk of retirement as though it has the same meaning for all elderly males. The probability of a retirement crisis varies considerably from individual to individual. And, in general, satisfaction during the working years predicts eventual adequate adaptation in retirement. Common

9

stereotypes of retirement do not fit the facts and are a poor basis for understanding this aspect of growing old.

PARENTS AND THEIR CHILDREN. For two decades it has been popular to worry about the changing functions of the American family, its mobility, and the isolation of parents from their children. The professionals whose job it is to worry about such things have been especially concerned about the adequacy of contact between parents and children and about the adequacy of filial responsibility for elderly parents.

Research findings have been somewhat surprising. First, if the highly visible minority of elderly people who never had children are excluded from consideration, the overwhelming majority of elderly parents have a child who lives reasonably close to them. Moreover, for the majority of elderly persons with children living, most of them have regular contact with at least one child. This is especially true in the Southern region generally and in the rural South particularly. The development of modern transportation and communication facilities, contact between parents and children even when they are separated geographically, and the probability that each succeeding generation of older people will increasingly use such means would lead us to expect even more intergenerational contact than we now observe. Second, intergenerational contacts typically involve an elaborate exchange of goods and services. Interestingly, goods and services have been observed to flow from the old to the young about as often as the reverse. In short, there is more contact and exchange between the generations than our earlier pessimistic guesses about the isolation of the old led us to believe. We still do not know enough about one important factor of intergenerational contact, however: we need to know more than we do about the expectations and the feelings of older and younger people about intergenerational contact and exchange. This leads to a third observation.

We are very prone to assume that older parents expect and want a great deal of contact with their children. Some recent evidence suggests that we may overestimate these desires and expectations. Both children and parents are typically trained to expect geographical and social mobility; it is also reasonable to assume that many parents as well as children learn to accept the psychological implications of mobility. One implication of this acceptance is the achievement of a sense of independence on the part of the old and young alike. Our welfare and security system has encouraged and sustained the psychological independence of both the old and young by decreasing the material dependence of the old on the young. These observations lead to some questions: How much contact between generations is perceived as desirable by older people? From the perspective of the older person, can the amount and kind of contact with children be too much as well as too little?

If we rely on sentiment rather than research, we might expect an older parent's desire for contact with children to be insatiable. Sentiment encourages stereotypes, but neither sentiment nor stereotype is an adequate substitute for research. What little evidence we have on this point suggests how little we know about preferred relationships between older parents and their children. In fact, on the basis of limited research it is possible to hypothesize that satisfactory and satisfying contacts between parents and children during the child-rearing years tend to produce psychological independence; in turn, this independence is associated with modest expectations about and dependence on parent-child contact in the later years. Moreover, there is evidence that neither parent nor child prefers to live in the same household if other arrangements can be made.

Again, then, our stereotypes of intergenerational relationships, like the stereotypes of retirement, do not quite fit the complexity of the facts. Intergenerational contact appears to be more extensive than our stereotypes about the isolation of the old suggest. And the desire for intergenerational contact may be less extensive and intensive than our stereotypes suggest.

LIFE SATISFACTION. "Grow old along with me!" says the poet. "The best is yet to be./The last of life for which the first was made." This optimistic idea of growing old hardly seems consistent with the dreary tales of the helpless and hopeless old which have pervaded the pages of professional journals as well as the popular press in the past two decades. The fact is that the middle-aged, middle class professionals who have described and evaluated what it means to grow old tend to see a highly visible minority of older people and, as a result, tend to have some identifiable biases which color their observations and confound their conclusions. For the middle-aged, middle-class American, successful adaptation involves activity, involvement, productivity, and a future orientation. Moreover, he contemplates death uneasily. Insofar as, with age, older people tend to become less active, less involved, less productive, less future-oriented, and more willing to contemplate the end of life, they invite the conclusion that they are hopeless and helpless. This conclusion is compounded by the reports of professionals whose clientele is composed of welfare recipients and the institutionalized old, who actually comprise only a minority of the old. In short, the less older people look and behave like middle-aged, middle-class folk, the more likely they are to be characterized as in need of help. The fact is that we know relatively little about what constitutes successful aging and the factors which produce and sustain successful adaptation to growing old. But there are some things that we do know.

For example, we know that there is more than one mode of successful aging and that the preferred mode for any given older person is related to his previous experience and resources. The aphorism—busy old people are happy old people—surely describes the preferred state of affairs for some individuals. This is especially true if they have been actively involved, resourceful people during their adult years and if their physical health remains good. But even in such cases successful aging is likely to involve decreasing activity, involvement, productivity, and future orientation. For others, lack of active involvement with life has characterized the adult years, and the later years do not really constitute a change for them.

We must not underestimate the reality orientation of older

people. For all our American fantasies about eternal youthfulness, growing old involves changes which must be dealt with. The changes are greater for some than for others; the personal and social resources which make the necessary adaptations easier or more difficult vary considerably. But my impression, in spite of the high visibility of welfare cases and the institutionalized old, is that the vast majority of older people (e.g., eight out of ten of them) adapt themselves to growing old with reasonable success. Moreover, even those older people who most violate our notions of what growing old ought to be like can and do distinguish between their current plight and the essential goodness and worthwhileness of their lives as they are reviewed. My optimism about the capacity of a majority of older people to age successfully is based in part on the reports of the current generation of older people. One can be even more optimistic about future generations of the old, who will be better equipped to adapt to change and who will have a more secure economic environment.

SOME IMPLICATIONS FOR SOCIAL POLICY

Stereotypes of elderly persons, such as the ones we have been discussing, are an inadequate basis for understanding what it means to grow old and are an even more inadequate basis for planning the ways and means of making the aging process as trouble-free as possible. Stereotypes ignore variations and tend to be inappropriately rigid.

What has been said here is certainly no basis for a systematic critique of current social policy or services for the elderly. Yet these observations do have broad policy implications. First, planning for *the elderly* is planning for everyone and no one at the same time. If we accept the proposition that older people are not a homogeneous mass but people who, like those of other ages, have a variety of needs and a variety of values, then there can be no single, simple, sovereign solution for *the elderly*. A single solution to their housing problems, their economic problems, their health problems, and so on, clearly will not do. The mass delivery of services to people of any age is difficult, and our defensive response, if we have the responsibility for policy-making or services for older people, is to think stereotypically and to propose standard solutions to complex problems. This tendency will remain no matter what we say or do. At best we can hope for corrective efforts to get behind and beyond the stereotypes as much as our understanding of needs and resources permits. A professional person or an informed layman should expect this much from himself and from others no matter what the pressure to find simple solutions to complex problems.

Second, we must continually remind ourselves that the old who are public welfare clients or who are institutionalized are an inadequate basis for describing older people in general, for generalizing about their needs, and for planning to meet those needs. A substantial number of elderly people, perhaps 20 percent of the total, do tend to be helpless, hopeless, or both. They need help of all kinds and they need it desperately. One is not overly optimistic in concluding, however, that our society has humanitarian values which are being implemented by welfare services. No services we can imagine will undo the lifetime of deprivation or the massiveness of needs which many of these people exhibit. But our social policy clearly commits us to ameliorate these needs as much as possible so as to increase their chances of living and dying with at least a minimum of human dignity. Moreover, we have only begun to explore the possibility that wise intervention which appears to be costly in the short run is in fact economical for the taxpayer's dollar in the long run. That is, we may be able to demonstrate the wisdom of the old adage, "An ounce of prevention is worth a pound of cure."

Less obvious but equally pressing needs of the great majority of older people warrant our attention also. Their problems are likely to be the general problems of our society, only more intensified. How, for example, do we get adequate medical attention at a price people with modest incomes can afford? How do we cope with the increasing amounts of enforced leisure as the work life is shortened and life expectancy increases? How do we distribute income over the expected life span of our citizens so as to guarantee an adequate level of living in the later years? How do we sustain an adequate level of social involvement and the related conception of one's self as an adequate worthwhile human being in the later years, when personal and social change is a constant threat to every individual's sense of personal integrity and to his opportunity to be socially involved if he is so inclined? How can we be professional people in the broadest sense in organizational environments excessively conscious of rules and, often, of rules which are quite punitive? These problems are peculiarly the problems of elderly people. But they are also the problems of all Americans. In a sense, the current generation of older people is on a frontier which each of us will visit.

Third, although the current generation of older people foreshadows the experience of the next generation, an important qualification needs to be made. Our stereotypes of those who are currently old, no matter how accurate they may be, potentially can mislead us if we assume that future generations of older people can be described in the same way. For example, our current concerns about leisure as a problem for a generation committed to work as its central life task may change drastically if, as now seems to be the case, subsequent generations of the old learn to give up work with pleasure and grace. Or, our definition of the common economic problems of aging will surely change as our developing social security system is elaborated still further and as new generations approach old age with twice the years completed in school as that observed in this generation of older people. In brief, adequate planning for the needs of old people will have to be based on stereotypes of older people which we construct with more or less accuracy as we imagine what older people will be like in the future rather than their current appearance.

One final but related point needs to be made. Where should our resources for improving life in the later years be concentrated? As we plan for meeting the needs of older people in the future, some attention needs to be given to whether much of the crucial work which will improve life for older people must be done with younger people. It is possible that every improvement we make in our educational system, every upgrading of job skills we achieve, and every success we have in improving the mental and physical health of the young in fact increases the probability that the later years of life in our country will be satisfying ones.

SELECTED BIBLIOGRAPHY

CUMMING, E., AND W. E. HENRY. *Growing Old.* New York: Basic Books, 1961.

MCKINNEY, J., AND F. DEVYVER (eds.) *Aging and Social Policy.* New York: Appleton-Century-Croft, 1966.

MORGAN, J., *et al. Income and Welfare in the U.S.* New York: McGraw-Hill, 1962.

SHANAS, E. *The Health of Older People.* Cambridge: Harvard University Press, 1961.

SIMPSON, I., J. MCKINNEY, AND K. BACK. *Social Aspects of Aging.* Durham: Duke Unversity Press, 1966.

2

SOME VIEWS ON HUMAN AGING
E. Grant Youmans

I would like to speak about "some views on human aging," drawing from current literature on social-psychological aspects of the field. In doing so, I realize there are serious problems of communication. Basic data supplied by a research person may leave the average individual somewhat frustrated, since such information may not solve practical problems.

As a background to my discussion, I wish to present some information on the aging process, as developed by some social scientists. These viewpoints should be useful, since they provide a bench mark to look at the work being done. Each of us carries in his head some idea about old age. Some persons take a very pessimistic view of old age, looking upon older persons as problems, as indigent, and as needy and helpless, requiring at best some assistance to see them to the grave. In my judgment, such a view is becoming out of date. According to the U.S. Department of Health, Education, and Welfare, only about 4 percent of the approximately 20,000,000 persons aged 65 and over in the United States are in institutions. Thus about 96 percent of the aged are living in the community. It is estimated that the status and well-being of older people will improve significantly with each decade. Older persons in the future will be better educated than older people of today, they will have larger incomes, and they will be in better health. Some biologists estimate that within a

E. Grant Youmans is professor of sociology, Department of Sociology, University of Kentucky, Lexington, Kentucky.

couple of decades the health of the average person age 65 will equal that of the average person age 45 today.

I wish to present three views about human aging. Obviously these do not give a complete picture of the aging process. One reflects a rather pessimistic orientation to old age. The second is more optimistic, and the third contains some elements of optimism and pessimism.

Cumming and Henry, in their book *Growing Old,* developed a rather systematic explanation of human aging as social-psychological phenomena. Their theory of disengagement was based on a study of 275 men and women between the ages of 50 and 90 who were in good health and not economically deprived. Their theory suggests that human aging involves an inevitable withdrawal from relationships with other people and that this withdrawal is associated with important changes in the goals, attitudes, and orientations of the aging person. This theory conceives the aging individual as being at the center of a network of social interactions, and, as he ages, his life space tends to constrict and he experiences a general curtailment of involvement in social life. The process of disengagement, these authors argue, is beneficial to society and to the individual.

One of the critics of disengagement theory is Arnold Rose, who offers an opposing and more optimistic theory of human aging called the "aging subculture." In his book, *Older People and Their Social World,* Rose argues that the process of disengagement is not inevitable, that nonengagement in later life may be a continuation of lifelong patterns of social participation, that disengagement is not beneficial to the individual, and that socio-cultural trends in American society serve to counteract the forces making for disengagement. Rose offered evidence that older persons in the United States, by virtue of being excluded from many groups and organizations, tend to develop interaction systems among themselves. The older people are integrated by their common interests and problems, and thus tend to develop an aging subculture.

The ideas stated by Arnold Rose have been criticized severely by some social gerontologists and by some social scientists. The term "subculture" carries a negative connotation in American society, and some practitioners in the aging field deny its existence. However, when one considers the many social clubs and organizations established for and by older people and the many retirement communities populated by older persons, it is apparent that these social structures provide opportunities for older persons to develop a "way of life" which may be called a subculture.

The third viewpoint I would like to mention, and one which intrigues me, is the "sociology of the life course." I do not want to give the impression that I am creating this term. Studies of the life course, or the life span, or the life cycle, are well established in the discipline of sociology. One of the men who has been influential in applying this concept to the aging process is Leonard D. Cain. Essentially, the sociology of the life course suggests that every person, if he survives, moves through various stages of development—infancy, childhood, young adulthood, maturity, and older age. This is a universal phenomenon, occurring in every society, at any time, at any place. To function effectively, a given society must provide the means by which a person can move in an orderly fashion from one status position to another, and a society also must provide the motivations for individuals to fulfill the roles associated with each status position.

In the United States, massive resources are directed to preparing young persons for adult roles, but relatively little attention has been given to preparing middle-aged persons for older-age roles. The transition from middle to older age is usually unplanned, and studies suggest that in many cases old-age roles are tragic and wasteful. The movement from middle to older age involves giving up the prestigious roles of adulthood and accepting those of old age. At a time in life when stability and security are desired, older persons are confronted with many changes and adaptations. ✓

The movement of a given individual through the life course is a normal process. Obviously, each phase or period is associated with preceding and subsequent phases. But each phase has a core set of values and behavior which distinguishes it from the others. Any individual can plunge himself into the activities of his current phase of the life course and gain satisfaction from them. In addition, the individual maintains a perspective. He can look back at his past experiences, and he can look ahead at his expected life in the future. He can organize and reorganize his life for maximum satisfaction in any period in his life course. For some, this may mean disengagement from some activities in later phases of his life, if he prefers this. A knowledge of the salient characteristics of each phase of the life course will help the individual obtain some of the satisfactions he desires.

Some popular writers have divided the life course into four periods or episodes and have labeled these spring, summer, fall, and winter. There is some merit in this classification, and it does indicate that each phase has its distinct possibilities and problems. Some persons prefer the spring of the year, and some prefer the winter. But perhaps we should not push the seasonal analogy too far. Perhaps more meaningful labels can be given to the four periods of life, such as the period of growth and preparation, the period of stabilization, the period of individual strategies, and the period of older age. These labels are rather arbitrarily selected for purposes of discussion. By examining some of the behavior characteristic of each period, one can gain a perspective on the life course in the United States.

The first period in the life course covers approximately the first 25 years of life. We know from psychoanalytic literature that what we are as adults depends to a great extent on what happened to us as children. This statement can be extended, of course, to include older age. The first episode in life is characterized as preparation for the roles of adulthood. It is a period of growth and development. A dominant motif of this period is the value of achievement. The young man or woman typically wants to get ahead in the world. He wants to achieve higher status and prestige in his career, in his family roles, and in his community roles. There is considerable testing and experimentation with various tasks, responsibilities, and roles. The young person looks ahead with anticipation to fulfilling the roles of the next period in the life course.

It is generally recognized that we have a youth-centered society in the United States, and this is evidenced in the many organizational structures which give support to the achievement activities of young people. In addition, society provides many models of heroes and successful men and women in American life which inspire young people to achieve. There seems to be a good fit between the social expectations of society and the abilities of young people to perform.

However, it is apparent that not all young people respond to these social expectations for achievement. Many rebel against the "establishment." Many drop out of school or fail in other ways to fit into the expected roles prescribed by society. Despite the strong supports provided by society, many young persons experience frustrations, unhappiness, and extreme psychological stress during their preparatory phase.

The second period in the life course covers roughly the years 25 to 45 and may be designated as the period of "stabilization." During this period the typical adult in the United States reaches the peak of his abilities. Most males reach the highest rung in their status achievements, although some professional persons continue in their achievements. During this phase of the life course the average person becomes aware of the limits of his abilities. He may experience a reduction in his drive for success, a sense of caution in the enterprises he will undertake, and an awareness of the pitfalls in overextending himself.

During the stabilization period of the life course, an interesting paradox occurs. At a time in life when the individual experiences slight detriments in abilities and energies, the expectations of society continue to press for achievement. There is pressure placed on the middle-aged man to keep on achieving. There is a painful disparity between rising social expectations and the ability of the man or woman to meet these expectations. The individual is caught in a press, and he must discover techniques for coping with it. Unfortunately, there are few institutionalized practices he can draw upon for guidance, and he is obliged to develop his own strategies to deal with his life situation.

The third phase of the life course, from about age 45 to 65, may be called the period of individual strategies. Abilities and energies continue on a gradual downward curve. But social expectations continue to press for achievement beyond and above these abilities. It may be said that society gives a poor fit between abilities of people and social expectations for performance. In this press, the executive, the businessman, the professional person, and the worker are confronted squarely with a dilemma: they must develop strategies to cope with the situation, and they must develop these on their own initiative. The individual wishes to retain his status and prestige among his associates, even though he lacks the energy and stamina he possessed as a younger man. This is the period in life when most people become aware that they are aging. If they resist the idea, it is called to their attention in subtle ways by persons in their environment.

Many examples could be cited of individual strategies which develop during the third phase of the life course. In the family setting, the husband may let his son or wife do most of the car driving or the shoveling of snow in the winter time. The businessman does not take the stuffed briefcase home at night, as he used to when he was younger. The executive may delegate more leg work to his subordinates, and he may concentrate on the development of skills in maneuvering, skills in decision-making, and skills in conserving his energies. He may pay greater attention to visualizing the sequence of steps in a given process, a skill difficult for young persons to master. In the third phase of the life course, the individual may become acutely anxious over the fear of failure, a state of mind bolstered by recollections of the sting of defeat.

A small proportion of persons in the United States reach the age of 65 (about 10 percent of the population) and thus enter the fourth stage of the life course—that of older age. Abilities and energies continue their gradual decline, as they did in the second and third periods of the life course. However, the older-age stage of the life course reveals a sharp contrast to all three previous stages. In the period of growth and development, society gives strong social support for the preparation of youth. In the second and third stages, social expectations exceed the abilities and energies of men and women. In the fourth stage, social expectations and social supports decline sharply below the level of abilities of older people. In this respect, there is an uncomfortable fit in our society between the potentials of older persons and the structure of society. There is a lack of organized group life to sustain the social functioning of older people, and the aged person in the United States, typically, is confronted with the prospects of a "roleless role."

The last phase of the life course is characterized by some dominant values and interests. In this period, the aging person becomes fully aware that there is a limit to his life span, and he typically holds the belief that he wants to live as long as possible. Not all aged persons share this motivation, but the huge majority attempt to preserve and safeguard their energies and their health. They may develop strategies to avoid inappropriate tasks or situations which might reveal their inability to perform as well as younger people. In this period of the life course, older people typically want to maintain some involvement with significant others, and they want to retain, so far as possible, their previous status, prestige, authority, power, and seniority.

The lack of social structures to provide opportunities for aged people to perform meaningful social roles offers a distinct challenge to older persons in the United States. Many private and public organizations are developing programs to meet this need in society. Older persons can play a vital role in this endeavor. The large numbers of aged persons who have relatively good health, fairly good incomes, and considerable education can participate meaningfully in the development of these organizations and these programs. In the second and third phases of the life course, the typical adult is obliged to develop individual strategies to cope with high social expectations in the face of declining abilities and energies. In the fourth phase of the life course, it is doubtful that individual strategies will suffice. Group strategies are probably required. The aged persons themselves can organize to provide for their social needs. This may mean the emergence of an aging subculture in the United States, but, if this is the case, perhaps older persons should make the most of it!

It is probably fitting that this essay might close with some critical thoughts about the discipline concerned with the social aspects of human aging—social gerontology. During the past decade or so, an increasing number of publications, conferences, seminars, and lectures have been devoted to the field. Some writers, such as Clark Tibbitts, maintain that social gerontology includes an identifiable set of principles and concepts about human aging. Some social scientists, among them Michel Philibert and Robert Kastenbaum, suggest that social gerontology is a mixture of findings made by older and established disciplines. These critics maintain that a collection of findings from psychology, sociology, and economics does not offer an adequate understanding of human aging and does not provide a suitable guide for action programs. There is need for a comprehensive theoretical framework to facilitate the collection of integrated and comprehensive knowledge about human aging. The social issues confronting American society in providing health services for the aging, in preparing people for retirement and for second careers, in providing suitable leisure time opportunties, and in providing rehabilitative services accentuate the need for this integrated knowledge. In devising homes, hospitals, recreation centers, and other services for the aged, there is the danger that applied social gerontology can foster patronizing and discriminatory attitudes toward older people, which can be decidedly detrimental to their welfare.

One possible solution to this dilemma would be a theoretical formulation of social gerontology that provides a full understanding of the aging process. A full understanding of later life and old age requires that the last phase of the life course be compared with earlier stages of life. Each stage in the life course presents the common problems of caring for the body, maintaining mental health, and coping with the sociocultural environment. Each phase of the life course must find ways to deal satisfactorily with "the soma, the psyche, and the socio." Old age in the United States follows former stages in human development, and each stage offers its own particular frustrations, problems, and difficulties, as well as its own satisfactions, challenges, and opportunities.

An examination of human aging as periods in the life course provides a model for placing a wide variety of discrete information in meaningful perspective. Examination of the life course suggests that human aging is a "normal" phenomenon and not entirely a misfortune. It permits insight into the allegations of biologists that aging and disease are different phenomena and that most illnesses and diseases are environmentally induced during some phase of the life course. It permits a feasible means of studying the differential life expectancy between men and women by pointing to the influences of the social environment on the masculine role throughout the life span. Sidney M. Jourard has labeled this phenomenon the "lethal aspects of the male role."

The study of the life course throws light on the emerging problems of generational differences in the United States. Each generation holds a somewhat different outlook on life, which adds to the many generational conflicts in society. The rapid technological changes occurring in the United States tend to produce a widening gap between generations. Many young people assert that no one over age 30 can understand them. Educational practices have failed to keep pace with the changes. Most school curricula are still geared to preparing the boy or girl only for the completion of early maturity and not for the longevity of old age. The perspective of the life-course approach to human aging provides a meaningful opportunity for society to cope with the many stresses and strains existing between generations.

Studies of the life course provide an opportunity to understand a universal phenomenon which in most instances is avoided—the phenomenon of death and dying. Some social scientists have recently conducted studies of death and dying and have documented some of the factors in operation throughout the life course—such as race, sex, socio-economic status, personality, and the attitudes and practices of the medical profession. One recent publication on this topic is that of David Sudnow, who examined the social organization of "death work" in two hospitals.

REFERENCES

CAIN, LEONARD D., JR., "Life Course and Social Structure" in Robert E. L. Faris (ed.), *Handbook of Modern Sociology*, Chicago: Rand McNally, 1964, pp. 272–309.

CAIN, LEONARD D., JR., "Age Status and Generational Phenomena: The New Old People in Contemporary America," *Gerontologist*, 7 (1967) Part 1, pp. 83–92.

CUMMING, E. AND W. E. HENRY. *Growing Old*. New York: Basic Books, 1961.

JOURARD, SIDNEY M. *The Transparent Self*. New York: Van Nostrand, 1964, pp. 46–58.

KASTENBAUM, ROBERT, "Theories of Human Aging: The Search for a Conceptual Framework," *Journal of Social Issues*, 21 (1965) 13–36.

PHILIBERT, MICHEL A. J., "The Emergence of Social Gerontology," *Journal of Social Issues*, 21 (1965) 4–12.

ROSE, A. M., AND W. A. PETERSON. *Older People and Their Social World*. Philadelphia: F. A. Davis, 1965.

SUDNOW, DAVID. *Passing On: The Social Organization of Dying*. New York: Prentice-Hall, 1967.

TIBBITTS, C. (ed.). *Handbook of Social Gerontology*. Chicago: University of Chicago Press, 1960, pp. 3–26.

3

THE FAMILY AND AGING
SEEN CROSS-CULTURALLY

Ruth Albrecht

There are many aspects to the sociology of aging. This chapter will concentrate on the meaning of age, certain factors dealing with the population here and in other countries, and the family picture.

THE MEANING OF AGE

One common mistake is the idea that people are old at the age of 65. Nothing happens to people when they reach this age; it is an arbitrary figure which was selected years ago as the main age for retirement from work. When we were studying older people, we found that most of the persons who were this age seemed so young that we were almost ashamed to interview them for our research. There is a good bit of evidence that a man or woman aged 65 years today is biologically as young as a person of 40 to 45 years was in 1900. Better medical care throughout life, better dental care, and a more varied diet helped, but easier work and more living comforts also contributed to the maintenance of health and energy.

Age itself is often maligned. When the newscaster for sports talks about "the old man of baseball" he may be talking about a man who is only 39 years old. Sometimes people

Ruth Albrecht is professor of sociology, University of Florida, Gainesville, Florida.

are told that they are too old to learn something. For example, when Rocky Marciano wanted to become a prize-fighter the managers told him he was too old. He was 24 years old at the time. He went on in spite of discouragement and became the World's Champion. Another thing is that at one time the scientists gave many intelligence tests to learn how much was lost in the later years. They gave tests which required speed and, as a result, obtained some unfortunate results. Recent tests have corrected this error.

Another idea which should be ruled out or should be dropped from our vocabulary is that age is "a time for resting." Children who mean well may say, "Mother, you must not do anything. You have earned a rest." If she is only 60 years old, she may have 20 or 30 years of living to do. For a healthy person to just sit and rest can become very dull and can lead to all sorts of problems. At any age people want to be needed, to be active, and to be in the swim of life. Of course, it is important to get enough rest, but, if you have ever been forced to sit for a long time with nothing to do, you know this can become very, very dull.

We should also omit the statement, "Be your age." Maybe people use this more often when talking to the growing-up group, but they still think it also concerns adults and older persons. Who knows how you are supposed to act when you are older? Some people are old at the age of 30; others are young as they near 100. One day I happened to hear the Art Linkletter program on television when a specialist in gerontology was a guest. People were invited to ask questions, and one woman said, "What can I do with my father, who is 95 years old and has so much pep that he wants to move into an apartment by himself? What advice do you have?" The specialist, who was in charge of an old-age community, said, "I don't think we could handle him in our place, he sounds as though he has too much life for us." Dr. Belle Boone Beard has been studying people who are at least 100 years old, and she says that these persons do not become senile in the usual sense of the word. They do not become absentminded but remain active and interested in things, events, and people.

AGING HERE AND IN OTHER COUNTRIES

The two countries which were the first ones to have many older people were France and Sweden. The increase of their elderly population started before the turn of the century. Since then all of the European countries and those settled mainly by Europeans are the ones with high proportions of older people. They are, of course, also the industrialized nations such as the United States, Canada, Australia, and New Zealand. The countries with the largest populations— Brazil, China, India, and others—have many people but only a small percent are old. While we were in India in December, we spoke to various officials about it and one said, "This is a problem we are just moving into."

In our country and in the European nations women live longer than men. This fact gained a great deal of attention, but the situation is not universal. The life expectancy for a man in India was 32.4 years in 1950; for a woman it was only 31.7. In Ceylon men can expect to reach the age of 57.6 years, women only 55.5 years. It is true that the differences are not great, but when we tried to find out the cause there were no answers. It seems to be a genetic factor, in that more boys than girls are born in the proportion of about 160 males to 100 females. Infanticide does not seem to be the cause. This has been outlawed in these countries. In studying the statistical information for other nations, we found that the differential in the life expectancy of men and women is rather small except in the nations that are developed.

In the summer of 1967 the National Center for Health Statistics reported the life expectancy for males as 66.9 years, which is a gain of 20.6 years since 1900. Females could expect to live 50.7 years in 1900, but gained 23.0 years to the current 73.7 years. When you think of the figures given for India, you will note that people here can live, or expect to live, just twice as long as the ones in India. Now we have the job of keeping more men alive longer, but so far this has not been easy. It may take more than medical science to bring this about.

There are many people who believe that the United States will become a matriarchal society. This could happen only in the older age group, where there are more women than men. Young people do not have to worry; the proportion of men to women is just about even during the main marrying years. In case any college students, children, or grandchildren try to put pressure on you to let them marry for fear there will not be anyone left, they have their facts wrong. Last year there were about 129 women for every man in the age group of 65 years and over. In the year 2000 there will be about 148 women for every older man. Most of these women are widows, but we shall say more about that later.

The majority of older people live in families. When you see the many institutions being built to house older people, it may seem that most of them are moving, but only 4.3 percent of the older women and 3.5 percent of the older men are in any kind of institution. We might point out that some persons have spent much of their lives in such a protected environment. When we visit schools for the feeble-minded, we learn that some of the residents have achieved long and full lives. While lengthening the life span in general, the specialists have also increased it for those with special illnesses. Some people have been in mental institutions for many years and, in fact, have grown old there. Our interest is more in the family picture, and we are told that 66.8 percent of the men live in husband-wife families, 13 percent live with family members, and a little over 16 percent live alone. Only a third of the women are married, about 30 percent live with family members and are the head of the house or live where some other person is in charge. Since women may be able to manage fairly well, about a third of them live alone, probably in their own homes or in an apartment.

There are certain social roles that we take in certain circumstances, as parents, grandparents, or even great-grandparents. We find some variation in the statistics, but in one study which included people in homes for the aged we found that 22 percent had no living children. They either had never had them or had outlived them, as happened to about 3 percent. In a recent study of the family picture made by Dr. Ethel Shanas and her European counterparts, it was reported that in Denmark and the United States 18 percent of the older people who are not in institutions have no children, and in Britain 24 percent have none. When the general population thinks of children taking care of aged parents, they often have no idea that from one-fifth to one-fourth of them are without offspring. In some cases older people have grandchildren; in fact, we found that 70 percent of one sample had them and 23 percent had great-grandchildren.

What kinds of roles should grandparents take? We did a study on that and found that we had to make a division between the white-collar and working-class groups. On the whole, grandmothers have more or less the same roles no matter how much money they have. However, men of the white-collar groups have more interaction with their grandchildren than do men with very little education who have been laborers most of their lives. People in the higher economic groups visit their grandchildren a good bit or have them come for visits. They have a lot more social interaction with them. It was not uncommon for older people to find the energy and noise of children wearing, and, as one grandfather said, "A visit of two days was enough." But there can be something very comforting for the child to have a grandparent who listens and cuddles and coddles him a bit. Perhaps I should not say this, since it is now popular to be thin, but I wonder whether a child does not gain a great deal of comfort on the lap of a well-padded grandparent. Actually, people in the higher status groups do not necessarily baby-sit with the grandchildren unless they really want to. Their children may hire baby-sitters when they go out rather than expect the parents to do this. In one case a woman's son had divorced his wife and remarried, all of this against his mother's wishes. She stayed with wife number one, kept house, and took care of the children while their mother worked. She even went to the Saturday morning movies with them, and that is the supreme sacrifice. There was a close relationship between her, the daughter-in-law, and the grandchildren.

Great-grandmothers tend to keep in touch with the great-grandchildren more than do the men, the great-grandfathers. This is probably because the women in our culture tend to be the letter-writers. Again, the people in the higher economic groups have more pictures of their descendants and see them more often, but do not take responsibility for them. Usually they are in their 80's, although we know one who was a great-grandmother when she was in her mid-sixties. There are younger people to take care of the physical needs of the children.

One of the big subjects for discussion concerns older parents living with their children. In the study mentioned comparing Denmark, Britain, and the United States, the researchers found that a daughter is more apt to give help, but that for some reason the white-collar people may have only one surviving child and are less apt to have a daughter than a son. These people also said that they give help to the children more than they receive help from them. In the working class in the United States the men give more help than they get. In Britain they receive more help than they give. This is not necessarily a difference in the size of the family—the older people in Denmark have an average of 2.8 children, those in Britain have 2.5, and the ones in the United States have 3.1 living children.

Many of the older people in our country came from Europe when they were young and may have left most of their relatives there. However, studies show that here, as well as in Europe, about 4 out of 5 older people have living brothers and sisters. This can be an important factor as far as the social life of the individual is concerned.

In some of our research we found that 2 percent of the people who were over 65 years of age still had a parent living. On one visit, the woman who came to the door had an odd look on her face when we said we were studying older people, until we asked about her father. He was 95 years old, and she became most cordial when we considered him eligible and relieved that we did not mean that she belonged in this group. After all, she was only 73, and glad to be free to go off to her bridge club.

In quite a few cases the older parent is in better health than the child. In other instances the child may be too feeble to take care of the aged parent. This is hard to understand until you get to know many older families. In one instance an 85-year-old woman came to visit her neighbors for a few moments but had to hurry home because she had left her 105-year-old mother alone. In another set of problems it may be difficult to learn exactly who lives with whom. Do the children live with the parents, or do the parents live with the children? But in some cases the parents are very independent and refuse to live with the children or allow anyone to move in with them. This can be very hard on the children, especially if they have to bring in all the meals and make many calls to see that the older person is comfortable.

As we look at the census reports to learn how the marital status of older people has changed, we note that in 1900 a total of 67.1 percent of the men were married, compared to 71.3 percent in 1965. While 34.2 percent of the women were married in 1900, 36.0 percent were married in 1965. The percentage of older widowed men and women decreased from 6 to 5 percent in the same period, and the divorced increased, more among the men than among the women. In 1900 only 0.5 percent of the older men were divorced, but in 1965 a total of 2.6 percent were in this status group. We now have more single, never married people. From 1900 to 1965 the percentage of unmarried men went up from 5.7 to 6.6 percent, and that of women from 6.0 to 7.7 percent. Men were more apt to marry in the later years regardless of whether they were widowed, divorced, or marrying for the first time.

In some instances older people encounter more opposition than do teen-agers when they wish to marry. The children may be the chief objectors, either because they do not wish to have a step-parent, because of possible inheritance, or because they may think the parent is becoming childish. In one such case the couple married in spite of objections from both sides of the family. They went ahead and set up their own home and lived a very happy life for more than 15 years. Instead of being the extra people in the households of the children, they were now sought as companions, because the parent-child relationships were much more adult on both sides. Romances blossom in some of the retirement homes, but the attitude of the administrator may discourage this.

One thing happened in 1966 which may have a wholesome effect on the lives of retirees. This was the change in the Social Security regulations so that a widow who had received a pension from her husband's work could continue to receive it even if she remarried. In certain cases, when each of two people has a pension, they may be able to manage much better if they are married to each other and both can contribute to the family income and home costs. They can take care of each other, have companionship, and may even relieve the children of some responsibility.

In closing, we might emphasize that children may need help to keep them from trying to do too much for the parents. They may mean well, but in their anxiety to take good care of the parents they may even deprive them of their independence, make them feel old too soon, and keep them from doing the things they want to do. This is more apt to happen in the middle and upper classes, but oversolicitousness must be guarded against by both generations.

REFERENCES

SHANAS, ETHEL, "Family Help Patterns and Social Class in Three Countries," *Journal of Marriage and the Family*, Vol. 29, No. 2 (May, 1967), 257–66.

UNITED STATES DEPARTMENT OF HEALTH, EDUCATION, AND WELFARE, *Facts About Older Americans*, AOA Publication No. 410, May, 1966.

4

EMERGING ROLES OF THE
FOUR-GENERATIONAL FAMILY

Rosamonde Ramsay Boyd

This chapter summarizes a study of seventy four-generational families. The purpose of the study was to assess the emerging social roles and their interrelationships in the intergenerational family system. To define the terms, a four-generational family represents a group of persons related by blood and marriage in which four living generations sustain contacts and interaction with each other and are conscious of family ties and relationships. The *local community* may be a city, a county, a rural settlement, a village, a suburban area, or a metropolis. Here it represents a city of 50,000 population in a county of 150,000 people, largely rural, but interspersed with agricultural and industrial villages and small towns. By *emerging social roles* is meant the social functions which are repetitive for each generation with regularity, to indicate a trend or an emergence which would appear to be developing in the direction of established and systematized parts to be played by each generation sequentially in the social context and social structure of the four-generational relationship system, and to be significant as parts of the complex of social roles constituting the four-generational family.

The study of the *interrelationship of these roles* defined above will deal with the reciprocity of the generations as they

Rosamonde Ramsay Boyd is professor of sociology, Converse College, Spartanburg, South Carolina.

interact and relate themselves one to the other. The evaluation includes answers to the free and open-ended question put to members of each generation and provocative of original rather than suggested answers: "What are the factors which have strengthened your relationship to Generations I, II, III, and IV?" And another question was posed: "What are the factors that have weakened your relationship to Generations I, II, III, and IV?" Further spontaneous comments were elicited by the question, "What do *you* wish from each generation to enhance your happiness?" A comparison question asked, "What could *you do* for each generation to enhance its happiness?"

The family relationship system is composed of the web of social contacts and social interaction established, regularized, and systematized into a functioning whole, or complex of roles, which gives character and uniqueness to the four-generational family as a distinct form of family and social relationship.

The method used to secure data for this study was the interview method aided by a questionnaire. Students in the course on the family at Converse College made appointments and visited representatives of three generations of the four-generational family, unless the fourth generation was old enough to be interviewed effectively. Under such circumstances, the fourth generation was requested to cooperate with the interviewer also. Representatives of the generations were interviewed and the interviewer filled out identifying information on the first sheet, the face sheet. Then she requested the representatives to answer the relationship questions of pages two, three, and four.

Four-generational families were found through the efforts of town students and the instructor, who were familiar with the membership of the leading churches of all denominations in the city. When the four-generational family was approached by an interviewer, members were asked to name *other* four-generational families of their acquaintance. Pastors and priests were questioned regarding four-generational parishioners. Members of the local branch of the American Association of

University Women furnished names. Since members of this organization are largely teachers, they knew the families of the community quite well. The names compiled in this way tended to represent the social, economic, religious, business, and professional leadership of the community. Forty-five families, 135 persons, seemed to be a fair, representative, and sufficiently large, sample of this class. It was decided to study this group intensively and to describe its four-generational family relationships and emerging social roles. Since this group sets the standards for the city and is the accepted pace-setting leadership, a study of it might become an ideal construct for a comparative study of the four-generational families of other social and economic classes of the community. The first part of the study will focus on the leadership class of four-generational families in this small city, with rural and agricultural hinterland and base, and on the working class of the industrial villages in the county. These latter will be represented in the study by the four-generational families whose names were furnished us by the personnel offices of three textile plants.

Before presenting the proximate social roles of the four generations to each other and to the relationship system, a description of the social milieu of the middle, upper, and working class samples of this study furnishes background material which may be significant. The same milieu is shared by these groups in a *general* sense. On the other hand, the middle and upper classes are specifically molded by the prestigious milieu of the leadership group, and the working class represents a more limited and restricted industrial community marked by some degree of separateness from the broader community in which the leadership group functions actively and influentially.

The dominant cultural pattern is middle class, affected by a strong artistic, educational, religious, business, professional, and industrial tradition and bias, with accelerating industrialization a characteristic of comparatively recent date, but with an agricultural and rural background providing a stable base from the period of the original settlement to the present era.

In 1950 the Community Research Associates of New York City recommended that in social planning this community should coordinate city and county. They form a unit. Both share the agricultural and textile interests of the wider community.

The middle- and upper-class families are characterized by home-ownership, college education, religious affiliation (predominantly Protestant), and steady income from business, profession, investments, savings, property, retirement income, and social security. Family income is from multiple sources. Their organizations are many and are middle class in type, such as civic and service clubs, professional and occupational groups, Community Fund and Council, P.T.A., music, art, book, and garden clubs, American Red Cross, Junior League, etc. Both males and females are active in the organizational life of the community, with female organizations slightly in excess of male ones, and with much joint participation through the same organizations or their auxiliaries. Church leadership is assumed by men and women cooperatively and according to their respective and collective needs.

The industrial working-class families are characterized by home-ownership, elementary and secondary education, religious affiliation (predominantly Baptist and Methodist), steady income from salary or wages in the mill, and social security at retirement. Approximately 50 percent of the earning generations have additional sources of income from savings, investments, property, and/or insurance. Their organizational participation, exclusive of the church, is minimal, with males more active in the few organizations than women. The organizations include the W.O.W., Masons, Ruritan Club, the Civitans, and the Veterans of Foreign Wars for men. Joint participation with women is largely confined to the P.T.A. Church organizations have the loyal support and active participation of men and women, respectively or jointly.

Turning from background to the emerging social roles of the four-generational family, it is appropriate to begin with Generation I, the great-grandparent generation. The generalized social roles as directed toward Generations II, III, and

IV are those of family *progenitor, symbol of family longevity* and *continuity, link* of the past with contemporary generations, *depository* of family genealogy and history, and *inspiration* for the continuation of family culture, tradition, ritual, and celebrations.

In the questionnaires several respondents of Generation III expressed as a strengthening relationship to Generation I, "She is my grandmother," or, "He is my grandfather." This was emphatic and sufficient tribute to Generation I's role as *progenitor* and *link* between the past and the present. Frequent mention of age and length of relationship to Generation I is testimonial of this generation's role as *symbol of longevity* and *family continuity*. The third generations sensed the role of *depository of family history* by several statements such as, "Grandmother made me aware of my family background." Another respondent said, "My mother used to tell me about my grandmother's activities and the interesting family of which she was a part."

Ritual and celebrations were focused around the great-grandparent generation, as almost one-third of the respondents mentioned regular visits, family and birthday dinners, holidays, and celebrations initiated by Generation I or more often inspired by the expectation of this generation's presence and participation.

Generation II feels a sense of filial duty, obligation, and responsibility for Generation I. This arises from love and affection, from custom and community expectations, and from memories of the family orientation provided by Generation I for the siblings of the home. Generation I reciprocates with *concern* for the well-being and continuing happiness of Generation II, referred to repeatedly by respondents.

To Generation III, the grandparent (Generation I) has been the indulgent friend and confidant, the "friendly equal" according to Alfred R. Radcliffe-Brown. This generation has also been the giver of gifts and the beloved narrator of children's stories and anecdotes of the family and its members, the baby-sitter par excellence. It has been teacher of skills and bestower of life's extras over and beyond the immediate family's spiritual and material services. It has been recognized as the perpetuator of culture and tradition—the model that has internalized the best from the past, harmonized it realistically with current behavior patterns, and is liaison between the generations. This generation is the maintainer of the family homestead, if there is one. Even when the homestead belongs to the great-grandparent generation, the grandparent helps in making possible its use as a family gathering point by responding over the years to requests for financial advice and monetary aid, by cooperating in plans for the get-together, or by assisting in entertaining.

But, paradoxically, the traits enumerated above actually constitute a description of the *generalized social role* of Generation II, for Generation I had previously functioned as Generation II when its grandchildren, Generation III, were unmarried and in fact continued to function in this role until the arrival of a great-grandchild, turning parents into grandparents and grandparents into great-grandparents. It is still through Generation III's experiences, however, that the role of grandparents becomes known, since Generation IV is generally too young to objectify this role.

When Generation II has assumed the above role toward its grandchildren (Generation IV), *then* the earlier and similar role of Generation I toward Generation III has been completed, and the great-grandparent generation has become stabilized to the more impersonal, generalized social role described at the beginning of the analysis.

Something remains to be said regarding Generation II's relationship to Generation III. No longer is the emphasis on parent-child relationship. It is not a dominant-subordinate type but one of approximate equality. Our respondents noted this by such remarks as, "With a child of my own, I am recognized by my parents as knowing and sharing with them experiences of responsibility and parenthood."

More than half of the respondents of this study included among the strengthening factors of four-generational interrelationships "proximity of residence," "keeping in touch," "phone calls," "frequent visits," "correspondence," and "sharing interests, friends, and trips."

The above responses were shared by the social classes of this study. The working class, however, recognized the assistance of older generations with child care, cooking, sewing, and other domestic services.

One advantage accruing from the four-generational family is that Generation II does not experience or sense the "empty nest"; that is, it does not feel unfulfilled and unwanted when children grow up and leave home. This is due to the opportunities and/or demands of service to Generation I, on the one hand, and to Generations III and IV, on the other hand. Generation II is the generation that is apt to invest the greatest amount of time and money in the others.

The generalized role of Generation III is that of learner, experimenter, and innovator. Learning to perform the roles of young husband or wife, father or mother, homemaker, breadwinner, and young adult is time-consuming. Fortunately, youth has the necessary energy and enthusiasm for success in these new roles. Independence is sought, realized, and emphasized. Noninterference from other adult generations is desired. A fair amount of sensitivity regarding any failure on the part of Generations I and II to accord this independence fully is apparent from such comments by third-generation respondents as, "My parents were too possessive in attitude."

The generalized role of Generation IV is that of the dependent, immature neophyte of the family and of society. The members of this group are to be loved, nurtured, trained, and enculturated. This is the obedient and submissive generation, the receiver of culture. This generation is being conditioned to the patterns of family, neighborhood, and society until the period of adolescence ushers in the inception of purposive efforts toward independence and young adulthood.

In more symbolic representation, each of the four generations may be presented as: Generation I, Bearer of Culture and Tradition and Inspiration for its Continuance; Generation II, Maintainer and Perpetuator of Culture and Tradition; Generation III, Innovator of Culture and Tradition; and Generation IV, Receiver of Culture and Tradition. It is obvious that there is some overlapping of generational symbols.

By and large, each role is performed by the appropriate

adult generation of the upper-, middle-, and working-class families of this study, each maintaining its separate dwelling, independent and apart from the other adult generations. This proved to be the approved pattern, as indicated by the results of this survey. However, association and family visitation, contacts by phone, letters, errands, gifts, shared trips to town, church, clubs, and parties were numerous and frequent. This leads to the conclusion that the four-generational family of this study is a segmentally coordinated family, that is, an intimate association between familial generations initiated by each generational segment or household when and as it wishes, according to the promptings of love, affection, and mutual respect and according to family custom, ritual, pleasure, and need. This assures a coordinated and partially shared way of life for all the generations or family segments while maintaining the independence of separate dwellings and a maximum of autonomy for the individuals and their respective households. The segmentally coordinated family represents an urban modification of the rural extended family, which usually did not represent four living generations but which accommodated under one roof or in one village an intergenerational family. Eugene Litwak speaks of the "modified extended family," and it approximates the conceptualization of the segmentally coordinated family except that it stresses mutual aid and reciprocal benefit to the family's occupational and social mobility. The segmentally coordinated family is a more adequate description of the four-generational family, since it emphasizes separateness, independence, and autonomy while it posits the mutual affection, close association, family sharing, and voluntary coordination of familial, social, religious, and financial interests and activities between the nuclear segments. It does not focus on reciprocal advantage but on preferred, affectional ties and association for satisfying, competent, interpersonal relationships and the ongoing of family heritage and values.

The unity in the segmentally coordinated family is more dependent on psychological and attitudinal expectations than it is on residential, spatial, and geographic location. However, two-thirds of the middle-class respondents named geographical distance as a weakening factor, but one which was definitely offset by being in a "closely knit family." The most significant indication of potential change from this cohesiveness was the frequent mention in the questionnaires of the existence of cultural barriers between the generations, expressed as, "We do not speak the same language." Other comments were, "The older generations do not understand us," and, "Our children live a different kind of life from ours."

This tendency toward cultural, social, and psychological separation was counterbalanced by emphatic and positive statements which maintained that family unity was unbroken and family ties were fundamentally strong. The inference of these statements was that no weakness of consequence could exist long in the four-generational family rooted in familism and in adherence to well-established and revered family roles, producing a systematized whole of interrelationships: the segmentally coordinated family.

A summary of the strengths and weaknesses in the four-generational family indicates that propinquity, personal attention and services, shared group activities, and desirable personal qualities loom high as strengthening factors; whereas spatial and social distance, differing beliefs and ideologies, preoccupation with affairs separate from the wider family connection, infrequent get-togethers and visits to one another, illness, age, and debility, are weakening factors.

Strengthening factors are twice as numerous as weakening factors in the segmentally coordinated, four-generational families of this study. A thorough description of these factors provides source materials from actual family life, useful for deliberate application of them for purposes of improving family relationships and of attaining competence in family association. In this respect the study is significant for laymen as well as for specialists. Its findings could be effectively implemented by individuals and could be incorporated into the theories and techniques of family counseling.

Data relating to the expectations of generations toward each other and to the means of contributing to familial and generational happiness could be applied in enhancing the value of the family and in strengthening the individual's sense of belonging, responsibility, and usefulness.

An understanding of family roles, both the traditional ones of grandparent, parent, and child and the emerging one of great-grandparent, will be of assistance to those of us who wish to sustain appropriate and satisfying interpersonal relationships with members of our families, to counsel others with similar desires, or to provide help to those seeking improvement in intergenerational contact and interaction.

The most significant data for the accomplishment of more constructive relationships in the four- or even five-generational family can be found in the descriptive material on the transition from grandparent to great-grandparent. This is because the differentials between the grand and great-grand roles have not yet been clarified by research. There have been few four- or five-generational families studied in the past. Since the White House Conference on Aging in 1961, emphasis on intergenerational families has grown, since such families are becoming noticeably numerous due to increasing longevity. The White House Conference on Aging, through its Committees on Family and Friends of the Aging and Social Services, on both of which the writer served, reiterated the intergenerational concern and the need for continuing research and counseling in this area.

Since our research revealed a clear-cut role for great-grandparents which is less active and more isolated from the day-to-day family interaction than had been the case in the former grandparent role, it indicated the necessity for preparation on the part of the grandparent for readjustment. In other words, the grandparent as liaison between the generations has an active role directed above and below the age scale. But the great-grandparent occupies the apex of the scale, is the bearer of culture and the inspiration for periodic family celebrations, but is somewhat disengaged from continuous participation in the full range of family activities.

Preparation for this stage and role in the family life cycle of the four generations requires a sense of humor and personal interests which may be pursued alone, with one's peers, or even with younger people, both within the home and, if physically possible, in the community, church, club, friendship groups, etc.

By far the chief concern has to be related to attitude and disposition. This study has underscored the fact that younger generations look with disfavor on unsolicited advice from oldsters. In this study 8.2 percent of those interviewed indicated that they could enhance family happiness by being more agreeable. It has been pointed out in another paper, "The Valued Grandparent," presented by the writer at the 17th Annual Conference on Aging, Ann Arbor, Michigan, in June, 1964, that today grandparents and great-grandparents are less apt to be awarded status by virtue of kinship and tradition. Rather, they earn their status through successful reciprocity with the younger people. They have to be liked by the younger generation because they are young in spirit and outlook, are cheerful and understanding, and have something to contribute to family solidarity and interpersonal relationships.

Turning next to the grandparent in the modern, urban society, we may apply the same traits of disposition, viewpoint, understanding, and solidarity, but there are other implications for counseling and social planning. According to Edith Neisser, active and functional grandparents are a source in "meeting emergencies." They also widen the social horizons and "the circle of security" for their grandchildren. This is of infinite benefit since "small persons" need to love and to be loved by several adults and, in addition, to experience life beyond the scope of the immediate family and its domicile. Educated grandparents who keep abreast of changing times and issues may prove to be interesting and dynamic companions for hours of leisure.

If the grandparent maintains his own home and makes of it an attractive center for family gatherings and vacations for the grandchildren, he possesses a strong asset that enhances his value as a grandparent. Our four-generational study underscored this fact as a cohesive tie and also emphasized the unifying force of trips shared with children and grandchildren.

As to the mental activity of grandparents, if they are alert to ways of increasing their intellectual contributions to the family, they stimulate discussions of family history and relate interesting and timely anecdotes of bygone days. This often results in greater family cohesion. To youth, such recountings sometimes provide an historical panorama that is correlated with an academic potential for literature and/or history.

An ingenious grandparent can organize family functions around common interests and rituals that bring zest and meaning to life and bind the generations together into a closely knit whole. Such an intellectually alive person will be valued as a grandparent and will not be considered an "old fuddy-duddy" as far as his children and grandchildren are concerned.

The Poverty Program of the Office of Economic Opportunity has provided funds for Foster Grandparents, assigned to children's institutions. This experiment has proven so successful that community leaders are becoming interested in widening the scope of the program. Senior citizens' information and referral centers are logical agencies for the organization, recruitment, orientation, and placement of foster grandparents in families bereft of grand and great-grandparents.

For families with junior and senior high school students, the grandparent-child relationships may be enhanced by arranging shared experiences such as youth-age banquets, periodic discussion groups in which the older citizens may be questioned about World War I, the Wilson Administration, Teapot Dome, the Depression, and other problems outside the direct experience of youth. On the other hand, youth might be called on to give the older generation impressions of beatniks, civil rights demonstrations, campus protests against war, administrative indifference, and tuition charges; the meaning of existentialism, the popularity of James Bond movies; and the rationale for mini-skirts, the bouffant hairdo, and pastel shades for men. The generations have much to offer each other. Understanding is not facilitated by separation but by sharing.

Finally, the modern, valued grandparent will accept with understanding the role of today's grandparent. It has been noted that the role is no longer that of "ally" with the child against the parents. The latter are more permissive in mid-century than they were in an earlier period. They are more companionable with their children, and, with the lowering age of marriage, they grow up with the youngsters, in a sense. Studies of working-class families by Peter Townsend and others indicate that the grandparent is a mother substitute, caring for the children of working parents. However, mobility and day-care services are weakening the role of grandparent as substitute mother. It seems that the grandparent role has undergone a two-fold change. First, the role is maternal for both men and women, and secondly, it is that of an *extended* parent rather than a parent substitute.

Ruth S. Cavan has developed the theme of the maternal role for grandparents irrespective of sex. She considers the father's role to be one that cannot be shared to the degree of the mother's role. There can be only one family head, authority, and breadwinner. The maternal role is *less* perfectly and explicitly defined, according to Cavan. She posits the assumption that the maternal role may be filled and performed "concurrently" or "successively" by several people who may baby-sit, feed, and trundle the child. For grandmothers this is often a natural function, since it conforms to the affectional and expressive role of women. For grandfathers it involves a readjustment in image and an untried and unfamiliar role, since it is not instrumental as the active male role of provider and decision-maker with authority and responsibility. However, if accepted gracefully as a new and satisfying experience, the grandparent role and its performance by a man will bring new respect and envy on the part of friends and relatives and will bring to the individual a new sense of pride and happiness.

There is, however, an alternative. Talcott Parsons and Robert Bales maintain that boys have greater difficulty in identifying with the father's male role than do girls in an identification with the mother's role due to the father's absence from home, the separation of home and office, and the fact that men's occupational roles are so diverse; whereas the mother-homemaker functions in a generalized, near universal role. Grandfathers have an opportunity to explain and demonstrate the world of work and occupations to their grandsons. If retired, they have time to spend with the boys and can take them around to see at firsthand many kinds of professions, vocations, and occupational activities, thereby enabling them to identify with men and to project themselves imaginatively into the world of work and activity that father and other men engage in when away from home and family. Such a shared experience and relationship between grandfather and grandsons would be mutually beneficial. On the one hand, it would maintain the instrumental role for grandfather; and, on the other hand, it would assist in establishing the boy's concept of an instrumental role for himself as distinguished from the maternal, affective role he observes daily in the home with mother and sisters.

The concept of the *extended* parent role is advanced by this writer. Margaret Park Redfield mentions the mother's role today as "extended," and Cavan describes the grandparent role as "maternal." Combining these two ideas with the knowledge that the modern mother abandons the maternal role with reluctance at any age, it is logical to conclude that mothers in our society and culture are unwilling to acknowledge a mother *substitute* but are apt to welcome *help* with their multiple, extended, current roles if their initiative and prerogatives remain unimpaired. In fact, it is my understanding that in New York City certain Jewish families have adopted a grandparent when this role was absent from the home because they have recognized the potential value of grandparents in our society.

The *extended* parent role presupposes close and congenial relationships with one's children and in-laws. A prerequisite for the successful fulfillment of this role of *extended* parent is to be recognized and accepted as an active and valued parent and grandparent. Then, and only then, can the grandparent identify with the children and grandchildren sufficiently to function as an extension of the parental role and to provide life's extras in the form of affection, companionship, useful services, shared skills, welcome gifts, trips, vacations, religious motivation, and family heritage.

It behooves those who would someday be valued grandparents to cultivate a disposition accepting of change, able to relinquish the parental role with one's children and to enter into a new role with one's grandchildren—a role that supplements the parental role and in no way conflicts or competes with it; a role that satisfies both parents and grandparents; a role that the younger generation will favor; and a role that will bring to the elderly the self-realization of being a valued grandparent whom the generations call "blessed."

SELECTED BIBLIOGRAPHY

BOSSARD, JAMES H. S., AND ELEANOR S. BOLL, "Ritual in Family Living." *American Sociological Review*, 14 (1949).

BOYD, ROSAMONDE R. *Self-Evaluation of Four-Generational Families*. Converse College: unpublished manuscript, 1963.

CAVAN, RUTH SHONLE, "Self and Role in Adjustment During Old Age," In A.M. Rose (ed.) *Human Behavior and Social Process: An Interactionist Approach*. Boston: Houghton Mifflin, 1962.

CUMMING, ELAINE, AND WILLIAM E. HENRY. *Growing Old*. New York: Basic Books, 1961.

DUVALL, EVELYN MILLIS. *Family Development*. New York: J. B. Lippincott Company, 1957.

FARIS, ROBERT E. L., "Interaction of Generations and Family Stability," *American Sociological Review*, 12 (1947).

KEPHART, WILLIAM M. *The Family, Society, and the Individual*. Boston: Houghton Mifflin Company, 1961.

LITWAK, EUGENE, "The Use of Extended Family Groups in the Achievement of Social Goals: Some Policy Implications," *Social Problems*, 7 (1959–60).

NEISSER, EDITH G., "What Grandmothers Are For," *National Parent-Teacher*, 51 (January, 1957).

NIMKOFF, MEYER F., "Changing Family Relationships of Older People in the United States During the Last Forty Years," *Gerontologist*, Vol. 1 (June, 1961).

REDFIELD, MARGARET PARK, "The American Family: Consensus and Freedom," *American Journal of Sociology*, 52 (1946).

SCHORR, ALVIN L. *Filial Responsibility in the Modern American Family.* Washington: Government Printing Office, 1960.

SIMPSON, GEORGE. *People in Families.* New York: Thomas Y. Crowell Company, 1960.

SUSSMAN, MARVIN B., "The Help Pattern in the Middle-Class Family, *American Sociological Review,* 18 (1953).

————, "The Isolated Nuclear Family: Fact or Fiction," *Social Problems,* 64 (1959).

SWEETSTER, DORRIAN APPLIE, "The Social Structure of Grandparenthood," *American Anthropologist,* 58 (1956).

TIBBITTS, CLARK, AND WILMA DONAHUE. *Aging in Today's Society.* Englewood Cliffs, N.J.: Prentice-Hall, Inc., 1960.

VOLLMER, HERMANN, "The Grandmother: A Problem in Child Rearing," *American Journal of Orthopsychiatry,* 7 (1937).

WINCH, ROBERT F. *The Modern Family.* New York: Holt, Rinehart and Winston, Inc., 1963 (Rev. Ed.).

PART II

HEALTH AND ILLNESS
AMONG THE ELDERLY

PART II

HEALTH AND ILLNESS AMONG THE ELDERLY

Three disciplines are represented in the chapters of this section. Adriaan Verwoerdt and Carl Eisdorfer are both physicians, but Dr. Eisdorfer brings to his medical practice and research a strong background in psychology. Charles Oakes is a sociologist who has taught in a medical school and conducted research in hospitals and outpatient clinics. This trio of perspectives is focused on three of the major areas of concern for the elderly: biological aging, illness, and medical care. Verwoerdt loses little time, however, in repeating the themes established by George Maddox and Ruth Albrecht as they pertain to biological processes: variation more than similarity characterizes the biological changes in the elderly. Biological aging begins and develops at different ages and rates for different people, and its commencement will vary from one body organ to another. In this sense Verwoerdt emphasizes that both health and illness are relative concepts, the real issue being the ability of the individual to maintain himself and to function in his usual environment.

The *relative* nature of health and illness becomes a major issue for Oakes, who cites variations in the definitions of these by individual, family, physician, and society. He draws from the literature which indicates how these variations depend on educational, occupational, religious, and residential histories.

Despite the confusion which exists concerning the properties of health and illness, Eisdorfer, again following the most pervasive theme in these readings, criticizes the popular misconception that "to be old is to be sick." This is corroborated by Verwoerdt's disquieting claim that we tend to overemphasize the pathological aspects of aging. He offers the alternative that "prompting the dignity of old age does not only benefit the elderly, but the entire community."

To the barriers to the public's adequate understanding of the changing biological status of the elderly Eisdorfer adds the built-in inadequacies of contemporary medical school curricula which stress the higher probability of cure among the young. Consequently, today's physicians are not prepared to cope with the frustrations associated with treatment of the elderly.

Although not specific to the aged, the physician's frustration is compounded by the sparsity of others in his own ranks and the limited amount of time available to provide the type of care that was characteristic of the "bedside" relationship older persons experienced in previous generations. By formalizing the contact with the patient in the office or hospital setting, the doctor-client relationship takes on a more impersonal air, which is not only foreign to the elderly patient but repugnant to one who is more likely to experience loneliness. To fill these vacancies in enjoyable social relationships, Oakes recommends the development of programs which include, for hospital care at least, bedside companions. The *healthy* elderly person could administer the traditional "tender loving care" to his ill counterpart and follow him back into the home after his discharge, where he could provide homemaker services.

Verwoerdt goes beyond the other two contributors to this

section in his elaborate descriptions of programs and practices to ameliorate the problems associated with health and illness. Some of the problems mentioned by Eisdorfer are provided only partial solution by Oakes, indicating that healthcare for the elderly is yet a virgin area for continuing research and exploratory programs to test the effectiveness of new techniques. The three writers agree on many facets of the area, though. Oakes makes an appeal for greater specification of the conditions under which we tend to call some persons sick and others well. Verwoerdt calls for a balance in the treatment of the elderly. For example, he says, "A very important consideration in advising the individual to eat less, to stop smoking, or to desist from alcohol is that any physical gains may be overshadowed and outweighed by the development of emotional distress."

5

BIOLOGICAL CHARACTERISTICS
OF THE ELDERLY

Adriaan Verwoerdt

THE CONCEPTS OF AGING, HEALTH, AND ILLNESS

The human being is a biological, psychological, and social organism, developing and moving forward in time. Over the life-span, there exists a continuously ongoing change of goals and interests: the awareness of changes results in a sense of becoming. During the various phases of the life-span (e.g., adolescence, parenthood, etc.), there are specific opportunities and challenges. With advancing age these tasks or problems may assume the proportion of crisis. Aging may be viewed as a process leading to increased vulnerability to stresses, such as disease, accident, widowhood, economic deprivation, or loss of status. It may be that people who reach extremely old age, e.g., centenarians, have an extraordinary capacity to cope with stress because of genetic endowment and acquired abilities.

Senescence connotes the process of becoming aged: that period in life which follows the so-called climacterium. Although the age of 65 is usually taken as an arbitrary cut-off point for the beginning of old age (the senium), the time of onset of senescence is variable. Although this onset is usually more or less gradual, one's perception of approaching the

Adriaan Verwoerdt, M.D., is on the staff of the Duke University Medical Center, Durham, North Carolina.

senium may enter one's conscious awareness in the form of a painful discovery leading to a crisis. The term senility is frequently misused and should be reserved for a psychopathological condition frequently occurring in late life which should not be confused with normal pre-death deterioration.

Longevity brings inevitable losses. Those who survive to old age must, of necessity, outlive many contemporaries. Loss and grief (the psychological reaction to loss) are integral components of late life. Such losses, as an intrinsic part of a life phase, usually begin to come to the individual's awareness at the beginning of senescence. In addition to interpersonal losses, there are loss of occupation, role changes in the family constellation, loss of status and prestige, as well as loss of real income. Consequently, the aged typically have multiple problems. Illness, loss of a job, or death of a spouse can occur at any time in life, but the elderly characteristically encounter many or all of these problems simultaneously—at a time that the energy and capacity to cope with loss and stress may be decreasing.

Health could be defined as a state of complete physical, mental, and social well-being, and not merely as the absence of disease or infirmity. If we take this definition strictly, few if any people would be really healthy or possess health for any length of time. Stresses and conflicts of everyday life affect us continuously and may interfere with our sense of well-being. As a matter of fact, a certain amount of stress and conflict are probably desirable, in that they stimulate growth and maturation through crisis resolution. From a dynamic point of view, we may consider a person healthy if his coping with stress is likely to be successful. The subjective experience of being involved in a struggle along with the anticipation of a successful outcome is the sense of confidence. Although present distress and hardship actually may interfere with complete well-being, the point is that there is not necessarily a state of illness. The maintenance of a dynamic equilibrium between oneself and his environment is the hallmark of health. Disease develops when the biological and/or psychological coping mechanisms of the individual are taxed beyond capacity. The important point is that health and illness are relative and dynamic, rather than absolute and static, concepts.

NEEDS OF THE AGED

Almost one in ten Americans is 65 or older, about 19 million persons. By 1975 there will be 22 million aged, and by 2000 at least 30 million people will be 65 or older. If dramatic progress should occur in the treatment or prevention of cancer and of cardiovascular and renal diseases, these figures will be even higher. In addition, people are living more often into the oldest ages. This does not mean that the outermost limits of the human life-span are expanding, but that more people are approaching these limits. Since there will be more of the aged, and more "older" people, the increase in the need for care will be greater than is suggested by the increase in numbers alone. Aging individuals are more likely to have multiple chronic conditions. In order to prevent undue disability, chronic conditions such as arthritis, heart disease, and high blood pressure will require continuous medical attention. The medical treatment of chronic diseases is more expensive than that of acute illness. The elderly, who by and large have chronic diseases, use more physician services and prescribed drugs; they have more hospital admissions, stay longer in the hospital, and more often use long-term care facilities. Medicare will result in more intensive utilization of these services.

The shortage of health practitioners is a major concern. In addition, there are increasing demands based on rising expectations on the part of the public. The balance between demand and supply will be decisively altered in the direction of increased demand. The greater number of old people, the greater emphasis on care for them, the upgrading of requirements of treatment and care, and the gradually increasing affluence of older people as a group—all this adds up to a greater demand for professionally trained health workers and scientifically based programs of care. But, besides these purely quantitative factors, there are other forces at work responsible for the discrepancy between the demand for care and the supply. The term "gerophobia" refers to a complex of personal-psychological factors: fear of old age, of the aged, fear of disease, disability, and death—a set of challenges with which every health worker in the field of aging has to come to grips.

Many health workers in general, such as physicians and nurses, have chosen their profession because of their wish to heal and to cure. In caring for the aged and the chronically ill, however, there is little, if any, satisfaction for this desire to cure. (Compare the satisfaction of a nurse in an obstetrical ward who shares, as it were, in the joys of motherhood, with that of a nurse in a geriatric unit of a mental hospital.) However, there is also considerable satisfaction in alleviating suffering. It is this challenge, i.e., the alleviation of distress, the preservation of function, and the maintenance of hope and meaning, which provide particularly rewarding satisfactions for those engaged in caring for the aged.

BIOLOGICAL ASPECTS OF AGING

Aging increases the susceptibility to illness and the probability of death. As a rule, biological characteristics show earlier maturation and decline than psychological capacities and functions. The pattern of age decrement is characteristic for each person, and the rate of decline varies from one function to another and from one individual to another. Some capacities decline early in life, but the decline becomes manifest only in the case of stress; thus, football players may be "old" in their late twenties. On the other hand, many creative musicians are still productive and "young" in their sixties. Health status of the aged should not be evaluated in terms of standards for young adults. If one takes the latter as criteria for health, then, indeed, most of the aged would have to be considered ill. The term "well" in the case of a 30-year-old person and a 90-year-old person has entirely different meanings.

Diabetes is an example illustrating the difficulty of distinguishing clearly between biological aging, pathological aging, and disease. If standards and values indicative of diabetes in young adults are indiscriminately applied to the aged, many of them would be diagnosed as diabetic. Still, older persons with a so-called "diabetic" type of glucose tolerance test show no evidence of diabetes on clinical examination. The blood glucose values in the fasting state may be quite similar in the young and the aged. The difference between the young and the old does show up under specific stressful circumstances, e.g., the glucose tolerance test. This test involves a stressing of the stability of the glucose metabolism, and it is here that the aged person manifests a decline in the capacity to keep the blood glucose level within certain narrow limits. Another example is body temperature: this may be entirely normal until and unless the aged person (and his heat-regulating system) are subjected to the stress of unusual heat or cold. Because adjustment to excessive temperature and temperature changes in the environment becomes less rapid and effective, the risk of hypothermia is a real danger for aged people, especially those living alone and without adequate food and heating facilities.

In developing medical programs for the aged, the emphasis should be on health maintenance. Many people, and especially older people, are reluctant to see a physician because they are afraid—afraid that a serious illness may be diagnosed, that they may have to be hospitalized, undergo surgery, or have to pay for expensive medications. Public campaigns or community actions should avoid emphasis on the detection of serious illness (cancer, heart disease, etc.), because the resulting fears and anxieties thus engendered tend to promote "avoidance behavior" rather than "approach behavior." An ongoing relationship with one physician provides a natural opportunity for regular contacts and medical checkups. Regular medical checkups can be encouraged by placing emphasis on the maintenance of health; by developing the corollary of the "well-baby" clinic and setting up "well-aging" clinics; and by maintaining a matter-of-fact attitude concerning medical examinations. "Well-aging" clinics aimed at prevention, early detection, and treatment of disease can operate under the aegis of the public health department or in the setting of a hospital outpatient clinic.

Since it appears that the lower income, lower social groups do not use available health facilities, special efforts should be made to reach and motivate them. The local welfare and public health departments should be involved and actively participate in such efforts.

We will now briefly review the age-related changes in various organs and systems of the body. Structural changes in organs, such as atrophy and degeneration, are accompanied by, or result in, alteration of function. The effects of aging are observed more clearly in those functions which require the coordinated activity of several organs or systems. The function of walking, for example, depends on the intact functioning of bones, joints, muscles, and nerves. Generalized damage to any one of these bodily structures will interfere with the performance of walking.

SKIN AND CONNECTIVE TISSUES: Changes in external appearance are due to age-related changes in the skin itself (e.g., loss of elasticity, pigmentary changes) and the loss of tissue immediately below the skin. These skin changes also contribute to the increased difficulty in maintaining normal temperature and to the tendency to develop bruises or skin sores.

Practical Implications: Aged people should be advised to avoid exposure to sunlight since this tends to accelerate aging of the skin. Chronic skin sores may be the result of falling and other accidents, or they may be due to prolonged immobility. These skin lesions represent a major nursing management problem in many institutionalized patients. Accident prevention and maintenance of the ability to walk are the best prevention.

MUSCULAR AND SKELETAL SYSTEM: Stiffened joints and changes in the structure of bone may cause reduction in height, a stooped posture, as well as limitation in mobility. There is loss of muscle power and a decrease in the ability to perform rapid movements at will. Changes in the muscular system make routine daily tasks more difficult and, even more important, tend to impair the efficiency of such vital functions as breathing, urination, and defecation. Although joints and ligaments become progressively more stiff, there is very often a good preservation of motion. Again, stiffening of the rib joints may add to respiratory difficulties. One common change in the bones is that of osteoporosis: the bone structure becomes more porous and lighter. This condition may be painful and disabling, but fortunately, it often can be successfully managed with proper medical treatment.

Practical Implications: Muscular insufficiency causes very common disabilities which are usually preventable and correctable. Generally, not enough attention is given to the patient's potential for physical training and postural exercise; likewise, the aged patient's capacity and need for moderate and regular exercise are underestimated. Lack of activity usually aggravates disability from musculoskeletal changes. This is best illustrated by the contractures (permanent joint contractions) of aged people who are bedridden. Maintenance of mobility should be a basic goal. Aged individuals should be encouraged to be physically active within the limits of their ability. Walking is one of the best types of exercise; it can be done alone or in groups. It might be useful to organize walking clubs for aged individuals. Others might be interested in activities such as gardening or nonstrenuous sports such as swimming or shuffle board. In planning urban development and housing for the elderly, special attention should be given to this very important aspect: safe sidewalks, parks, and places to rest (e.g., simple benches) make a community more liveable for everybody, especially for the elderly. Also, many aged people like to live within walking distance of a shopping center or the center of town.

CARDIOVASCULAR SYSTEM: The heart and blood vessels are affected by such age-related changes as degeneration and "wear and tear." The heart, that remarkably strong muscle, gradually becomes less capable of responding to the extra

61

demands involved in the stress of heavy work. Narrowing of the blood vessels (generalized or localized arteriosclerosis) is one of the most important conditions in the aged. Arteriosclerosis leads to increased resistance to the flow of blood, and the heart compensates for this by an increase in the systolic blood pressure. Essential hypertension is characterized by increased peripheral resistance and elevation of diastolic and systolic blood pressure. Drug therapy is usually effective in reducing the pressure gradually and in preventing blood-flow complications in the heart, brain, and kidney. Peripheral vascular disease which may affect the legs is especially a condition for which the physician usually advises the patient to stop smoking. The coexistence of peripheral vascular disease and diabetes is, in particular, likely to interfere with adequate supply of blood to the legs. Many and different signs and symptoms are related to cardiovascular changes; for example, coronary arteriosclerosis may lead to heart disease; sclerotic changes in the vessels of the brain may cause a number of psychological symptoms. It is emphasized that there is no direct and simple cause-and-effect relationship between the degree of arteriosclerosis on the one hand and the presence of actual disease on the other hand. Thus, for example, on autopsy it is not unusual to find rather extensive changes in the brain vessels while there was no evidence of serious psychological or intellectual impairment prior to death.

Practical Implications: Medical progress in this area will reduce morbidity and mortality rates among the aged. Adequate medical supervision and proper attention to optimal physical activity and diet are also essential. One of the major goals of medical research is prevention and treatment of cerebral thrombosis (stroke). Although little can be done to prevent actual cerebral thrombosis, many disabilities can be avoided by intensive treatment and by vigorous rehabilitation. The rehabilitation of cardiac patients should be based on a comprehensive psychosomatic approach. Special efforts should be made to avoid the development of undue disability from heart disease (e.g., a cardiac neurosis). The physician and his co-therapists (e.g., the physical therapist, dietitian, social caseworker, visiting nurse, etc.) should keep in mind that a great number of factors influence the patient's condition. These factors include negative emotions (anxiety, depression, and hostility), stressful family relationships, personal habits, and living patterns (sleep, nutrition, physical activity). Rehabilitation of cardiac disease must begin with the very onset of the illness, should be continued from then on, and is best carried out by a team of health workers.

RESPIRATORY SYSTEM: The function of breathing serves the exchange of oxygen and carbon dioxide between lungs and blood. Respiration may be less efficient due to changes in the muscles and joints of the ribs and chest. In addition, there may be arteriosclerosis of the lung vessels as well as changes in the elastic fibers of the lung (emphysema).

Practical Implications: Lung cancer has become one of the most frequent malignancies, and this again underscores the significance of regular physical examinations. Tuberculosis of the lungs is another condition to which one should be alert: it appears that tuberculosis occurs relatively more frequently in the older age group. In many instances, difficulties in breathing and shortness of breath result from excessive or inappropriate exercise. Only in clear-cut and severe lung and/or heart disease is shortness of breath present in the resting state. Psychological problems, such as anxiety, frequently cause discomfort in the chest or difficulties in breathing. These symptoms may then occur in the absence of organic disease, or they may be out of keeping with the severity of organic illness which happens to be present.

Climate is not a significant factor in the maintenance of good health, and generally older persons do quite well in colder climates, although respiratory diseases are less prevalent in warm climates. Since the aging person has a reduced ability to adjust to extreme temperature variations, he should be advised against extreme heat, extreme cold, extreme dampness, and heavy winds.

GASTROINTESTINAL SYSTEM: Older people become more interested in and preoccupied with food, eating, and elimination. There are both physical and psychological reasons for this. Physical factors involve a decrease in the sense of smell and taste; loss of teeth and problems with dentures; reduced motility of the stomach and intestines; a decrease in production of the digestive juices of the stomach. Some of these factors are also responsible for the constipation which frequently occurs in aged persons. Hemorrhoids may further complicate elimination. Extreme constipation as well as its counterpart, i.e., bowel incontinence, represent serious nursing management problems in healthy aged persons. The usual age-related changes in eating patterns include a decreased fluid intake and an increased liking for sweets. Since the body's overall metabolic rate normally decreases with aging, the amount of calories needed for maintaining the body tissues and for the production of energy is less.

The psychological aspect of food and eating is extremely important. Food means many different things to different people. It may symbolize affection, security, strength, pleasure, etc. Food and food intake is not simply a matter of calories, but is also intimately related to social experiences. Thus, we often observe that people who live alone begin to neglect their meals; or, conversely, the lack of company may lead to greater emphasis on the satisfactions of eating, with overeating as a result. The social satisfactions of mealtime are lacking for those aged persons who are isolated, alone, or lonely. In keeping with this, they are not motivated to plan or to prepare meals adequately. The result of these poor eating habits is a decreased sense of physical and mental vigor which, in turn, aggravates the poor eating. Interpersonal deprivation and social isolation, however, may create a situation in which eating is the only pleasant experience in a bleak existence. (Alcoholism may develop on a similar basis, especially in large metropolitan areas.) Of course, there are many other possible causes, both physical and psychological, for the development of obesity.

Practical Implications: Certain programs such as "meals on wheels" and the "friendly visitor" program aim at preventing or breaking up a vicious circle leading to progressive undereating or overeating. Older people have a tendency to prepare and to eat meals that take the least effort; the result may be vitamin deficiency, especially vitamin B deficiency. Homemaker-housekeepers, "friendly visitors," visiting nurses, and others can play an important role in altering such deficient eating habits. Special booklets or pamphlets describing attractive and adequate menus for older people could be prepared and made available to various community agencies for distribution (the departments of welfare and public health, the information and referral center, the hospital out-patient clinic, etc.). Such booklets could also be sent to the medical practitioners in the community. Perhaps even local restaurants and cafeterias might be interested in this direction. Specific attention and primary effort in the area of nutrition should be directed toward aged people who live alone and to those who require special diets due to illness. Finally, it would be useful to have regular meetings between a "geriatric" dietitian and boarding house operators, nursing home directors, and representatives of other institutions in order to discuss the nutritional, psychological, and social aspects of meals for the institutionalized aged.

Obesity has certain harmful consequences, such as increased risk of heart disease, stroke, and arthritis. For this reason, caloric intake and food habits should be adjusted. A weight reduction program in the aged must be strict but not drastic. A very important consideration in advising the individual to eat less, stop smoking, or to desist from alcohol is that any physical gains may be overshadowed and outweighed by the development of emotional distress. For example, a cardiac patient who is somewhat overweight may be told to go on a low fat, low cholesterol, low salt diet and to stop smoking. His cardiac status may improve on this regimen, but such a person may now develop a depression that cripples him more than his heart disease ever did. The important point is to treat the whole patient, that is, to evaluate both the physical and the psychological aspects, to assess their relative importance and their mutual effect on each other, and to treat both of them simultaneously.

GENITO-URINARY SYSTEM: A common urinary problem in the aged is more frequent urination. In men this is frequently caused by enlargement of the prostrate gland, while in women infection of the urethra and bladder is responsible. Urinary incontinence, like bowel incontinence, is a major problem in nursing management and may be a source of considerable embarrassment to the aged patient as well as his family. Intensive retraining of incontinent patients may be successful in re-establishing continence.

The menopause is the cessation of the menstrual cycle and signifies the end of the childbearing capacity. The menopause, which occurs at the average age of 47, is frequently associated with a variety of physical and psychological symptoms (e.g., hot flashes, irritability, and depression). The female reproductive organs show atrophic changes due to decreased production of the sex hormones. The "change of life" for the man (the climacterium) usually occurs later than the menopause, i.e., in the 50's and 60's. The climacterium is characterized by greater variability in time of onset, duration, and intensity of the changes. The psychological reaction to these age-related changes in the reproductive organs may represent a strain on marital relationships. Unmarried persons, likewise, may react, sometimes even more markedly than married individuals. Although the pattern of sexual behavior changes, the capacity for various sexual functions, except reproduction itself, may remain intact until advanced age. The maintenance of good physical and mental health, and the removal of negative personal and social attitudes and misconceptions, will contribute to making the later years more "golden" in this important area as well.

FREQUENT MISCONCEPTIONS ABOUT AGING AND SOME PRACTICAL IMPLICATIONS

By way of summary some frequent misconceptions about aging are covered here. These will be seen to be in sharp contrast to many points dealt with in the more accurate descriptions of biological changes typical of the elderly. Further, there are offered practical suggestions on how to "correct" these erroneous views.

> *(1) "The aged are all alike." Aging proceeds not only at different rates in different individuals, but also at different rates in different systems of the same person. Thus, older people are more different than alike. Changes in the body take place at different rates of speed and begin at different times in various people. Personal needs, health status, and social conditions vary among the elderly as they do among young people.*

Practical Implications: Programs for the aged should be flexible and should provide alternatives which offer the individual a choice. Treatment approaches should be individualized likewise. Generalizations about the aged and uniformity of service programs should be avoided. For example, in planning activities or group experiences, it is necessary to keep in mind that some aged individuals prefer to keep a certain distance from other people. Not all isolation and disengagement are necessarily pathological.

> *(2) "Most of the aged live or should live in an institution." Although many aged persons have a chronic condition, the resulting physical disability usually is not to the degree that institutionalization is necessary. Only about 5 percent of the aged actually reside in nursing homes or mental hospitals.*

Practical Implications: Hospitalization and institutionalization are not usually the best solutions to the needs of aged people. Rather, they should be viewed as last resorts. It is worthwhile to make an effort to keep the elderly person in his usual habitat. It is there that he is likely to function best and to have the greatest sense of well-being. Remarkably often, aged persons vigorously resist being moved out of their familiar surroundings. The statement, "I want to go home," is the one most frequently heard among institutionalized agents. A great variety of services is aimed at enabling the aged to remain in their own environment, e.g., home care programs, friendly visitors, meals on wheels, visiting nurses, and so on.

(3) "Most of the aged have little or no contact with relatives." Recent research indicates that older people with children, whether living alone or not, keep in physical proximity with at least one child and see him often. Most older people prefer to live apart from their children but close enough to see them often.

Practical Implications: Family relationships, by nature, are complex, and this is especially true in the case of intrafamily conflict. Disturbed relationships between the aged and other family members frequently are long-standing. In some cases, the disturbed family relationships are passed on from one generation to the next. In the case of "family pathology," special professional assistance (e.g., social case work, family service) is indicated. Well-adjusted families and their aged family members usually pose no problems which call for special services. Most of the aged usually place high value on remaining independent, and they are reluctant to become dependent on their children. Not infrequently, a widowed person moves in with his children, and sometimes this continued closeness to each other may lead to friction. If the family relationships used to be basically sound, then such a specific situational problem is likely to be resolved quite readily by way of counseling. Such counseling can be carried out by physicians, the clergy, visiting nurses, welfare workers, and so on.

(4) "Older people are not able to make decisions." This misconception may lead to the mistake of planning for the aged instead of planning with them. It would be useful, if not actually necessary, to develop plans and programs for

the aged in collaboration with a number of representatives of the aged community. Thus, one could invite aged individuals who represent specific groups and segments in the community to be "in" on the planning and implementation phases of program development. Different socio-economic, ethnic, religious, and occupational backgrounds should be included.

(5) "Old age is a second childhood." This misconception is related to the foregoing one and may lead to the tragic result of "infantilizing" older people. In fact, learning ability and intelligence remain relatively intact provided no major illness develops. The pathological condition of senility does show phenomena that are "childlike" but this has very little to do with childhood.

Practical Implications: The older person should be treated with the respect to which he is entitled. Promoting the dignity of old age does not only benefit the elderly, but the entire community. If the "image" of old age can be changed in a positive direction, then the attitudes of younger people to aging and the prospect of their own old age may be altered favorably. True and authentic dignity of the aged excludes any attempt (on the part of the aged and others) unduly to cover up the effects of aging (e.g., by trying to act or appear much younger than one really is). A community can make a deliberate and planned effort to enhance the "image" of the elderly, for example, by occasionally including pictures of older persons in advertisements and commercials.

(6) "Most of the aged are in poor health." Illness and disability are not simply the result of aging alone. Most of the aged are not in poor health, and in spite of certain chronic conditions, they continue to function well. Health and illness are relative concepts. What really counts is the ability to maintain oneself and to function in one's usual environment.

Practical Implications: The practical point to be made here is emphasizing an important principle: essential in maintaining adjustment in the aged is adjusting the environment. A diminished ability to cope with stress can best be met by removing stress by way of environmental manipulation. For example, a husband and wife, both in their 80's, were regularly hospitalized at the same time, although for different reasons. The husband suffered from recurrent heart failure, the wife from malnutrition and depression. One important contributing factor causing these hospital admissions was a gradually worsening martial conflict: the husband, once strong and powerful, reacted to his decline in power by becoming increasingly dominating and demanding of his wife. The latter, unable to cope with this, became increasingly depressed, thus "depriving" the husband even more. This vicious circle was finally broken when both moved into a boarding home where they felt more secure. There were no more hospital admissions for either of them. It would have been useless in this case to treat the marital discord itself; what was needed was a different and "protective" environment.

(7) "Aged persons have no sex life." Recent studies show that sexual desires and capabilities, although altered and modified by the aging process, may remain sufficiently intact in late life. In the absence of illness, sexual activity can be maintained into the 70's and 80's.

Practical Implications: It may be useful to have available to aging individuals counseling services (e.g., physicians in a hospital outpatient clinic; or medical social workers in an information and referral center) in the area of sex and sexual adjustments. Specific pamphlets or booklets could be prepared as well. Older persons may suffer unnecessarily from marital misery if they fail to understand that spouses may age at different rates. A brief series of talks with the counselor may help the elderly couple to re-open channels of communication between themselves; to face each other more realistically without the need to put up a front; to find new ways of intimacy and of being together; and, last but not least, to cherish the memories of shared experiences.

REFERENCES

BIRREN, T. E. *The Psychology of Aging.* Englewood Cliffs, N.J.: Prentice-Hall, Inc., 1964.

COWDRY, E. V. (ed.), *The Care of the Geriatric Patient,* Chapter 2, "Psychologic Aspects," by W. Donahue and R. Stoll. St. Louis: C. V. Mosby Co., 1963.

ENGEL, GEORGE L., *Psychological Development in Health and Disease.* Philadelphia: W. B. Saunders Company, 1962, Chapter 23.

LINDEN, M. E., AND D. COURTNEY, "The Human Life Cycle and Its Interruptions: A Psychologic Hypothesis." *American Journal of Psychiatry* (1953), 109: pp. 906–15.

SHANAS, ETHEL. *The Health of Older People.* Cambridge, Mass.: Harvard University Press, 1962.

VERWOERDT, ADRIAAN. *Communication with the Fatally Ill.* Springfield, Ill.: Charles C. Thomas, 1966.

WIGGINS, JAMES W., AND HELMUT SCHOECK, "Profile of the Aging: U.S.A.," *Geriatrics,* 16 (July, 1961), 336–42.

"Working with Older People: I. The Practitioner and the Elderly" (prepared by the Gerontological Society), U.S. Department of H.E.W., Division of Chronic Diseases, Gerontology Branch, Washington, D.C., 1966.

ZETZEL, E .R., "Dynamics of the Metapsychology of the Aging Process," *Geriatric Psychiatry,* edited by M. A. Berezin and S. H. Cath. New York: International Universities Press, 1965, pp. 106–11.

6

OBSERVATIONS ON MEDICAL CARE
OF THE AGED

Carl Eisdorfer

Among the significant changes of our civilization during the past few decades has been the rising number and proportion of aged persons in the population. To many, this change has been identified as a product of advances in medicine or, perhaps more accurately, advances in public health and prenatal care. The results of such advances in health have not been an unmixed blessing. Ignoring for the moment the implications of an uncontrolled "population explosion," we will proceed to the subject of ongoing medical care for increasing numbers of persons who require such care. The concern with good health and maintenance of the best level of functioning has generated a great amount of attention, particularly in view of rising medical costs and shortages of medical personnel.

The scope of medical care and the factors relevant to the delivery of medical service to the aged are sufficiently complex that I am tempted to observe that it is virtually impossible to develop a coherent report here. This is by way of introduction to what may emerge rather as a series of comments concerning the problems and some of the relevant issues.

Perhaps the most poorly understood difficulty in caring for the aged ill resides in the problem of expectation. The prac-

Carl Eisdorfer, Ph.D., M.D., is on the staff at Duke University, Durham, North Carolina.

tice of medicine or any other clinical discipline requires that the professional develop an appraisal of the situation including some estimation as to deviation from normal or "healthy," and that he also attempt to modify the problem to enable a return to an expected level of adaptation. Through his training the physician is educated to determine a host of etiologic agents and factors that modify the health of his patient. The science, or perhaps the art, of reasonableness of expectation as directed toward patients in general and aging patients in particular has not been taught, to the best of my knowledge, in any medical or social work school nor in any clinical psychology unit or other professional training program. This, perhaps, is the salient advantage to professional experience and a history of having worked with individuals over long periods of time. In short, we must deal with the problem of having our clinicians develop expectations which are too low or too high, thus either placing pressures on the patient to meet an impossible standard or setting the standard so low that we allow the patient to deteriorate to that level. In my opinion, this problem is magnified with the aged individual.

Expectations involve a significant attitudinal component, in part because of a paucity of good normative data. Comments such as, "What do you expect from someone your age?" and similar remarks reflect this sliding scale of good health. Thus, one is not expected to be as healthy—normally—as age progresses beyond the fifth or sixth decade of life.

In the recent studies of Eisdorfer and Frances Wilkie, it seems quite clear that the concept of "old" is intermingled with the concept of sick and that there is on the part of undergraduate college students an expectation that "old" persons are "sick." This expectation is probably not solely that of the younger person but may, in fact, be true of the aged individual, that is to say, of the patient himself as well as his physician. The point at issue is that if no one expects the patient to be healthier than he is, there will be little effort devoted toward attempting to restore or regenerate good health. As a consequence, there is a violation of one of the cardinal rules of the physician's practice, i.e., early detection and treatment. This is compromised even more by numbers of patients who wait too long before seeking help because their problems are attributed by them to "old age."

By way of introducing the next issue, I must confess a degree of discomfort. We are living in an awkward era when altruism is in poor repute. Despite the vulnerability of my position, however, I would like to state that I believe strongly that, for the medical student and physician in practice, helping the patient, i.e., curing people, is a most significant motive. Physicians are indeed human, however; they have the same foibles and follow the same laws of personality dynamics that all other members of the population share: when they expend a considerable amount of time and energy and do a good job, they expect to achieve their motives and want to be appreciated. Observing medical students, young physicians, and senior physicians in practice, it appears that one of the most frustrating and upsetting events to them is not the failure of the patient to pay his bill but rather the failure of the patient to get well. This difficulty *could* be directed toward virtually every professional dealing with clients. In the case of the aged sick patient, a major difficulty resides in the fact that it is impossible to "cure" many of the difficulties he presents to the doctor. Typically, he has the kind of disease that has no medical cure; his illness tends to be chronic. Thus, the role that the physician must take is not a curative one; rather, he must help the patient develop the best possible adaptation given the existing circumstances. This means that the physician caring for the patient has to accept the illness, despite the fact that he is trained not to accept illness but to combat it. To complete this point, then, the personality of the dedicated individual who will train himself for ten or more years to go into practice is also the kind that would be very frustrated by dealing with a situation he sees as hopeless. A parallel problem is the communication barrier between physician and aging patient; the latter has difficulty comprehending the instructions and observations of the physician. In this context, too, not only does the doctor want to cure his patient but the patient expects a cure. Often he is hard pressed to accept "learning to live with" his difficulties, especially where pain or limitations of activity ensue. He then severs relations with his own physician and may look to many others for a cure, often resorting to charlatans or wasting his money on worthless drugs. In many instances he can hardly be blamed for this, yet it is likely to be a futile search.

An issue of considerable consequence is the intimate relationship between the physical and emotional expressions of diseases which we see in the aged. In a number of observations made on the first admission of psychiatric patients past the age of 65, it has been demonstrated that approximately 75 percent of the sample are found to have some underlying physical disease of a serious magnitude. The reverse is equally true. That is to say, serious emotional illness is manifested in physical symptomology. What this suggests is that the physician is often not sure of the scope of the illness he has to treat. The patient presents himself as a person with an emotional problem and the physician in practice, particularly if he has not had a long history of having worked with the patient, will find himself dealing with a communications barrier that is characteristic of persons with emotional problems. As a consequence, the physician may never get to hear the underlying physical complaint. Only by very intensive investigation can this problem be elucidated. Alexander Simon of the Langler Porter Institute at the University of California demonstrated that of a large group of aged first-admission psychiatric patients more than two-thirds had some primary medical problem. Doubtless many of these persons were seen by physicians who could not cope with the physical problem because their patients were having frank hallucinatory or delusory symptoms and so had to be sent in for psychiatric examination with diagnoses of senile psychosis or chronic brain syndrome. This intimate relationship of physical and emotional states is a significant facet in the office management of the aging patient.

As I indicated, the reverse is also true. The patients present us with a physical problem, and quite often we tend to treat the symptoms without being able to cope with the fact that the primary illness of the aged person needs to be redefined. Dr. Amos Johnson, a well-known general practitioner in Eastern North Carolina and past president of the American Academy of General Practice, suggests that we ought to identify a new disease and call it "loneliness." Dr. Johnson feels that this may be one of the most crippling diseases of the older person and a more serious neurologic agent than any virus or autoimmune phenomenon. Psychiatrists over the past two decades have been talking about the "grief" reaction, and it is interesting that the observation has been made, particularly among children. The probability of losing a beloved individual such as a spouse or friend is, of course, markedly increased with age. Such patients may present themselves to the physician not with complaints of sadness or depression, but more typically with concerns about digestion, elimination, and fatigue. Again, the physician who does not know the patient well and who has 40 other people in his waiting room often does not take the time to question and appreciate the factors in the life situation of the elderly person. In too many instances he is forced to treat such symptoms with drugs designed to affect the gastrointestinal system rather than the underlying etiology. In a situation such as this, the resultant cycle of symptom—inadequate examination and return of patient to his doctor with new symptoms—will continue until the patient's underlying depression is identified and treated. Too often this is not done; the physician remains "too busy" or the patient "goes shopping" for another physician who starts the cycle again.

On several occasions I have alluded to the communication barrier between the doctor and the patient. What are the factors in such communication difficulty? Not only are the expectations of young and aged patients markedly different with respect to their health, but the aged patient's use of the physician as a confidant often runs counter to the expectations of today's practitioner, who sees himself primarily as a specialist in the practice of scientific medicine. An additional concern frequently is the generation gap between physicians and patients. Young and middle-aged patients will see physicians who are likely to be older than the patients are initially. The probability is high that the physician may die before these patients, and, as a result, late in life patients are requested to look for a new physician. As in every other dyadic relationship, there is no immediate rapport, and, as a consequence, the patient may find himself in the situation that he and his physician do not "make it" together. Very often for financial or physical reasons the patient is unable to go to a physician who is better suited to his personal needs. The result is a poor team for generating and maintaining good health.

In yet another way the aged person is a casualty of the changing pattern of medical care. For example, the house call, once so sacred and still enshrined in the hearts of many, now appears, for some very valid reasons, no longer sanctified. Physicians have learned through many sad experiences that they require a substantial amount of equipment, medication, etc. in order to be really effective agents in an emergency. This equipment cannot be carried in a black bag. Furthermore, the number of general practitioners has been declining in proportion to the number of physicians and the population of the community at large. The specialist is even more dependent on complex equipment and is reluctant to practice outside of the hospital or office, having little doubt that hospital and office practice has resulted in a substantial improvement in medical care. The aging individual who wishes to see the doctor in his home is, of course, in the position of attempting to sustain a pattern which is becoming less and less viable for the overtaxed practitioner. The apparent result during this period of change is that, as medical care gets better, interpersonal relations with physicians are getting worse.

I have been avoiding statistics, but there are some facts which should be reviewed. By 1970 the aged will comprise 10 percent of the population, or approximately 20 million persons aged 65 and over. These individuals tend to seek medical care at a rate about 2½ to 3 times that of the population at large. For aging individuals who suffer various assaults on their integrity, including the death of people who love them, the loss of important social roles, etc., their bodies often become sources of great concern. This, coupled with the fact that they are indeed more prone to physical illness, makes their relation with the medical care facilities of the country of more immediate concern. What must be recognized is that aged individuals need medical care more than any other portion of the population (except, perhaps, very young infants). In addition to his real need, it seems likely that the aged person also uses the physician for a host of nonphysical concerns more than other persons, because such concerns are expressed in physical symptoms.

Another facet to this problem is the source of information available to the physician. Not only does he obtain his information from the aged patient, but very often from the relatives of such patients. Sons and daughters who may have difficulty in coping with the problems of an aged parent at home very often take a defensive posture, and the resultant history may be distorted. The physician, therefore, often has no recourse but to go along with the material presented to him.

One final issue concerns the response of society. Aging individuals traditionally have been seen as surplus commodities. Western society has never had to cope with considerable numbers of the aged and so has not evolved clear patterns of extended care except on a family basis. The situation now exists, and we must take into consideration the facilities available. Thus, we have a variety of extended care facilities which in many instances are not subject to the usual kinds of controls. This is not to imply that we do not have laws, but simply that the laws are so loosely implemented that all we can do is provide minimal maintenance facilities. Aged persons are fed, clothed, and bedded down, and most of the institutions are as sanitary as an average home. The responsibility for doing something beyond that is missing except in a few of the larger, better staffed, and better funded installations. Medical care in many such facilities is on a consultative basis and frequently is based on telephone conversations between the doctor and the nurse. The result is custodial care: keeping the resident from becoming so agitated that he disturbs the other patients. What is the criterion for better care? All too often the answer is financial status. It is important to recognize that the shortage of physicians, nursing homes, and extended care facilities and their level of functioning are simply not a medical problem; they are a social problem.

It is unfortunate and somewhat absurd to blame physicians because of their sparsity, while simultaneously medical schools are losing thousands of dollars per year per medical student. Similarly, our emphasis on children and youth and beauty has detracted from our recruitment of qualified people to work with the aged.

In the overview, there appears to be lacking a total system of care for the aged, a system, incidentally, which requires preliminary analysis and rather dramatic changes. The approach to the aged patient today is to infantilize him. We have what Kastenbaum has referred to as the zoo or pet model of hospital care; it is easier for the doctor or nurse to take care of a patient than to teach him to care for himself. We have seen professionals walk up to patients, pat them on the head, and refer to them as if they were cocker spaniels instead of people. By so doing, we cut them off from the community. A few of them we elevate to the status of pets, which, if they are completely passive, learn to purr for us.

Our culture has not yet considered the significance of the contribution that the aging can make. In order to make room for the young, we are requiring early retirement and getting rid of the older, those 45 to 65, who are more vulnerable to physical and mental disease. To what extent this vulnerability would be minimized by continued employment is yet to be explored.

I have presented a number of problems and have done very little to suggest solutions. It is necessary, however, to appreciate the exciting and dramatic advances in science and technology, and the social conditions which have resulted in growth of the population, thus increasing the probability that a child will live out his life and grow into the category of "the aged." Indeed, we must do more to capitalize on the developments of recent decades. I have no doubt that these problems are soluble; my only concern is that we not wait too long before we attempt to tackle them.

SELECTED REFERENCES

DAVIS, FRED (ed.). *The Nursing Profession.* New York: Wiley, 1966.

FREIDSON, ELIOT. *Patients' Views of Medical Practice.* Philadelphia: Russell Sage Foundation, 1961.

SCHOECK, HELMUT (ed.). *Financing Medical Care.* Caldwell, Idaho: Caxton Printers, Ltd., 1962.

SKIPPER, JAMES K., JR., AND ROBERT C. LEONARD. *Social Interaction and Patient Care.* Philadelphia: J. B. Lippincott, 1965.

WHITE, KERR L. (ed.). *Medical Care Research.* New York: Pergamon Press, 1965.

7

SOCIOMEDICAL PROBLEMS AMONG THE ELDERLY

Charles G. Oakes

INTRODUCTION

The interest in gerontology as an academic pursuit and the concern for the elderly by practitioners and policy-makers have increased considerably in recent years. With this interest and concern has come a confusion over what constitutes the *true* state of the elderly. This is especially so of the social aspects of health and illness of elderly people.

The confusion which exists should not be surprising. In the early periods of research on any new subject, the discovery of yesterday frequently is antiquated by the one of today. The scientist, hopefully, is more used to this contingency of research, but the practitioner and policy-maker wish that life were more consistent so that social problems, where they exist, could be attacked with an underlying logic that does not fade into irrelevance by the time an ameliorative program gets underway. Accordingly, the material which follows is based on the hope that a greater appreciation of the multifaceted aspects of this area of interest will result. Where appropriate, suggestions will be offered for means of trying to solve some of the problems that exist.

The involvement of many disciplines concerned with the elderly, while encouraging in one sense, has disadvantages in another. Rapid proliferation of research findings runs the risk

Charles G. Oakes is on the faculty of the Duke University Medical Center and also Director of the Division of Planning and Evaluation, North Carolina Regional Medical Program.

of lack of coordination of these findings. And lack of coordination frequently results in conclusions which are only "partially valid." A carefully contrived research project in sociology, for instance, resulting in statistically significant findings describing or explaining the behavior of elderly persons, is modified appreciably when the sociologist is "enlightened," much to his dismay and embarrassment, by discovering that certain economic, biological, and psychological factors, of which he may be relatively ignorant, were not taken into account and were shown to be of crucial importance. When this happens, we realize that a sociological perspective by itself is only partially true. By the same token, partial truth is the outcome in any discipline when the results represent but a small slice of fact out of the broad spectrum of reality.

Recognition of the shortcomings of uncoordinated research by some students of the health and illness behavior of elderly persons has led to some sincere efforts to arrive at a broader perspective. Appreciation of the biological, economic, psychological, and sociological dimensions is greater when it is seen how each contributes to the other. One such example is that of Stanislav V. Kasl and Sidney Cobb, and some attention will be given here to their work. These writers have distinguished among three levels of behavior related to our subject: health behavior, illness behavior, and sick-role behavior. Each level, in turn, is described in biological, psychological, and sociological terms.

Health behavior is what one does when he is well for the purpose of staying that way. Taking vitamins, getting a good night's sleep, visiting the doctor for periodic physical checkups, and getting vaccinations or "booster shots" are all methods of keeping well, and, biologically speaking, the person is well. Psychologically, the person *sees* himself as a well person, and, sociologically, he is able to maintain his usual level of activities in various roles—husband, father, employee, club member, etc.

Illness behavior, again beginning with the biological, refers to such things as self-medication, going to a doctor for the diagnosis of unusual symptoms, or seeking counsel from friends or relatives on how to treat a physical problem. In illness behavior the individual perceives himself in a new light—"I feel ill"—and he often expects others to take this into account in their relations with him. Sociologically, this new image of self is compounded by an increasing deterioration of routine duties or activities.

Sick-role behavior signals the summation of early symptoms into a defined disease in which the individual truly sees himself as sick, is unable to participate in his usual roles, and takes on a new one of dependence on others—relatives, friends, doctor—for assistance.

These three descriptions are listed here in their ideal or pure form, which is to say that in illness behavior, for instance, the biological condition is supported by a set of corresponding psychological and sociological factors. Life is not always so simple, however, and this is especially true when we look at the health, illness, and sick-role behavior of elderly persons who grew up in a generation in which the definitions of health and illness, and the manner in which they responded to them, were different from today.

Take as an example "dear old Granddad," now 75, who has lived through periods of hunger and several flu epidemics, and, in his younger years, has plowed the field or tended the store despite possible poor health. Granddad says to himself, "I don't feel too well, but an aspirin or some tonic should help out." His children with whom he is living insist that he go to the hospital and even pack his suitcase for a two weeks' stay. But when the doctor finally examines him, he reports: "Look, for a man of 75, you're in excellent shape; what do you expect anyway?" Psychologically and biologically, Granddad was displaying illness behavior. His grown children felt that he should have taken on the sick role, but the doctor disagreed with both. Such an example is supported from many of our own experiences with old people.

The problems that confront us in understanding adequately the health, illness, and sick-role behavior of the elderly are contributed to by a number of factors in addition to the difference in generations which was suggested above. Religious, educational, socio-economic, and residential backgrounds, among others, have prevented ready access by the scholar, practitioner, and policy-maker to *general* conclusions about the elderly. As George Maddox said in Chapter 1: We cannot stereotype the elderly any more than we can say that all teen-agers are alike or that all middle-aged persons can be described by a similar list of characteristics. To appreciate the present behavior of the elderly person, we have to consider the types of experiences he has had in the past, for these will determine to a great measure how he keeps himself healthy, how he defines illness, and how readily and in what manner he assumes *and* leaves the sick role.

HEALTH BEHAVIOR

In their discussion of health behavior, Kasl and Cobb suggest that there is a relationship between *perceived threat of disease* and *health behavior.* That is to say, to the extent that an individual has been sick in the past, to the extent that he considers himself susceptible to specific diseases or disease in general in the future, he will occupy himself with methods for decreasing the probability that he will get sick again. In the light of this proposition, do elderly persons see themselves as becoming sick, and what evidence do we have for this attitude?

The studies of participants in free community-wide health examinations indicate that those most frequently represented are the young and middle-aged. In studies of participation in free polio vaccine programs, those who accepted the vaccine, again, were younger people. Why are the elderly underrepresented? The answer may lie in the fact that for younger persons illness signals greater loss in terms of position, income, and family stability, issues which are not as important for the elderly person. If he has survived contagious diseases until his later years, the elderly person has a right to assume that they no longer pose a threat.

There is, however, a certain irony in this lack of response to programs which prevent contagious diseases, for the real threats to the elderly are not the contagious diseases but rather the chronic ones—rheumatoid arthritis, diabetes, and the various cardiovascular diseases. For these there are few, if any, preventive measures in which the individual can engage, and little evidence exists to suggest how the middle-aged individual prepares for the almost inevitable chronic diseases of later years. What are the implications of this condition for community programs devoted to the welfare of senior citizens?

In the City of Memphis hospitals, for instance, outpatients who are diabetics are enrolled in a program the purpose of which is to educate them to the nature of their disease so that they can identify sudden changes requiring immediate professional attention. The participants in these programs are not highly educated persons, and the majority are indigent, yet they continue to live relatively healthy lives because they have been informed of the details of their illness. Significant about many similar programs throughout the country is that those enrolled in them did not suspect anything wrong until *after* they had first participated in community-wide screening or detection programs. If such programs were established in your community for detecting diabetics, or those in the early stages of glaucoma, arthritis, or hypertensive heart disease, the problem of controlling.chronic diseases would be made considerably easier. Also, early detection of disease results in treatment which frequently is much less expensive than that for well-advanced illnesses.

Where one lives also makes a difference in how one acts in regard to health and illness. E. Grant Youmans has devoted considerable attention to these differences. While the rural elderly have more sick days per year and are more restricted in their activities than elderly persons living in the large cities, they tend to complain less about their infirmities. Our information on the reason for this is sparse, but a suggested answer lies in the traditional image of the rural dweller. We view him as an exceptionally independent and resourceful person, self-sufficient, and used to adversity. Couple with this the possibility that poorer health may be accepted as a *way of life,* and we have a clue about the difficulty public health officials will have in elevating the general state of health of the rural elderly or in controlling their already existing chronic diseases.

One of the sad truths about this description of rural residents is that there are fewer physicians in these areas to care for them, and, judging from the continuing trend in medical education toward specialization, we can reasonably predict that few young doctors will be recruited by small rural communities where the practice of medicine is not as attractive as in the cities, where the conveniences of sophisticated diagnostic techniques are more in evidence. One of the attempted solutions has been the development of peripatetic medical units—mobile teams of physicians and nurses who periodically visit rural areas to treat those who will not or cannot come to the city. There are problems in organizing these teams which must be faced. Who will be recruited for the team? Will the staff always consist of the same persons, or will there be some type of rotation system drawing from volunteer doctors in the community? And how much equipment will be necessary to provide adequate diagnosis in the field? How expensive is such a program?

Working out the mechanics of such a program will depend first of all on the resources presently existing in the community, and, since these resources usually vary from city to city, we cannot expect peripatetic teams always to assume the same structure. As to cost, we can expect from the beginning that it will be great. But community health officials and leaders have to weigh the economic alternatives. If elderly persons living in rural areas cannot or will not come to community clinics or private physicians, the alternative may be the progressive worsening of chronic diseases among the elderly, culminating in their becoming wards of the county or state. When this happens, entire families frequently end up on the welfare rolls. The choice is between expensive but controlled outpatient care or more expensive and permanent inpatient treatment.

One of the areas in which our information is lacking has

to do with the preparation that middle-aged persons make to guarantee good health in the later years. There is some indication that religious affiliation is of importance here, and one group in particular is singled out for comment. Orthodox Jews seem to be much more sensitive to indications of illness than are members of most other religious groups. Jewish parents, more than parents belonging to other faiths, tend to notice and respond to the complaints of their children, whether these be of a physical or psychological nature. Also, during adulthood, Orthodox Jews are much more regular in having routine physical examinations. These patterns indicate an appreciably greater preoccupation with matters of health, and it has been suggested that Orthodox faith, as related in the Old Testament, does not distinguish between problems of the body, mind, and spirit. A physical problem is just as likely to be interpreted by Orthodox Jews as having consequences for one's mental and religious health; accordingly, more attention is paid to disturbances that would escape the attention of members of other faiths.

The lesson in this for all parents, whatever their religious beliefs, and for organizations concerned with health is that preparation for adequate health behavior in the elderly years must begin prior to their arrival and, reasonably so, as early as childhood, a point mentioned by Adriaan Verwoerdt in Chapter 9. It has been said that the elderly person stands on a threshold of life over which all of us must pass. To this can be added that *how* we will pass over that threshold is determined by our preparation long before it is reached.

ILLNESS BEHAVIOR

The interrelationships between the biological, psychological, and sociological aspects of human behavior are magnified, it is proposed, to a greater extent at the level of illness behavior. It is sometimes difficult to determine which of these aspects is the causal factor and which is effect. Psychiatrists have distinguished between *psychosomatic* and *somatopsychic* illnesses. Dr. Verwoerdt illustrated the distinction by saying that a person who becomes very excited or anxious may begin to breathe abnormally heavy—hyperventilate—and this condition can result in a change in the cardiovascular processes. Abnormal breathing following some psychological causal factor is a classical example of a psychosomatic syndrome. On the other hand, the individual may have a persistent pain, not psychogenic in nature, from which follows a prolonged (somatogenic) period of depression. If we add to this the idea that one's social relations, once disrupted, can result in excessive excitement or anxiety, as mentioned above for the first case, then it is understandable that some physical problems arise because of our relations with others. By the same token, referring to the somatogenic example, one's relations with others can suffer from the state of depression which followed the persistent pain.

One of the types of illness behavior mentioned earlier had to do with an individual's visit to a physician following the appearance of symptoms. When the appraisals of elderly people about their health are compared with those of their physicians, we find that older persons are much more optimistic about their health than younger persons are. But to a greater degree elderly men disagree with their physicians on the status of their health; that is, they feel they are healthier than they really are. Even when they perceive symptoms, older persons in general, and older men in particular, tend to disagree with the doctor's objective diagnosis. Why this is so we are not sure, unless there is something akin to anxiety over decreasing health and virility and a refusal to admit their presence. There are exceptions, and it is important that the conditions under which these occur are spelled out.

Recent studies by Maddox show that elderly persons are more objective about their health, whether good or poor, if they have a history of extensive contact with others their own age. Those who are socially isolated do not as frequently *perceive reality validly*. It is as if relationships with one's peers, seeing how others like oneself really are, provide a standard for a more objective appraisal of oneself. In this sense, the old adage, "There is no fool like an old fool," is modified when the older person associates with others his own age and finds that he cannot "pull the wool over their eyes" or the eyes of others.

Frequent contact with other persons of the same age among the elderly has relevance for community program-planning. Going to a doctor for diagnostic purposes and agreeing with the doctor will be seen more frequently among those who maintain more extensive peer relationships. These persons will be more willing, we predict, to admit illness when it exists and will be more likely to do something about it. The implications of this for the ease of the treatment process are obvious. To the extent that groups exist in the community for the senior citizen, the more likely it is that participants will respond objectively to changes in the physical state common to many elderly citizens.

At this point I wish to raise a question that has certain ethical overtones. We have said that, psychologically, illness behavior requires that one recognize and admit illness. In other words, one's conception of himself as an ill person requires that a label of illness be ascribed to him, whether the individual does this himself or someone else forces it upon him. If Grandmother, for instance, says she is *not* ill, but her children say she is, and the doctor agrees with the children, is it then mandatory that Grandmother get a physical checkup as well as treatment whether she wants it or not?

Raised to a general and more far-reaching level, are practitioners, social reformers, and policy-makers justified in developing programs for all persons, including those who say they do not need them? The question is by now well known, and no little debate has resulted, accompanied, naturally, by considerable antagonism in both the private and public realms. In a recent study of reform programs, Peter Marris and Martin Rein carefully point out in their conclusion that the failure of many programs at the public level results from the inability of reformers to control (i.e., to change in the direction of *their* views) either the views of directors of competing programs or a strong tradition of individualism characteristic of Americans generally. (Evidence that the question raised here is *not* in any way an isolated one is found in the fact that the 1967 annual meetings of the American Association for the Advancement of Science devoted an entire day to the presentation of papers dealing with *voluntary* participation in publicly supported health programs.)

The rapid growth in the number of elderly persons in our country and the increase in knowledge among medical researchers on the nature of chronic diseases in the later years suggest that in terms of community planning we have to distinguish between two types of persons: (1) the elderly person who does not ask for help and does *not* need it, and (2) the elderly person who does not ask for help but who, according to the best information available, *does* need it. Medical knowledge has progressed so rapidly that it is possible now to detect many medical problems in the early stages of their development. Health is too vital and personal to each of us to think that early awareness of disease will result in a refusal to accept assistance in favor of a continued posture of so-called self-sufficiency. Self-sufficiency itself is dependent on how long we remain healthy.

As can be inferred from the above comments, the group which should be of greater concern to us is the second one—those who do not ask for medical assistance but nevertheless need it. How can services be provided for these persons while at the same time we respect the right of the individual to either accept or refuse such services? The key to our answer is in the word "provide." It is proposed that policy-makers and those interested in reform strike a middle ground in their concern for the interests and welfare of the elderly. By middle ground is meant a procedure that serves to enlighten but not to coerce the public, leaving the decision to act in the light of newly acquired knowledge up to the individual. Through programs held in senior citizen centers, the churches, continuing education courses in the schools, and through the mass media —television, radio, and the newspapers—senior citizens can become informed of the possibilities that pertain to them.

The value of continuing education for the elderly in this area cannot be underestimated. Practically every study on the subject supports the conclusion that the more educated a person is, the more accurately he will recognize the significance of early symptoms and seek counsel from a physician. What a manual laborer may define as a "sprained back," the business executive may define as a possible "slipped vertebral disk." What a craftsman claims is a "simple case of persisting heartburn" or constipation, the middle-class white-collar worker may suspect as an ulcer or early appendicitis.

Because they lack the appropriate labels for their illnesses, and because they tend to minimize the significance of symptoms, lower-class, poorly educated persons are more often considerably sicker by the time they reach the hospital than more educated persons. This is not because the lower classes just happen to be more sickly, but rather because the lapse of time between initial appearance of symptoms and arrival at the hospital is longer.

The reference to lower-class, uneducated persons does not imply by any means that the older generations are either lower class or poorly educated. But the mere difference in generations renders the more recent ones more sophisticated in medical matters, if for no other reason than exposure to "popular medicine" articles found in newspapers and magazines.

SICK-ROLE BEHAVIOR

With increasing age, the individual sees his physician or visits a community outpatient clinic more frequently. We are not sure at present, judging from the literature on the subject, whether this frequency is because medical care is really needed or whether the doctor or nurse provides for the elderly person a kind of personal relationship which may be lacking in other places. Evidence both for and against either possibility exists, but in a study conducted several years ago in Memphis of welfare clients attending a community clinic comparisons between older and younger persons showed that the former kept a significantly greater number of their scheduled appointments. This tendency was true when subgroups having similar severity of symptoms were compared. This is not to say that a larger proportion of *all* elderly persons, as compared with younger ones, came to the outpatient clinic, but rather that those who came did so with greater regularity.

Further analysis revealed that older persons who were unemployed and no longer had children living in their homes with them attended more frequently than the ones who had greater responsibilities. It was as if loneliness provoked a gravitation to the doctor's office, or at least to a clinic where the outpatient could come in contact with others his own age. If this interpretation of the findings is accurate, then sick-role behavior had become a way of life not necessarily related to health problems of the elderly! Some of the outpatients, it was observed, remained for hours after the completion of their appointments, sitting and talking with others with whom they had struck up friendships.

Most hospital administrators will confirm that this practice is not an isolated example, but is rather typical of the outpatient clinic culture. It becomes a place for fellowship, a haven for the lonely, and this often results in crowding and inefficient movement in and out and treatment of patients. We have been told that loneliness is more prevalent among the elderly, and, while not universally true, loneliness is more characteristic of the elderly than of the younger. Are hospital clinics, then, condemned to serve a function for which they were never intended? If not, what is the answer?

In many communities senior citizen centers are planned for location in the central portion of the city, easily accessible by public transportation. Many of these centers are multipurpose facilities, and one answer to the problem just described would be to establish a small medical clinic in the center so that the visitor to the clinic could enjoy his fellowship with others, but in that portion of the facility devoted to recreation and the like. Also, with careful planning, a senior citizen center could be located near an already established health clinic so that, following treatment, the elderly outpatient could merely walk to the center without disrupting the clinic schedule.

A discussion of sick-role behavior among the elderly would

be incomplete if some mention were not made of elderly patients in hospitals, and I call your attention to Eisdorfer's earlier comments. Because of the close relationship with doctors that older people enjoyed in their earlier years, many older persons expect such rapport to continue.

There are few of us who do not welcome a close personal relationship with the one who is caring for our health needs, whether we are old or not, and the research bearing on the subject supports the greater benefits accruing to the patient who is not only informed of the nature of his illness and the results to be expected from his medication, but who has the opportunity to converse with the physician and other members of the hospital staff. In other words, the receipt of benefits from a close relationship with one's doctor in the hospital is not idiosyncratic to the elderly patient.

To repeat an earlier phrase, however, life is not so simple. The psychological and sociological soundness of such a proposal welcomes any effort that will allow the doctor graciously to sit and chat with the patient. This practice assumes, though, that the doctor is free to engage in such a relationship, which is not at all the case. I wonder whether it is economically feasible—from the standpoint of the doctor's personal limitations (i.e., his time and energy), and from the standpoint of the hospital's financial situation—to expect the same type of care for the elderly patient that existed a generation or two ago. We will never in the near future have sufficient doctors to provide this type of service.

In some circles, an answer to this problem has been found, as evidenced by the "foster grandparents" programs that are emerging on pediatric wards in large hospitals and have been effective in raising the spirits of the patients. Would it not be possible, by the same token, to develop "bedside companion" programs geared specifically to the needs of elderly patients? These programs could be organized by senior citizen centers or by churches. By using elderly persons to minister to the elderly, both the patient and the companion would benefit, the latter in gaining a sense of worth through contributing to the welfare of the community in which he lives. Similar to the role played by the foster grandparent, the trained elderly bedside companion could care for minor needs, but most important of all, he could keep the patient company.

The implementation of a companion program assumes that the patient will remain in the hospital for a long period of time, and in such cases the toll of loneliness is greatest. Hospitals attempt in every way possible, on the other hand, to move patients out as quickly as they can to make room for new ones, but discharge of the patient when he is medically ready is frequently prevented by the failure to find persons who can care for the patient in his own home. Few would deny that, for both patient and hospital, care in the home is more practical. Sometimes home nursing care is required for months after discharge, and public health nurses, the visiting nurse associations, or hired practical nurses fill this need if they are available. Once a bedside companion program is established, it could be extended to provide services in the home; thus a continuity of care *and* friendship would not be broken once the patient leaves the hospital. The value of this service is seen in the fact that the culmination of the sick role results in either death or a return to a more healthy state. To the extent that friendship itself is valued and maintained, renewed health is more eagerly anticipated.

CONCLUSION

More effort has been expended in the foregoing on the manner in which programs or individual efforts can be focused to understand and be of assistance to the elderly during health and illness than there has been on a thorough understanding of the intricacies of health, illness, and sick-role behavior. For the purpose of this presentation it is appropriate that this emphasis resulted. After all, in the disciplines which today concern themselves with the elderly, an abundant amount of information is available to provide, in modest proportions at least, a more rational basis for ameliorative programs than if the knowledge of these disciplines is ignored. This is not to imply that I am retracting my earlier statements concerning the confusion which abounds because of "half-truths," the frustration of practitioners or policy-makers over the fickle outdating of "scientific logics" basic to reform programs, or the lack of coordination among scholarly findings. These deficiencies still exist, and they must constantly be kept in mind by all of us as we search for more complete knowledge in this important area.

SELECTED REFERENCES

"Age Patterns in Medical Care, Illness, and Disability: United States—July, 1963–June, 1965," National Center for Health Statistics, Series 10, No. 32, Public Health Service, U.S. Department of Health, Education, and Welfare.

"Attitudes Toward Co-operation in a Health Examination Survey," Health Statistics from the U.S. National Health Survey, Series D, No. 6, Public Health Service, U.S. Department of Health, Education, and Welfare.

ELISON, JACK, ELENA PADILLA, AND MARVIN E. PERKINS. *Public Image of Mental Health Services.* New York: Mental Health Materials Center, 1967.

FREEMAN, HOWARD E., SOL LEVINE, AND LEO G. REEDER. *Handbook of Medical Sociology.* Englewood Cliffs, N.J.: Prentice-Hall, 1963.

KASL, STANISLAV V., AND SIDNEY COBB, "Health Behavior, Illness Behavior, Sick-Role Behavior, I: Health Behavior, Illness Behavior," *Archives of Environmental Health,* 12 (February, 1966), 246–66.

————, "Health Behavior, Illness Behavior, Sick-Role Behavior, II: Sick-Role Behavior," *Ibid.* (April, 1966), 531–41.

KNUTSON, ANDIE L. *The Individual, Society, and Health Behavior.* New York: Russell Sage Foundation, 1965.

MADDOX, GEORGE, "Self-Assessment of Health Status: A Longitudinal Study of Selected Elderly Subjects," *Journal of Chronic Disease,* 17 (1964), 449–60.

MARRIS, PETER, AND MARTIN REIN. *Dilemmas of Social Reform.* New York: Atherton Press, 1967.

OAKES, CHARLES G. *Social Psychological Factors in Outpatient Attrition.* Spartanburg, S.C.: Converse College, 1967.

"Planning Welfare Services for Older People," papers presented at the Training Institute for Public Welfare Specialists on

Aging, Cleveland, Ohio, June 13–24, 1965, Bureau of Family Services, Welfare Administration, U.S. Department of Health, Education, and Welfare.

"Retired Couple's Budget for a Moderate Living Standard," Bureau of Labor Statistics, Bulletin No. 1570–4 (Autumn, 1966), U.S. Department of Labor.

ROSE, ARNOLD M., AND WARREN A. PETERSON. *Older People and Their Social World*. Philadelphia: F. A. Davis, 1965.

SHANAS, ETHEL. *The Health of Older People*. Cambridge, Mass.: Harvard University Press, 1962.

YOUMANS, E. GRANT, "Pessimism Among Older Rural and Urban Persons," *Journal of Health and Human Behavior*, 2 (1961), 132–37.

————, "Health Orientations of Older Rural and Urban Men," *Geriatrics*, 22 (1967), 139–47.

PART III

PSYCHOLOGICAL AND PSYCHIATRIC
ASPECTS OF AGING

PART III

PSYCHOLOGICAL AND PSYCHIATRIC ASPECTS OF AGING

Chapter 8. THE PSYCHOLOGY OF AGING
Chapter 9. PSYCHIATRIC ASPECTS OF AGING

Almost everyone feels that he would be happier and more successful if he "understood people" better. The need to understand the elderly is no smaller than the need to understand the young. Increased numbers and proportions of the aged show clearly that the need is greater today than it was in the past. Even without the facts, the "problems of the aged" have been variously drummed into the public, and constant reminders via the mass media urge greater knowledge and appreciation of the senior citizen.

The field of psychology and its medical sister psychiatry show several avenues to an understanding of the individual. Were we all to become psychologically sophisticated, we are told, the problems of understanding might be eliminated. Most of us, though, are not so knowledgeable and lack the time to become so.

Frances Carp and Adriaan Verwoerdt, in presenting a variety of psychodynamic processes found among the aging and aged, perform an important task in correcting the stereotypes that nearly everyone acquires at one time or another. But despite this individuality, certain patterns exist.

Psychological patterns, stressed more by Miss Carp, include the expected changes in sensation and perception, vision and hearing, and mechanisms of response and locomotion.

Changes in learning ability, motivation, and intelligence, on the other hand, will vary from person to person depending on his past educational and other social experiences, a point repeated by Verwoerdt when he advocates that the preparation for old age begins in one's youth.

On learning, Carp says that the old person can learn new things, but this depends largely on whether it is a meaningful experience. Meaningfulness is more likely to have its roots in the past and not in the contemporary society of one's children. If the elderly person is "allowed" frequent reference to the past, motivation to learn is likely to be higher.

How does the oldster adjust to age? Carp claims that there is considerable advantage in seeing oneself in a temporal perspective, something referred to by Verwoerdt as the "life review." The life review is an autobiographical activity, an attempt to tie together the meaningful strings of the past. For those who are younger and devoted to a "more objective" view of life, there appears between the lines Verwoerdt's admonition that for the storyteller even the *invalid* tale is a way of making the present a successful culmination of all that has gone before. Here he echoes Rosamonde Boyd's classification of the elderly as that generation which bears the culture and tradition and gives inspiration for their continuance. Grandparents are the *oral* family historians.

Verwoerdt is not wholly optimistic in his description of the aging process, particularly regarding the organic disorders. In senile psychosis, for example, deterioration of the brain cannot be cured, and little can be done for the individual outside an institutional setting.

Like the subjects covered in each of the chapters, psychology and psychiatry do not operate in a vacuum. Part I, we are reminded, sets the social and cultural context which mediates the psychological and psychiatric findings and generalities, and influences not only the variations in response to changes in personality but also how others define and respond to these.

The insight provided by these chapters will be magnified for the reader who looks ahead to those by Nola Spain and James Ailor and learns how recreational and church programs may be practical settings for implementing the knowledge of the psychologist and psychiatrist.

8

THE PSYCHOLOGY OF AGING

Frances M. Carp

Before you read any farther, take a piece of paper and write down quickly the first thing that comes to mind when you hear the word "old." More will be said of this later on.

WHO IS OLD?

When does one become old? There is an interesting variety of answers. When the National Institute for Child Health and Human Development was started some four years ago, it was necessary, for administrative purposes, to divide the life-span. There was to be a Child Development Program, and there was to be an Aging Program. Where should the division be? There were spokesmen for age 16—not 60. (At 16 the person is too old for the pediatrician.) After much discussion, the dividing point was set at 21. So, for Institute purposes, aging begins at 21.

On the other hand, many persons who are studied by gerontologists insist that they are middle-aged. This is true even for persons who are quite old according to the calendar. For example, the group I am studying in San Antonio generally claimed middle age when they were first interviewed. At that time, in 1959, their average age was 72. We have just completed a re-interview in 1967, and many still identify themselves with the middle-aged!

Frances M. Carp holds the Ph.D. degree in psychology and is associated with the American Institute for Research in Palo Alto, California.

THE ROLE OF PSYCHOLOGY
IN UNDERSTANDING AGING

The National Institute of Child Health and Human Development, the NICHD, has as its mission improvement of the quality of life for persons of all ages, principally by providing scientific information on development throughout the lifespan, to provide a factual basis for action. In this enterprise, psychology lies between biology and medicine on one side; sociology, economics, and community action on the other. Psychology focuses on the experiencing and behaving person —who cannot be understood apart from the physiological human processes which are part of him, or outside the physical and social context in which he lives.

Unfortunately, it might fairly be said that there is, as yet, no psychology of aging. The need for one is great. In general, the older the age group, the more numerous are the determinants of behavior, and the less we know about those determinants. Obviously, regarding any level of development, there are gaps in scientific information, but beyond the achievement of maturity, that is, shortly after the development crisis of adolescence is resolved, there is very little information and a very large gap. The farther one looks on the age scale, the sparser become the data, the more primitive the theoretical formulations to guide investigation, and the smaller the repertory of techniques for data collection. Conceptualization and systematic investigation of the developmental stages of adult life have received little attention.

However, some research has been done, and some information is available about the psychology of aging. Hold in mind, therefore, the following guiding idea. We need to separate aging and damage. Even when the biochemists stop biological aging, every individual will continue to age psychologically in the sense of living longer and of being changed by that living. Also, the longer a person lives, the more opportunity he has to be damaged, physically, physiologically, socially, and emotionally. To develop a psychology of aging, we must distinguish trauma and damage from normal processes. Another way to say the same thing is that we need to separate context effects from essentially age-related changes. Many things so regularly accompany aging in our society that we mistake the effects of these other variables for those of age itself. Poverty, loneliness, poor health, and substandard housing are common among the old today. How differently would people age in conditions of affluence, sociability, good housing, and good health?

In turning to a consideration of some psychological processes involved in aging, some general statements should be made. First, developmental processes, both progressive and retrogressive, go on at all stages of life. Degenerative processes occur in the individual even before he is born. He would not be normal if they did not. Second, these processes of growth and retrogression go on at different times in various functions. Third, they go on with some consistency from person to person. These tendencies among the processes of development result in a similar pattern for almost every characteristic: in general, improvement or growth to early adulthood; a plateau; a period of disturbance about the time of retirement; and then decline, very gradual for most factors until 70 or so but, nevertheless, decline.

Attention was focused first on the decline. Now investigators are turning to studies of the potentialities which the individual has at any point in his life-span, and even to consideration of the possibility of finding some trait which may continue to improve with age. Currently there is interest in the possibility of defining unique and positive characteristics of *every* stage of life.

In defining the general viewpoint of psychology toward aging, we might say that psychology is interested in how the person, as he moves through time, adapts to the situation in which he finds himself, with the capacities he has available. Then we must consider many things, in order to talk about the psychology of aging. We have to talk about sensation and perception—the avenues of awareness of the self and of the situation; the mechanisms of response—the ways in which the person reacts to the situation; his capacities for learning and remembering and thinking. These coordinate experience and reaction and provide the self, which is continuous through time and through very extreme changes. You know that you are the same person you were when you were 12. You know that you are you, regardless of where you might be. We have also to consider motivation and emotion—the power sources of action and reaction, the power sources of learning, and of performing or not performing learned behaviors. Also we must consider attitudes—the residuals of past experience which orient persons to new ones; the adjustment techniques —the habits of performing life's tasks, of solving problems, of meeting challenges, and of withstanding stress; and personality—the self which grows and develops and recedes, and which mediates experience and behavior.

SENSATION AND PERCEPTION

Increasing age generally is accompanied by a loss in sensory acuity. It takes a stronger signal to get through to us. It takes a greater difference between two stimuli to be recognized as a difference. However, there is not a one-to-one relationship between the amount of loss and the consequences in behavior. People compensate. We extend our arms to great lengths and we wear glasses. Much less willingly we put on hearing aids. We can increase illumination. We can pay better attention. Some people learn to read lips and do not even know they are doing it. People use other modes of perception which help them perform better. Older people, even though their vision is getting worse, often check on what they are doing with their body parts by looking at them. They have to have this additional signal to let them know for sure where that foot or that hand is. These are positive things which help to compensate for loss in visual acuity.

However, all of the everyday habits of reacting have been built up on the basis of earlier levels of visual and auditory acuity. A lifetime of habit has been based on 20–20 vision, and now you do not have it. Information is received incorrectly or partially, which leads the person to make mistakes.

This makes the person, as he ages, become hesitant. He loses confidence in himself. Sometimes he denies the sensory loss. This is perhaps the saddest thing to do. People refuse to accept the fact that they no longer hear things, and they become withdrawn. They think that people are not trying to include them or even that they are trying to exclude them. They think they are left out of things, and consequently they become so.

In summary, everybody must expect to have visual and other sensory losses, but there is no one-to-one relationship between the loss and the consequences in behavior. This depends on other characteristics of the person.

In addition to the loss in sensory acuity, the aging person experiences increasing difficulty in dealing with complex stimuli. For example, it becomes increasingly difficult for the person to "see" the two possible pictures in a reversible figure, which looks one way when you look at it once and differently when you look at it again, or to find hidden figures —as in the child's puzzle in which the task is to locate so many lions in the drawing of a tree. Sensory input is further impeded as we age, because we have greater difficulty in keeping out irrelevant stimulation. As a consequence, an older person is bothered more by noise than is a younger person. It intrudes on his perception of the task. Fourth, and very importantly, perception is hampered by the person being rushed. These statements hold true generally for all sense modalities.

VISION

Now, to look at some of the senses separately. Vision is often considered the most important. We use it by far the most. This is a visual world. If any of you have ever had anything to do with blind children, and the very hard task of helping them to develop normally, you must be impressed with the importance of vision. This is getting away from age, but to stress the importance of vision I want to tell you about a youngster. At age three he was a little vegetable who had absolutely no behavior, no response, no nothing. He could not sit in a chair, he could not walk without being supported on both sides, his head hung down, and the only thing that he did was sort of crunch down on the floor and rock back and forth, and once in a while bang his head on the wall, and that was all. He had been blind from birth. It was thought that he also was hopelessly mentally retarded, and he was about to be institutionalized. Following years of patient, insightful work on the part of his parents, this child is now in high school and has been with a normal-sighted class of his own age for many years. He bowls, he rides horseback, he swims, he dives, he competes with sighted children in the regular classrooms. Without very specially designed stimulation, his development would not have proceeded beyond vegetable. Loss of visual capacity is a very great handicap.

Paradoxically, though their vision becomes less accurate, aging people become more dependent on vision. They begin to use visual cues to augment or correct kinesthetic, proprioceptive and auditory cues, which they are also losing.* For example, as I said a minute ago, some old people start lip-reading without knowing it. When they are about to step down off a curb, they look at the foot, because they are not really sure where it is.

What are some of the changes that go on in the eye which make it a less effective instrument? The size of the pupil grows smaller with age, and so less light is let in to the retina. Focusing becomes less accurate, and this reduces accuracy of vision. Sensitivity to glare increases. Lens opacity increases, and cataracts are increasingly common with age.

To give you an idea of what aging might be like within a few years, I would like to mention the work of the Doctors Colombré. This is a husband-wife research team which has recently come to the NICHD. They are observing now that if you take a chick embryo and remove the lens tissue and

---

* Kinesthesia refers to the sensation of movement or strain in muscles, tendons, or joints. Proprioceptive cues are those excitations which originate in muscles, tendons, or joints and are important in giving a "sense of balance."

mash it all up and scramble it around and put it back in, and if you do this at the appropriate time in development, it will sort itself out and develop into a fairly accurate lens. If you take a mouse embryo lens and mash it all up and scramble it about and put it in the chick eye, you will get a fairly good chick lens. Someday, they are going to figure out what causes this and perhaps learn how to instruct the aging human eye to replace its opaque or cataractous lens. "Aging" will change for many persons on that day!

Another thing that happens to the aging eye is that dark adaptation becomes slower and less effective. Perhaps some of you have noticed when you walk into a movie that it takes you a few more minutes standing at the back before you can see the room and people around you.

What do all these things mean for the person who is undergoing them? This is the important thing. Somebody has said it's too bad that little girls start putting on makeup just when their mothers need glasses and don't know it. More serious things than that occur because of sensory and perceptual changes. For example, one of the things which is not so well known is that color vision holds up better than visual acuity. There is a story about a very elderly man who was in a nursing home. The staff and his family were becoming quite concerned about him because he used his water jar interchangeably with his urinal. They thought this indicated serious deterioration of character. Finally, somebody said, "They're differently shaped, true, but he's pretty old and his vision is pretty bad. Why don't we try making one of them red and one of them green, and see what happens?" He never confused them again. He was not disorganized or deteriorated; he just did not see very well!

HEARING

As we age, our audition also becomes less acute. We have hearing loss especially for high frequencies, but also for low ones. Men have a worse time than women. We do not know whether this reflects an occupational damage factor, whether it's genetic, or what. Maybe it is *the latter* because men are not as highly motivated to hear what is going on!

The level at which auditory loss is handicapping to a person depends on many things. For one thing, it depends on how bright he is. A more intelligent person can interpret speech sounds even though he is quite a bit deafer. He does not do any better with pure tones, but he does better in communicating with people. The behavioral effect of hearing loss depends also, of course, on one's listening habits. Perhaps the most serious effect of hearing loss is withdrawal from others. For some reason, people find it hard to acknowledge hearing decrements. Eyeglasses are accepted much more readily than are hearing aids. Some old persons become suspicious and reclusive as a result of hearing failure.

KINESTHESIS

Perceptions of changes in body position and of orientation in space become less accurate with age. Ordinarily we are not aware of these sensations and perceptions. We orient our bodies and know where our parts are without thinking about it. If you want to become aware of them, get somebody to put you in a swivel chair and spin you around. You used to do it as a child. You would sit in a swing and twist the ropes and then let go and spin and be all giddy. After spinning in a swing or chair, your eyes go back and forth from side to side, and you cannot stop them. If you think you are too big for a swing, put some cold water into one of your ears. Then have somebody watch your eyes. These reflexes are at their strongest—and nobody knows why—between 40 and 50 years of age. This is one bit of behavior that matures and comes to its peak very late. I could not tell you what good it does at that stage of life, but there it is.

Falls may be related to the changes in proprioceptive and vestibular senses, and falls are a serious problem with older people* Body sway also increases with age. When people

---

* Vestibular refers to the "balance mechanism" contained in the chambers of the ears.

stand up, put their feet together, and shut their eyes, the older ones fall over more quickly.

These proprioceptive and kinesthetic perceptual changes probably cause the increased use of visual checks. Together with reduced visual acuity, they contribute to the increased tendency to fall.

OTHER SENSES

In regard to the other senses, much less work has been done. There is probably not much change in taste until at least 50 and not very large changes until after 70. The same is probably true of smell. There is very little change shown in sensitivity to pain until past 70. Generally, we find sensory-perceptual decrement with age, and we find more marked change at about 70 years of age. As we age, we can expect the world to impinge on us not quite as strongly.

MECHANISMS OF RESPONSE

And, then, how about the response side? With age, there is a loss of strength and agility. Perhaps the most impressive change in the response repertory is the slowing. We do not really know why this slowing occurs. Reaction time, that is, receiving the stimulation and making a simple action, starts slowing shortly after age 20. On the other hand, movement time, for example, tapping as rapidly as you can between signals, does not decline until after age 70. Spontaneous speech speed holds up also. People aged 70 can talk as fast as those who are 17, as you probably already knew! However, other complex tasks slow down. Writing is slowed with age. Anything unfamiliar that is introduced into the task further reduces the speed. Any extraneous stimulation that does not have to do with the task slows it also. Pressure for speed—trying to get the person to speed up—tends to make him slower and more prone to make errors. If the task cannot be completed in a certain amount of time, the older person seems to lose the instructions, and he may not complete the task at all.

Young adults are more adaptable in changing speeds and changing behavior. For example, if you tell people to write very slowly, then to write very quickly, then to write at their normal speeds, young adults and children will write at quite different rates. The older people give you the same speed, no matter what you tell them!

With regard to getting older people to respond, we might make some general statements. First, they need plenty of time for preparation, and they need a signal to let them know that the task is just about ready to begin. They need an adequate reminder of what the task is, particularly if it extends over a long period of time. They need to have plenty of time to respond. Ideally, they should be allowed to perform at their own rate, to self-pace rather than to be paced from the outside. They will do less well with unfamiliar material. We must remember that because of sensory-perceptual changes they will need a strong, clear signal and an environment which is without distractions.

LOCOMOTION

So far this has been a fairly abstract discussion. Now let us turn to what we might call personal skills, things like locomotion, getting around in the world. There is a very high accident rate past the age of 65, especially from falls. Most of the falls are at home, so they are not because of unfamiliarity. Also, there are many pedestrian accidents. You can see from what we have said about perception becoming less acute, about response becoming slower, and about habit patterns which were built up on perception and reaction capacities of younger years, that the person can have quite a lot of difficulty. He can really get out of phase with himself. There is what Dr. Lawton calls "convoy behavior" among older pedestrians. Have you ever seen an old person at a corner tentatively start and then pull back, and then start and pull back again, and then finally spot a younger person who looks competent and follow him across the street? Well, they do this because they cannot get all of the signals and necessary motions timed together and proceed across the street before the signal changes. Either we will find new ways to design traffic patterns, or we will kill many old people as signals increase in complexity and as traffic demands increase pressure for speed.

In driving automobiles, accident rates decline until about age 50. Then they start up, but they are not closely related to age until about 65. However, by the time a person is 70, he is more apt to have a wreck than is a teen-ager. There are different types of accidents at different ages. Under age 30, most accidents are caused by going too fast. Over 65, speed is not a factor, but other things are. Older drivers tend to get in trouble over right-of-way. They tend to get confused with complex stimuli such as several traffic lights. If there are three lights, two of them for people going straight ahead, and the left one for those making a left turn, an older driver may go ahead when a left turn is signaled, or he may turn left when it is appropriate only to go straight ahead. He has three lights to watch in a complex visual and temporal pattern, and apparently he cannot cope with this situation, particularly because there is time pressure. Older adults also have accidents involving turning. Apparently, again, there is difficulty in pacing and in coordinating the stimulus-response patterns that are involved in turning an automobile.

OCCUPATIONAL SKILLS

Some studies done in agriculture report what you might expect about occupational skills. The kinds of accidents that can be avoided by using good judgment tend to occur among the young farmers. The older farmer tends not to have accidents that could be avoided by good judgment, but he does have the kind that could be avoided by rapid evasive action.

Industrial accidents are lowest among older workers. People 65 and older have a very low rate of industrial accidents. However, the industrial worker past 65 is a highly selective phenomenon. He probably is among the best, and was all his life. On the other hand, he probably has the oldest machine, which is most likely to have accidents. Old workers have high accuracy rates and low absenteeism rates. They are a select and highly motivated group. This is a very special group.

Another interesting group is pilots. "Old" pilots are between 40 and 60, because it's hard to find pilots past 60. During this age range, from 40 to 60, the accident rate goes down. A pilot aged 40 is more likely to have an accident than is a pilot aged 60. If you take a group of pilots all of whom have the same number of hours of flying, you find a negative correlation between age and the accident rate. I cannot explain it, but there it is—among pilots with equal experience, greater age is associated with less likelihood of accident.

LEARNING

I used to have my students in General Psychology imagine for a minute what it would be like if everybody in the room walked through a little black box and came out the other end with every effect of learning gone. Would I know that I am me? Would I know that this is an object and not a person? Or that this table is not me and this hand is me? Would we know what to eat or how to eat? Imagine what it would be like if everything you had learned were gone.

Imagine, even, that at some point in the life history we were to lose only the capacity to acquire *new* knowledge. Even that seems pretty disastrous. Does such a loss occur with age? Though we have thought there was such a tendency, actually there is little evidence of change in learning itself. What is learned is effected by sensory input. If the signal is too weak, the person cannot learn from it. Learning scores are affected by slowing of responses. Learning in older people is also blocked by anxiety in the learning situation. It is reduced by a lack of interest in what we give them to learn, and by a lack of motivation to learn. It is reduced by disease processes. There are problems in regard to the learning of older persons, in signal strength and interference, pacing and motivation, which for a time made it appear that learning itself declined with age. Now, we are not so sure. Here is some anecdotal evidence from the old people I studied in San Antonio: Some of them moved into a fancy new apartment house that had stoves that it would take an engineer to run. They were push-button affairs. Everybody was very worried that these people would starve to death because they would never be able to learn how to use the stoves. A woman from the service department came out and gave one demonstration, and there was no problem. Motivation was strong, and the task was easily accomplished.

There is better evidence than that. An Englishman named Belbin has extremely interesting research to report. He compared 12-year-olds with older workers in two kinds of learning tasks. One was rote learning, just memorizing, and the other was problem-solving, in which they had to think a bit. He gave them two different approaches to this learning task. In one he told them exactly how they had to do it, and in the other he said, "Here's the problem, go do it." He found that with the problem-solving, if you prescribed absolutely how the learner had to go about the problem, the 12-year-olds did much better than the older workers, but if you allowed them to approach the problem in any way they could, the old workers did better. Dr. Belbin suspects that these old workers were less docile than the 12-year-olds and that this may have had something to do with it.

Dr. Belbin found another very interesting thing. Among his old workers, any kind of continuing education—making baskets, baking pots, studying engineering, it did not matter what—was definitely associated with good capacity to learn in old age. Maybe we should get back to that concept psychologists have been telling people to forget, the idea of "strengthening the mental muscles." There are no "mental muscles," but there is something up there that needs to be used. If it is used, persons may continue to learn, perhaps as well as they did at any age, perhaps better. Learning can be facilitated in older persons by chemical means, and learning can be facilitated by putting the older person in a learning situation which does not scare him to death.

INTELLIGENCE

Closely related to learning ability is what we call intelligence. At present, we really do not know what the relationship is between IQ, that is, intelligence test scores, and age. Partly, this is because we have absolutely inadequate instruments for older persons. Look at the basis on which intelligence tests are standardized. They should include material that is familiar to everyone who takes the test; each person should be at ease and motivated to do his very best on the test; and each person should find the material interesting. The tests are not applicable to people who are not just like the standardization group. On whom did we standardize intelligence tests? Well, not on old people, to any great extent.

Old people do not have experience in common with standardization groups on most of our tests. People in my San Antonio study absolutely refused to do the arithmetic subtest. They said they simply would not do it, and they had a lot on their side. They would tell me, "Look, nobody had even thought of the new math when I went to school." They would not expose themselves to looking ignorant. This does not mean they were unintelligent. This group, even without the arithmetic subtest, scored higher than the typical adult aged 40 to 45.

Intelligence tests are not interesting to old people. If they are honest with you, they will tell you that they think tests are silly. And they are! Old people are not motivated to take these tests, or, if they are motivated, they are usually threatened by the experience. We keep equating the *do do* with the *can do*. The whole basis of intelligence tests is that we are getting a person's best effort, when he is comfortable in the situation. We certainly do not meet these requirements with old persons.

One other thing in comparing test performance of older people to that of younger people today—test-wiseness. People who are old today have not been put through test after test after test after test, all of their lives. Youngsters are test-wise. Old people are definitely not.

In attempting to summarize, it can be said that most studies on intelligence show a declining score with age. But there are some equally good studies that show a rise. Some show no change. We do not have the definitive study. We do know that factors other than age enter into the figures. For example, education—years in school—is more closely related to IQ than age is. Studies of age differences in IQ confound chronological age and education. Most people now complete high school, and college attendance is common. On the other hand, people who are past 65 have, on the average, about eight years in school.

We know that the original level of intelligence affects the score in old age. The "haves" get, and the "have-nots" lose. People who were originally brighter tend to hold up their scores better than those who were less intelligent. Nevertheless, Dr. Carl Eisdorfer found a drop in IQ score, even among a very high-level group of professional men who were well motivated to perform for him.

We also know now that IQ drops with serious illness. A very clear drop in intelligence test score usually heralds death. Actually, a drop of IQ score is the best predictor of death that there is today. In some sense, the decline in IQ with age is an artifact. The older the age group, the higher the death rate. So, when we take averages of IQ scores, the older the group, the more of these suddenly dropped scores are included. If we eliminate from the average those people who are within a year of death, intelligence score does not change very much.

MOTIVATION

Not a great deal is known about the needs and motives of older persons. Research investigators and practitioners generally agree that one driving need among older persons is independence, self-reliance, freedom. Another is the need to be useful. One clear-cut characteristic of persons as they age is accentuated individuality. Individual differences increase with age. Along with this, there seems to be a strong need to be oneself, and a deep satisfaction in maintaining one's identity and usefulness.

ADJUSTMENT TO OLD AGE

One facet of man's "higher mental processes" is the capacity to see himself as he moves through time. This is a great advantage in adjustment because it allows man to profit from past experience and to anticipate the future. He can try out possible solutions mentally and wait to act upon the best one. However, this capacity also subjects man to regret over what is past and gone, to anxiety over what may lie ahead, and to hopelessness.

As the person moves through life, his adjustment tasks change according to the developmental period; his capacities and situations alter; the rewards and satisfactions differ. All are related to society's "norm" for that age.

Now let us turn to the point raised in the beginning—that the intrinsic processes of aging must be differentiated from the effects of damage, and that context effects must be distinguished from essentially age-related change. Many other changes so regularly accompany aging that their effects may be perceived as those of aging itself.

How does our society define old age? To be old is probably to be poor (one-third of those past 65 exist below the poverty line). To be old is almost surely to be, at least, poorer than in earlier years. (Even good retirement incomes are sharply less than working incomes.) This relative and absolute poverty affect all aspects of life—housing, transportation, hobbies, community service, church attendance, contact with friends. It limits all aspects of freedom, individuality, and usefulness. It makes dependence an ever-present threat.

To be old is to have more ailments and less adequate medical care, because the old are poor, and because they have chronic ills and do not know that they can feel better. The doctor's "What do you expect at your age?" is taken too literally. This situation may change with medical research, with provision of medical services, and with concern for their utilization.

To be old is to be useless to others and to be devalued by them. Now look at the word you jotted down. Studies show consistently that people of all ages—old people, too—hold negative views of old age. No one wants to be old. Few want to serve the old. A small fraction of the national resource dollar is spent toward improving their lot.

CONCLUSION

The extending years of life—and of life beyond work—are for many people today a degrading and demeaning span. However, the years of later life provide opportunity for attainment to higher developmental levels than mankind has yet reached. It is said that a person and a society achieve "higher" goals such as self-realization only when subsistence needs are easily met. Just when they achieve leisure, which is also requisite to "higher order" development, we thrust our old people back to primitive concern with subsistence. When society defines and accepts aging as a normal developmental process, involving new levels of experience and behavior, and deserving of value—only then will we be able to understand the essential processes of psychological aging—because only then will we see them.

SELECTED REFERENCES

BIRREN, JAMES E. *The Psychology of Aging.* Englewood Cliffs, N.J.: Prentice-Hall, Inc., 1964.

BOTWINICK, JACK. *Cognitive Processes in Maturity and Old Age.* New York: Springer Publishing Co., Inc., New York, 1967.

9

PSYCHIATRIC ASPECTS OF AGING

Adriaan Verwoerdt

Geriatric psychiatry (geropsychiatry) is a psychiatric discipline which aims at the study of the normal and abnormal psychology of aging, as well as the treatment of psychological disorders associated with growing old.

THE PHENOMENA OF SENESCENCE

Although old age is usually defined as the phase of life beyond age 65, it is better understood as a psychosocial episode. It is "a period of withdrawal from usual occupational roles, progressive loosening of ties with others, and depletion of physical and psychic energy." It is characterized by changes in the balance between the individual and his environment, as reflected in retirement, enforced or voluntary, gradual or sudden; in decreasing energy due to aging or illness; and in separations and losses inevitably associated with longevity. Decline, withdrawal, retirement, and disengagement—all these concepts point to the central issue of involutional change.

AGING AND HUMAN DEVELOPMENT

PERSONALITY: Healthy old people apparently show no dramatic personality change with age. When, however, certain

Adriaan Verwoerdt, M.D., is on the staff of the Duke University Medical Center, Durham, North Carolina.

psychological tests (projective techniques) are used to study ego function, a difference emerges between the responses of middle-aged and aged individuals. The middle-aged perceive themselves as assertive and energetic, but the aged person tends to see the world as complex and perhaps even dangerous, and he responds by being more mild or conforming. Thus, as certain coping abilities become less effective in dealing with inner drives and external stresses, the overall personality pattern may undergo certain changes. Again, it is important to remember that there are marked individual differences, and that any glib generalizations about the "aged" should be avoided. Some people are psychologically old at the age of 50; others become creative, for the first time, in their 60's or 70's (e.g., Grandma Moses).

Different personality types have been described, each with a characteristic pattern of adjustment to aging. Some are considered well adjusted; e.g., the "mature," who take a constructive rather than an impulsive or a defensive approach to life; the "rocking chair" group, who take it easy and lean on others; and the "armored," who have a well-developed system of defenses against anxiety. Others are considered to be poorly adjusted: the "angry men," who blame others, and the "self-haters," who blame themselves for their frustrations.

Practical Implications: No attempts should be made, in general, to alter lifelong character patterns as they occur in aged individuals. The effort, time, and money involved in such attempts would be better spent in preparing younger age groups for that phase of human development which is senescence and the senium. Such "educational" efforts include a great variety of activities: retirement counseling for the middle-aged; training in leisure activities for all ages; enhancing the "public image" of old age; adequate general education for all young people; efforts to combat poverty; community mental health activities. In conclusion, preparation for old age should begin in the younger years. It has been said that a happy old age is the reward of a life well lived.

SENESCENCE AS A PHASE IN HUMAN DEVELOPMENT: When we speak of the psychological experiences of the last phase of life, the emphasis here is on the word *last*. Although we may conceive of aging in terms of decline, this decline is a movement toward a final end. It is this that distinguishes senescence from all previous life phases (e.g., adolescence). The latter have a beginning and an end which, at the same time, is a new commencement. Besides being a temporal determinant, the term "the end" also connotes the element of purpose, goal, or task. In previous developmental stages, the end of a phase is, at the same time, the goal and task toward which development is aimed. Toward which end is the stage of senescence aimed? Can we speak of a goal or task in senescence, as we do in previous life phases?

The progressive series of losses which the aged person faces foretell the final end. Grief and anxiety concerning losses may also be experienced and seen as dimensions of grief and fear concerning one's own death. Although the fact of death is an objective "fact of life," one's own position vis-á-vis death is an intensely personal matter. It is here that we may speak of a developmental task and of mastery, in the sense that a person comes to view his own death as the appropriate outcome of his life. Death is then not the submission to a blind fate, but the acceptance of life's end in terms of its fulfillment. The mental activities involved in the attempt to integrate an overall perspective of one's life have been described by R. N. Butler and James E. Birren as the life review.

LIFE REVIEW: A person's life may be reviewed by looking backward from the end toward its beginning. Those who deny that death might be imminent have no need to review. The task of the life review is to integrate one's life as it has been lived in relation to how it might have been lived. The life review is not a passive process, but a constructive effort to achieve a purposeful form of reminiscence. These reminiscences of older persons serve not primarily to recall facts, but to weave them into a harmonious perspective. Fantasy and confabulation may even be utilized, to reconcile the past, present, and expected future. The aged person wants to write a revised or corrected autobiography, as it were, to be left with those who survive him. The forms of the life review may range from a nostalgic recall to severe depression with anxiety, guilt, and suicidal tendencies. In general, the life review should not be viewed as a psychopathological phenomenon, but as a common normal experience. The lifelong personality of the individual is likely to influence the way in which he handles the life review; also, whether he feels he has much time or only a few days to get his psychological house in order. The person's characteristic patterns of coping with conflict may be used to resolve his terminal conflicts. (For example, does he tend to involve other people, or does he try to think things out by himself?)

Practical Implications: Any program of care for the aged (physical, psychological, social, economic) is, to a large extent, meaningful only to the degree that it assists the aged individual in his final quest for meaning. Of course, this is stating the case in terms of what is ideal; the ideal being the attainment of a final perspective (Eric H. Erikson's concept of "integrity"). In reality, many persons may not be sufficiently introspective or concerned about "meaning"; or they may be preoccupied with the comforts and discomforts of the present. On the other hand, persons with a lifelong religious faith are likely to have some preoccupation with the meaning and the "rightness" of their life. Also, individuals who suffer from more than average illness or disability tend to struggle with the question, "Why does it happen to me?" It is obvious that the minister, priest, or rabbi has an important role in this area. Because the reminiscences may be annoying to others, they are often deprecated as a sign of deterioration of the aged person, or as aggressive behavior to "capture the ears" of others. In counseling with relatives of aged persons, it is important to explain the function of reminiscing and to give advice concerning how to react to it, i.e., that it would be "poor technique" to try to correct the "wishful fantasy" element in the reminiscences, and that rather acceptance and listening are called for. Reminiscing and the life review may be carried out in the privacy of one's mind, or it may involve an audience. A certain degree of "audience participation" would be extremely desirable, because the issue, "Who am I and what have I been," is closely related to the notion of what one is and has been for others. In view of this, opportunities may be created that facilitate the sharing of reminiscences (e.g., the day care center, walking clubs). Even more desirable, but more difficult to arrange, are those situations in which the aged person can transmit his own personal experiences (or the insight and wisdom derived from them) to members of younger generations, as discussed in an earlier chapter by Dr. Rosamonde Boyd. A natural setting for this is the relationship between aged persons and their grandchildren. Perhaps, in a careful and experimental sort of way, other opportunities could be explored for selected aged members of the community to tell younger people "what things were like in bygone days." Such endeavors, if successful, would enhance a sense of continuity between generations. It would not be necessary to involve all of the aged citizens in this; the more eloquent and verbally gifted individuals can speak in behalf of their fellow aged—the latter obtaining a sense of satisfaction by way of identification with the speaker and by way of "vicarious gratification." The considerations that underlie the shaping of one's final will are probably closely related to the psychological processes of the life review. In the life review, there is much concern with the image the individual wishes to leave behind. This may lead to deathbed gifts, forgiveness, reconciliation of lifelong feuds, and the transmitting to others of one's own interpretation of the meaning of life. In some cases, there will be a need for protective services, for example, when serious emotional disorders or impaired brain function have undermined the aged person's ability to evaluate reality correctly. Such a person may squander his money and resources in the false belief that he should make up for past shortcomings. Successful resolution of terminal conflicts usually has important implications for the surviving relatives and friends. From this, it is obvious that there is a need for skillful counselors to help the dying, the relatives, and friends, lest past interpersonal conflicts get increasingly distorted and perpetuated for another generation.

OLD AGE AS A CONSUMMATORY PHASE: Returning once more to the notion of "goal" in that phase of human development designated as senescence, but, interestingly, also as "the golden years," the following question is posed: In view of so much decline, how can old age be called "the golden years"? Is this a deceptive euphemism, or does the phase contain an element of truth?

Talcott Parsons suggests that, as a kind of counterpoint to the basic instrumental emphasis of our culture,* old age should come to be viewed as a consummatory phase. It should be the period of "harvest" when the fruits of previous instrumental commitments are gathered in. The tendency has been to think of the enjoyments of youth as the prototypes of consummation (the pleasures of exhibiting physical prowess, of sexual gratification, etc.) and to think of old age as entailing a renunciation of the "best" things. In contrast, the last phase of life could be viewed as a reward for a life well lived. What is needed is a reward system offered by society which makes it clear that for most persons it is good to be old. This reward system needs to be delicately tailored to the highly differentiated and specific styles of life which it is to reward. In addition, there is the task for older people themselves to learn to interpret their own life situations in appropriate terms, and to view old age as an opportunity for the sheer enjoyment of the consummatory phase of life.

Practical Implications: These notions, of course, lead us to the concept of leisure and leisure-time activities. Leisure

---

* Instrumental activity refers to "how things are accomplished," and has meaning for the types of skills required for various social roles and for the ways in which different social roles are coordinated to accomplish some cooperative activity.

refers to "private time," the time one has for oneself and during which one is free to engage in "private activities." The latter can be described in terms of "hobby," recreation, or private work (in contrast to the occupational work role). Training in leisure-time activities would seem to be an essential part of any retirement counseling. In addition, specific advice and counseling services could be made available to the post-retirement aged. Certain programs can be developed to acquaint the aged person with a variety of recreational activities and to provide a training experience in the area of his interest. Such a program can be carried out by a day care center, church groups, the Golden Age Society, a local school or college, community art groups, etc. Of course, any continuous education for the elderly is basically a specific instance of "high level" re-creation.

EMOTIONAL REACTIONS TO STRESS AND LOSS

Fear is the normal emotional reaction in response to impending injury or damage. *Anxiety* represents the danger signal in response to stresses that arise from within and which are anticipated to cause conflict and distress (e.g., loss of control over unacceptable impulses). *Grief* occurs when damage or loss actually has taken place. The danger, injury, or loss which is anticipated and to which the person is reacting may be either actual (real) or imagined (existing in fantasy only). The more a person reacts to imagined dangers and losses, the more the psychological capacity of reality evaluation is impaired. In a neurosis there is only a mild to moderate impairment of contact with reality, while in a psychosis the impairment is severe or total. Thus a psychotic patient may live entirely in a fantasy world. A number of aged individuals tend to withdraw from reality and to retreat into their inner selves in order to "live off" their memories. In senility (advanced senile regression) there is frequently a complete break with present reality, the patient being totally engrossed in his past and the people contained within his past. Such a complete withdrawal into fantasy is the final outcome of a long process—a process which frequently begins with the experience of significant losses.

GRIEF AND DEPRESSION: As was mentioned earlier, aging is associated with the inevitable experiences of loss. Normally, the emotional response to a loss which actually took place is a grief reaction. This should be distinguished from "depression," which, although difficult to define in exact terms, is generally considered as a pathological emotional reaction. A grief reaction may or may not merge into a depression; conversely, a depression may or may not be preceded by a grief reaction. A grief reaction, then, is characterized as follows: it involves a clear and conscious recognition of an actual loss; following the initial emotional "shock," there is an increasing realization of the significance and of all the ramifications of the loss; during this period there are recurring episodes of specific physiological sensations of distress and "waves of sadness"; finally, toward the end of the grief reaction (which may last from 3 to 12 months), there is a resolution which involves a redirecting of energy and interest toward new people, goals, or activities. Important for our discussion here is that a successful resolution may become difficult or even impossible under certain circumstances. This happens when the individual used to have mixed feelings toward that which was lost. The term *ambivalence* designates such a coexistence of both positive and negative feelings. A person who has mixed feelings about having something will also have mixed feelings about not having it. On this basis, the resolution of one's feelings concerning a loss may become too difficult, so that the grief reaction, being prolonged and gaining in momentum, merges into a depression. In such a depression, guilt feelings are likely to be relatively prominent. Most depressions in the aged, however, are characterized by feelings of apathy and "emptiness" rather than guilt. The reason for this is that an accumulation of many losses of all kinds can deplete the individual's inner resources.

Since the experience of loss is inevitable in old age, grief and depression are common in the aged. But there are other psychological responses to losses and stressful changes. These behavioral responses may be either healthy (adaptive) or pathological (maladaptive). The latter are characterized by the fact that they lead to a vicious circle by aggravating the very problem they are directed against. A number of maladaptive psychological reactions will be mentioned.

First, the individual many deny, to himself and/or to others, that a particular loss has occurred or that a particular problem exists. A cardiac patient, for example, may deny the seriousness of his condition or minimize the extent of the limitations imposed on him by the illness. If such a denial is excessive, it may seriously interfere with medical treatment.

Secondly, a person, when faced with a loss or problem, may develop a reaction of anger and protest. (Why does it have to happen to me?) Anger usually seeks a scapegoat, and certain people, especially those who are aggressive by nature, have no trouble finding something or someone whom they can blame for their predicament. This behavior is mal-adaptive because it keeps the individual from seeing the true state of affairs and also because his angry and accusatory behavior alienates those around him.

Third, the aged person may respond by withdrawing from other people. He may feel, for example, that closeness to others involves too many risks. Thus, he retreats into a state of protective isolation and insulation. Such a move away from others is maladaptive because it entails, at the same time, a move away from reality itself. Thus, the stage is set for a proliferation of inner fantasies and, finally, senile regression.

Lastly, the individual may react to a loss by becoming overly helpless and dependent. A certain degree of increased dependency on others is normal and desirable following a loss or during a state of illness. But excessive helplessness and dependency create new complications all their own. If such undue helplessness is allowed to persist for some time, the individual's image of himself changes accordingly. Consequently, rehabilitative efforts toward increased self-care will become more difficult.

Practical Implications: In any depression which is associated with strong guilt feelings, there is a risk of suicide. In aged men, suicide occurs relatively frequently. The recognition and diagnosis of depression can be rather difficult because the depressive feelings may be hidden behind a facade of hypochondriasis and physical discomfort (lack of appetite, insomnia, constipation, etc.). The "case findings" and diagnostic efforts in this area should be developed in the framework of community mental health services organized by the mental health team under the supervision of a psychiatrist (who is well versed in community psychiatry and/or geropsychiatry). It is probably useful from a practical point of view to consider the possibility of some type of depression in any aged person who comes to whatever agency for whatever type of help. As a screening device, a simple questionnaire (specifically designed for this purpose) can be used routinely to detect the possible presence of depression. Most depressions respond fairly or even quite well to proper treatment. When a depression is characterized by "emptiness," apathy, and lack of responsiveness, it is easy to make the mistake of considering the depressed aged patient as being "senile," that is, suffering from the effects of irreversible brain changes. This is a serious diagnostic mistake, because, rather than treatment of the depression, the patient may be given only custodial care instead. Another serious mistake would be to continue treating only the physical symptoms of a person whose physical distress is really the manifestation of an "underlying" depression. The best cure, of course, is prevention. More or less complete prevention of depression on a community-wide basis is not feasible with currently available means and techniques. But a logical initial step would be to acquaint key people in the community with the basic concepts and manifestations of depression.

This knowledge would enable them to be alert to potential "trouble areas," to recognize situations that may produce depressions, and to initiate proper intervention where actual depression is suspected. Space here does not permit a review of the phenomena of depression. What could be done in the community is to organize seminars, a conference, or "institutes" that are specifically devoted to this topic. The seminar could be in the form of an annual one-day meeting; or it could take the form of a more or less continuing, on-going training or consultation program. Whatever form it takes, the participants should include social caseworkers, public health nurses, clergymen, welfare workers, operators of boarding homes and nursing homes, etc. Of course, it would also be possible to have seminars on other kinds of emotional disorders which may occur in aged persons (e.g., schizophrenia, senility, organic brain syndrome).

An example of a regular ongoing seminar series on the psychological and psychiatric aspects of aging is the Duke Geropsychiatric Consultation Program for the North Carolina Department of Public Welfare. This statewide program that provides in-service training to a total of 180 welfare workers became effective in the spring of 1966. The state has been divided into eight areas; each week there is a one-day conference in a particular area for the welfare workers in that area. The morning sessions are taken up by didactic presentations on the psychology and psychopathology of aging as well as the various treatment approaches. In the afternoon session, there are presentations of cases (prepared and submitted ahead of time by the welfare workers). These cases illustrate specific psychological or pathological phenomena and are discussed by the geropsychiatry consultant. Audiovisual materials (video tapes and films) and specially prepared reading materials have been used all along. It is our aim to develop a "canned course" that consists of a manual (comprising the didactic presentations and illustrative case material) and an "audiovisual library." The entire course could be taught in about eight sessions of four hours each. Different instructors would be able to utilize the same basic course materials. Such a training project can be developed for various groups, both professional and nonprofessional.

PSYCHIATRIC ILLNESSES IN LATE LIFE

Mental disorders in the aged that begin in old age fall into two major groups: (a) disorders in the absence of brain damage (psychogenic disorders); and (b) disorders in the presence of brain damage (organic disorders).

Of course, any of the mental disorders of youth and early adulthood, such as schizophrenia or alcoholism, may persist into old age, to be modified or complicated by events in the senium. Many of these individuals may have escaped long-term hospitalization (due to good physical health, economic resources, or family protection). In addition, there are a large number of persons who have grown old in hospitals (chronic schizophrenia, recurrent mood disorders, mental deficiency, chronic alcoholism, etc.). Many exemplify the "institutional syndrome": their symptoms are related to having been removed from normal social interactions. If such persons behave in a meek and quiet manner or appear to be well adjusted to institutional life, they are considered candidates for transfer to nonhospital facilities or for discharge. Often this does not result in a return to the community but simply a shift in institutions.

PSYCHOGENIC DISORDERS: These are related to psychological causes and interpersonal factors rather than organic brain damage. A psychogenic disturbance (neurotic, behavioral, or psychotic) may persist from youth into old age, or may appear for the first time in the aged person. In *psychotic reactions* the disorganization of the personality is extensive, and adaptive efforts in the social, intellectual, professional, and religious spheres are often ineffectual. Failure to evaluate reality correctly is a cardinal feature. The psychotic disorders include:

(1) Involutional psychotic reaction *is a depression (without previous history of depressions) and usually occurs in the 40's or 50's and in individuals of compulsive personality type. Most cases are characterized chiefly by depression. Sometimes the depression is manifested by preoccupation with diet, bowel movements, or general health. Agitation or psychomotor retardation, loss of appetite, insomnia, and constipation are frequent. An outstanding characteristic may be clinging and ingratiating dependency on another person, but this dependency may be so burdensome as to provoke hostile rejection by others. Delusions of extreme poverty or having committed grave and unpardonable sins are frequent. Auditory hallucinations, e.g., accusatory voices, may occur. Regardless of the symptom picture, the disturbance in mood is the outstanding sign; hence, the phrase "mood disorder." Mood disorders are characterized by a marked disturbance of mood and a secondary disturbance of thought and behavior.*

(2) Manic-depressive reaction: *Alternating, marked mood swings from depression to elation, remission, and recurrence comprise the essential features of this mood disorder. The manic type demonstrates increased verbal and psychomotor behavior. Rapid flow of ideas may be noted. During this phase the individual may engage in unwise business deals and extramarital romances. The depressed type manifests depression of mood. Psychomotor retardation is prominent; agitation or stupor may occur.*

(3) Schizophrenia, *by and large the most significant and malignant mental disease in general, usually begins in early adulthood and may, of course, be carried over into old age. Schizophrenia is a psychosis characterized by emotional, intellectual, and behavioral aberrations. There is an incongruency between the individual's thought content and ideas on the one hand, and his emotional responses on the other hand. The emotional feelings tend to be inappropriate or, at other times, seemingly absent. Thought and speech may be profoundly disturbed and bizarre. The schizophrenic patient may have absurd beliefs (delusions) and suffer from hallucinations. There are various types of schizophrenia, and one of these, paranoid schizophrenia, may have its onset relatively late in life. Compared with other types of*

schizophrenia, the overall personality organization remains comparatively intact in paranoid schizophrenia. The central feature is a disturbance in thinking with paranoid delusions (e.g., the false belief that one is persecuted).

The person suffering from a *neurosis* does not grossly distort reality or exhibit great personality disorganization. Anxiety, either consciously felt or unconsciously controlled by the utilization of certain psychological defense mechanisms, is a cardinal feature of the neuroses. The anxiety is caused by an "internal" threat, such as threatened breakthrough into awareness and expression of certain unacceptable urges, e.g., aggressive impulses. The various coping and defensive techniques for handling the anxiety give rise to the neurotic disorders. In a neurotic *anxiety reaction,* the anxiety is not controlled by a defense mechanism and the individual experiences a nameless dread. This differs from fear in that neurotic anxiety arises in the absence of a specific external fear-provoking or threatening situation. In a *conversion reaction,* anxiety is "converted" into symptoms in organ systems; the psychological conflict is converted into physical problems, which decreases anxiety. In a *phobic reaction,* anxiety is displaced from one idea or situation onto a substitute or symbolic one. The individual then attempts to control his anxiety by avoiding the phobic (substitute) situation. In an *obsessive-compulsive neurosis,* persistent undesirable ideas are associated with the compulsion to perform certain ritualistic acts. The person may realize the unreasonableness of his behavior but is compelled to perform the acts anyway. In a neurotic *depressive reaction,* self-condemnation and guilt partially relieve the anxiety. Absence of psychosis and lack of malignant symptoms distinguish this disorder from the psychotic depressions. As was mentioned earlier, depression in the aged is characterized by relatively little guilt; hypochondriasis and bodily overconcern, on the other hand, are very common.

Typical for *personality disorders* (or behavior disorders) is that internal discomfort and a sense of anxiety from within are singularly lacking, in contrast to the neuroses in which anxiety plays a paramount role. Disturbing and/or maladaptive behavior patterns and interactions with the environment are prominent instead of neurotic or somatic symptoms. Lifelong personality disorders may either become aggravated or alleviated in the course of the aging process, depending on many factors. A person who, for example, is characteristically aloof and suspicious (a schizoid or paranoid personality disorder) may become more so as the years go by. Such a person may finally present a clinical picture which is difficult to distinguish from paranoid schizophrenia. On the other hand, certain personality disorders characterized by poor impulse control, such as alcoholism or periodic violent behavior, may ameliorate in the course of the aging process. Perhaps this improvement is related to an age-related decrease in the strength of inner drives and impulses.

BRAIN DAMAGE (ORGANIC) DISORDERS: *Organic brain syndrome* constitutes the largest group of institutionalized older persons with mental disorders. Most of these patients are physically impaired, and they are the stereotype of old age posing the most immediate problems of medical, psychiatric, and social care of all groups of aged persons. If masked by physical complaints and illness, the mental impairment may not be recognized. Since complete social recovery of persons with brain syndrome cannot be expected, the condition calls for continued supervision and protection. Also, these persons require continuous or intermittent general medical care which they are often unable to afford or to find.

Organic brain disorders are characterized by impairment of orientation, memory, intellectual functions, and judgment. Lability of emotion is usually present. The syndrome may be *acute* (potentially reversible) or *chronic* (irreversible brain damage); and it may be mild, moderate, or severe in its manifestations. The psychotic reactions most commonly associated with chronic brain syndrome are paranoid states and depressions, with or without agitation. The causes of organic brain syndrome include infectious processes, either within the nervous system or elsewhere in the body; drugs, alcohol, or poison; trauma; circulatory disturbances; convulsive disorders; disturbances of metabolism; and neoplasms.

(1) Cerebral arteriosclerosis *is a chronic brain syndrome resulting from recurrent episodes of* focal brain damage. *The most frequent cause of focal (localized) brain damage is thrombosis of cerebral blood vessels or carotid artery blockage. The person with cerebral arteriosclerosis is initially aware of losing his physical and mental powers, and he usually reacts to this loss with feelings of depression. Attempts to ward off or defend oneself against the threat of disintegration may involve the use of certain defensive maneuvers such as regression, denial, etc.*

(2) Senile brain atrophy *is the causative factor in chronic brain syndrome when* no focal neurological signs *are present, and when there is no history of stroke. This disorder (senility) is most common after age 70 and occurs at a later age than cerebral arteriosclerosis. It is often insidious in onset; its progression may be introduced by ill-defined emotional disorders or by clear-cut depression. When environmental circumstances are supportive, the individual may be able to compensate for functional loss with relatively little emotional upset. Good early education, high occupational and economic status, and the early acquisition of socially acceptable patterns of behavior tend to protect against troublesome behavior. Social behavior may be so well preserved as to mask severe memory deficit and disorientation.*

RELATIONSHIP BETWEEN PHYSICAL AND PSYCHOLOGICAL FACTORS: Into most, if not all, illnesses, psychological factors enter sooner or later: either early as a contributing etiologic factor or relatively late as a complicating factor. This is particularly true in geriatric illnesses, which represent psychosomatic problems par excellence. In a psychosomatic sequence of events, for example, latent organic illness may be precipitated, or existing organic illness aggravated, by psychogenic factors. Thus, for example, anxiety may lead to hyperventilation (abnormally fast breathing), and this in turn may upset a delicate cardiac-pulmonary balance in a cardiac patient. Following the psychosomatic approach, one would, in such a patient, evaluate and treat the physical and the psychological signs and symptoms at the same time. The psychosomatic approach is of special practical significance because of the many specific psychotherapeutic and rehabilitative techniques which it entails. Clinical skills in this area require thorough acquaintance with geriatric pathophysiology and an understanding of psychological processes supplemented by and integrated with clinical experience. Such skills are a necessary prerequisite for effectively implementing the principles of comprehensive treatment programs for the aged.

Psychological reactions that result from alterations or losses of structure and function of organs depend on the personal meaning of the illness to the patient, the changes in the body image, and the vicissitudes of the illness situation (the doctor-patient relationship and the changes in the patient's social role). In fatal illness, the life-threatening nature of the disease may override all other aspects. The existence of these secondary psychological reactions is responsible both for suffering per se and for aggravation of the primary physical illness.

Not infrequently, a patient may complain of symptoms that suggest physical illness, but careful examination reveals no organic pathology. These patients are "psychosomatic" in the sense that their physiological distress is a manifestation of a psychological disorder such as hypochondriasis. The management of these patients is difficult and requires a careful balancing of psychotherapeutic techniques and regular medical attention.

SOME PRACTICAL IMPLICATIONS FOR COMPREHENSIVE SERVICES

Comprehensive services are based on the recognition that the condition of a given aged person is influenced by physical, psychological, interpersonal, cultural, economic, and environmental factors. These factors interact with each other in a complex manner, and, in view of this, comprehensive services should have a built-in element of flexibility. If one wishes to implement the principles of both comprehensiveness and individualization of service, then any rigidity in organization should be avoided. For example, a person with a serious economic problem should be in a position to receive assistance just as quickly as a patient with a serious physical illness. Likewise, a person with an emotional problem or psychiatric illness should receive adequate and appropriate help as soon as possible without having to go through all sorts of unnecessary "channels." In order to attain this goal of combined comprehensiveness, flexibility, and speediness of services, essentially two major primary community services are needed: a central agency that gathers and distributes information; and the entire spectrum of agencies, facilities, programs, etc., concerned with the various specific aspects of medical care and health maintenance.

THE CENTRAL AGENCY: This collects and distributes information relevant to aging and can be likened to the senses and the brain of an organism. One appropriate name for such a service would be Information and Referral Service (IRS). Its basic functions include the following:

(1) To make itself highly "visible" and well known to the entire community, especially the aged. This can be done with the aid of local newspapers, radio, and television, as well as by the distribution of special brochures and pamphlets.

(2) To initiate, facilitate, and organize local meetings for the purpose of planning for new services and review of existing services. A broad and representative cross section of the community, including a number of aged persons, should participate in this planning monitoring.

(3) To initiate appropriate channels of contact and communication between important local services and facilities. For example, the moving of aged individuals from their own homes to boarding homes, nursing homes, the general hospital, or the mental hospital (or subsequent moves between these various places) is not well regulated in many communities. To a large extent, this is due to lack of coordination between these institutions.

(4) To make special efforts aimed at locating those aged persons who have problems. Such "case finding" is facilitated by regular local publicity about the existence of the Information and Referral Service; in addition, it requires the active interest and participation of key people in the community, such as physicians, the clergy, social caseworkers, the Department of Public Welfare, and the Department of Public Health.

(5) To provide aged persons with information about existing community resources, to make proper referrals, and to help the older person find his way through "the system."

To these basic functions other services can be added depending on specific local needs and conditions. Thus, if the Information and Referral Service is located in the outpatient clinic of a hospital, certain medical services may be incorporated into the basic structure. Be that as it may, the IRS should have clear channels of communication and collaboration with all other agencies and services that are relevant to the aged. Actual physical proximity of the IRS to other facilities is desirable from a practical point of view.

THE SPECTRUM OF COMPREHENSIVE SERVICES: These will now be reviewed briefly.

(1) Diagnostic centers or well-aging clinics, *located in the outpatient clinic of a general hospital, in the local Department of Public Health or Public Welfare, or associated with a day care center or a high-rise apartment for the aged. Specific attention should be given to the problem of* transportation *to the diagnostic center. Some aged people have trouble driving; others have no car or live far away. Transportation for and of aged people can be organized by several community groups, for example, the church, the Welfare Department, the Golden Age Society, etc. Perhaps there may be some merit in considering the idea of using one or more buses (of the school bus variety) for the purpose of transporting aged persons to such facilities as the diagnostic center, the hospital clinic, the day care center, the recreational center, etc. The expense of operating such a specific transportation system for the aged will have to be solved by the community as a whole.*

(2) Extended care facilities *include, by and large, nursing homes and the geriatric units of mental hospitals. Some general hospitals have facilities for chronically ill patients. Also, a relatively large home for the aged may be in a position to develop an infirmary associated with the home. It is difficult to make generalizing statements about the question of which type of facility is the most desirable. The answer frequently depends on local conditions. This caution in generalizing also applies to the statement frequently heard today that "elderly patients in a mental institution should return to the community as soon as possible." Indiscriminate application of such generalizations leads to "passing the buck" from one institution to another and passing the patient from pillar to post. Frequently such moves only represent administrative (pseudo) solutions, and the aged patient is the victim of the resulting confusion. It is well known that aged people have a low tolerance to repetitive change of environment. Again, mutual understanding between institutions concerning each other's goals and methods might prevent much of this confusion. Representatives of the local hospital, departments of Public Health and Public Welfare, the mental hospital or mental health clinic, nursing and boarding homes—all of these might be involved in such policy planning.*

(3) Home care programs *may be developed by local hospitals or the Department of Public Health. These programs are aimed at keeping certain patients at home, thus preventing the need for more expensive hospitalization. The home care team consists of a physician, a visiting nurse, and various auxiliary therapists (physical therapy, dietitian, social caseworker, etc.). Such home care problems can be combined with other services such as "meals on wheels," "friendly visitors," or church volunteers. Again this points up the need for a central agency that can coordinate the various services for a given individual and determine which "package" of services is indicated.*

(4) Homemakers *can provide some basic assistance to the aged in their own homes. Certain aged persons have specific limitations in various areas which make it impossible for them to carry out basic activities at home. For example, an arthritic patient may be able to care for himself at home except in such things as shopping, doing the laun-*

dry, and washing dishes. In such a case, a homemaker-housekeeper who visits regularly may make the difference between the individual's staying at home and being institutionalized. Attendants *actually live in with the older person or the older couple, or they may spend only part of the day. Attendants may be recruited from among the aged person's relatives, his neighbors, etc. The attendant receives free lodging and in addition some compensation for her services in the home. The total expenditures involved are likely to be less than in the case of admission to an institution.* "Friendly visitors" *are trained volunteers who visit the aged in their home or in the institution. Aged individuals who are in reasonably good health may be encouraged to become friendly visitors themselves.* "Meals on Wheels" *refers to the service of bringing meals to the home. This would be especially useful for aged persons who are isolated, who require special diets, or who are physically incapable of preparing meals.*

(5) The day care center *is a facility at which an aged person can remain during the daytime. Such a center may offer a number of services and opportunities. The older people have a place to meet and to get to know each other. Group activities such as games can be carried out with the help of a recreational expert, or independently. Associated with the center may be also a physician, psychologist, or social worker who could provide counseling and guidance, or who might conduct group therapy sessions. Medical-geriatric facilities may be included as well. In planning a day care center, careful attention should be given to the question of types of services that will be needed to make the center maximally effective in view of the local conditions in the community. Ideally, there should be enough space around the center to make gardening possible (each person his own little garden area); to keep pets on the premises; to go outside for walks on the grounds, etc.* Recreational *activities can be organized by interested volunteers, or by specifically trained recreational therapists. These activities include games, sports, discussion groups, plays and role-playing, music and dance, and so on.*

(6) Mental health services *can be made available through the facilities of the local mental health clinic, a nearby mental hospital, the outpatient clinic of a general hospital,*

*the day care center, etc. These services are extremely
important in view of the frequent emotional disorders associated with physical illness, isolation, or deprivation. Effective mental health services can be offered by a team of
professionally trained individuals; the psychiatrist, the psychologist, and the social caseworker represent the core of
such a team.*

Preventive mental health services are perhaps *more* important than the treatment of chronic mental disorders in
the aged. What is needed in community mental health programs is: (a) methods of finding and treating acute situational problems such as crises due to death of spouse or due
to physical disability; (b) counseling and guidance with
regard to such problems as retirement, social role change,
altered family relationships, and leisure-time activities; (c)
assistance to families who are caring for disabled or emotionally disturbed aged relatives; (d) consultation and collaboration with other community agencies, e.g., with regard
to release planning for institutionalized aged patients; and
(e) organizing institutes, seminars, or conferences for other
professionals in order to transmit information about emotional aspects of aging.

REFERENCES

BEREZIN, MARTIN A., AND STANLEY H. CATH, "Geriatric Psychiatry," *The Boston Society for Gerontologic Psychiatry, Inc.*
International Universities Press, New York, 1965.

BIRREN, J. E. *The Psychology of Aging.* Chapter 12. Englewood
Cliffs, N.J.: Prentice-Hall, Inc., 1964.

BUTLER, R. N., "The Life Review: An Interpretation of Reminiscence in the Aged, *Psychiatry,* 26 (1963), 109–14.

CATH, STANLEY H., "Some Dynamics of Middle and Later
Years: A Study in Depletion and Restriction," *Geriatric Psy-
chiatry,* ed. Martin A. Berezin and Stanley H. Cath (New
York: International Universities Press, 1965), 21–72.

COWDRY, E. V. (ed.). *The Care of the Geriatric Patient,* Chapter 2, "Psychologic Aspects," by W. Donahue and R. Stoll.
St. Louis: C. V. Mosby Co., 1963.

CUMMING, E., AND W. HENRY. *Growing Old: The Process of
Disengagement.* New York: Basic Books, 1961.

ERICKSON, E. H., "Identity and the Life Cycle," *Psychological Issues*. New York, International Universities Press, 1959.

LINDEN, M. E., AND D. COURTNEY, "The Human Life Cycle and Its Interruptions: A Psychologic Hypothesis," *American Journal of Psychiatry* (1953), Vol. 109, pp. 906–15.

PARSONS, T., "Old Age as Consummatory Phase," *Gerontologist*, Vol. 3, No. 2 (June, 1963), 53.

REICHARD, S., *et al. Aging and Personality*. John Wiley and Sons: New York, 1962.

VERWOERDT, A., AND C. EISDORFER, "Geropsychiatry: The Psychiatry of Senescence," *Geriatrics*, 22 (July, 1967), 139–49.

ZETZEL, E. R., "Dynamics of the Metapsychology of the Aging Process," *Geriatric Psychiatry*, ed. Martin A. Berezin and Stanley H. Cath (New York: International Universities Press, 1965), 109–19.

ZINBERG, N. E., AND I. KAUFMAN, eds. *Normal Psychology of the Aging Process*. New York: International Universities Press, 1963.

ZINBERG, N. E., "Geriatric Psychiatry: Need and Problems," *Gerontologist*, Vol. 4, No. 3 (September, 1964), Part 1, pp. 130–35.

PART IV

THE ECONOMICS OF BEING OLD

PART IV

THE ECONOMICS OF BEING OLD

Chapter 10. HIGHER INCOMES FOR OLDER
AMERICANS
Chapter 11. PROBLEMS OF THE AGING IN
WORK AND RETIREMENT

*Are there problems any more tangible than those resulting
from the lack of an adequate income? When the two papers
included in this section were first presented at their respective
institutes, conferees responded more emphatically than to
any other single paper or group of papers. Not only is the
picture of poverty repugnant to most people, but the experience of a drastically reduced income upon retirement is a
feared encounter. In these chapters, one is required to recognize the dramatic basic and essential importance of money
in influencing many other areas of life.*

Juanita Kreps exposes the fallacy in assuming that present
guarantees of retirement income will be sufficient for an adequate level of living at the time retirement is reached. If
inflationary trends continue, the purchasing power of the
dollar now will be appreciably decreased by the time the
individual retires. Further, if the retirement period lasts for
a period of twenty years, which is not unlikely considering
the increasing longevity of the American population, then
what may even be adequate at the beginning of retirement
could be miniscule at the conclusion of the retirement years.

The answer, says Miss Kreps, will come, in fact has now

arrived, with increases in payroll taxes, which will be further increased in the future. To what extent continued increases in payroll taxes will be required will depend on the overall state of the American economy, as well as on a more basic question: how much will the public willingly underconsume during the years of employment in order to be consumers during the period of retirement?

Miss Kreps bases much of her discussion on the statistics of *median incomes,* and for this reason the more elaborate discussion by Ida Simpson aids in specifying the degree to which we should be concerned about *different* segments of the older generation. Mrs. Simpson, in some respects as pessimistic as Miss Kreps, does not paint an attractive picture of employment practices which are viewed by many today with much consternation: compulsory retirement is not only recommended but practically mandatory. The economy cannot cater to the elderly to the detriment of the younger population which must support itself. Industry, we know, cannot discriminate in its hiring practices on the grounds of age, and, as mentioned by Frances Carp earlier, older persons can still perform many economically useful jobs. But much more research is needed to increase the list of occupations capably handled by the old in order to circumvent the inconveniences of obsolescence of abilities due to rapid modernization of work opportunities.

However, Mrs. Simpson carefully points out, in a manner similar to authors of previous chapters, the inappropriateness of generalizing to all the elderly those conditions that characterize a visible disadvantaged group frequently the focus of reformers and policy-makers. These are the lower strata of blue-collar workers who will require some kind of continuing part-time employment following retirement, for which they are not financially prepared.

Mrs. Simpson's solution to the problems caused by forced retirement is based on the contention that older people do not change their basic patterns of living after they retire. Knowledge of an individual's work life is a means of predicting his style of retirement: the executive and professional groups have resources and interests that extend beyond the necessity for community planners to plan for them; the middle strata, because of their occupational backgrounds, will probably be able to assume various positions on a temporary and intermittent basis; the lower blue-collar workers seem the most in need of help to cope with retirement; however, they are the least likely to know how to get it or, if it is available, how to use it. This last group is most in need of community services, and Mrs. Simpson suggests a public registry which would put individual employers in contact with elderly persons who could do gardening, handiwork, etc.

10

HIGHER INCOMES FOR OLDER AMERICANS
Juanita M. Kreps

I believe in materialism. I believe in all the proceeds of a healthy materialism—good cooking, dry houses, dry feet, sewers, drain pipes, hot water, baths, electric lights, automobiles, good roads, bright streets, long vacations away from the village pump, new ideas, fast horses, swift conversation, theatres, operas, orchestras, bands,—I believe in them all for everybody. The man who dies without knowing these things may be as exquisite as a saint, and as rich as a poet; but it is in spite of, not because of, his deprivation.

—FRANCIS HACKETT, IRELAND

Materialism, as Francis Hackett has described it, can be discussed without apology. And it is particularly relevant to the status of the aged, who, accustomed in the past to sharing both the production and consumption of "things," may now find themselves denied both roles. It is perhaps more painful to suffer a sudden drop in income than never to have tasted the benefits of materialism. While it may be better to have earned and lost than never to have earned at all, it is also more unsettling. The transition from a full-employment to a retirement income can be a difficult one, for it will probably involve a severe change in living standards. A comparison

Juanita M. Kreps is professor of economics, Duke University, Durham, North Carolina.

between income figures for the elderly and those for under-64 members of the population confirms this.

INTRODUCTION: MONEY INCOMES OF THE AGED

The median income in the United States for all persons aged 65 and over is less than half that of those who have not yet reached 65. In 1966, families headed by a person over 65 had a median income of $3,645 or only 46 percent of the median ($7,922) for families with younger heads. For single persons the difference is even greater. The median income of aged individuals was 42 percent that of younger individuals: $1,443, compared with $3,443.

While incomes of both groups have been rising since 1960, that of older persons has not increased as much as that of persons under 65. The median incomes for families with heads under 65 has increased by $2,000 in the last six years, but families with heads over 65 have seen an increase of only $750. The income of the unrelated individual under 65 has risen almost $900 during this same period, while that of the older person has gone up less than $400. These figures indicate not only that older Americans are living on less than half the money income of younger persons, but also that the income gap between the older and younger segments of our population has been widening over the past several years.

RETIREMENT INCOMES AND EARNINGS

Comparison of the median income of the old with that of the young is useful for some purposes; it is important to know where in the life-span poverty is most frequently found. But a more meaningful comparison may be between the income received during the latter part of work life and the income received during retirement. For it may well be the magnitude of the drop in income, on retirement, that is relevant.

Along with the problem of the income drop at retirement is the equally pressing question: what happens to the retiree's relative income position during the years of his retirement? The retirement span is now long enough to permit a significant worsening of his income relative to that of persons still at work. At age 65, a man's life expectancy is about 13 years, and that of his wife, who is probably slightly younger, is almost 20 years. If there is any lowering of retirement age or increase in life expectancy, the couple's nonworking period may extend to two full decades.

During these 20 years dramatic changes are likely to occur in the income position of those persons in the labor force. If the economy's real rate of growth were as high as 4 percent annually, the total output of goods and services would roughly double in two decades. Active persons and their families would thus enjoy a 100 percent increase in real incomes, while the bulk of the retirees continued to live on incomes that were fixed. To the extent that prices rose, the aged's income position would be worsened even further.

Offsets to their relative decline in income would be available only insofar as older persons were able to continue working, at least on a part-time basis, or retirement benefits grew in some rough accord with the overall growth of the economy. Arrangements for tying the Social Security benefits to the cost of living, although an important safeguard in periods of inflation, would not meet the need to keep retirement incomes in line with the incomes of persons still at work. The central question comes to be, then, to what extent (and through what mechanisms) are older people to share in the growth in national output?

SOURCES OF INCOME: It is important to remember that growth in real income for persons of all ages comes from the same source: increased output. The rate of economic growth thus sets the limit to the pace at which we can raise incomes. The better our technology, the more efficiently we use our manpower and other resources, the faster incomes can rise. But whereas productivity will provide the goods and services with which to raise future levels of living for all age groups, persons share in this growth in accordance with their income claims—claims which accrue to retirees via the tax mechanism (and Old Age Survivors and Disability Health Insurance benefits) or through private saving. If we would raise the income of the future retiree, we must therefore increase his capacity to save during work life or raise the Social Security benefit by transferring a larger income claim to him through the taxation benefit scheme. In either case, consumption is foregone during work life in return for consumption during retirement. For the present generation of retirees, further private savings are not possible; their incomes can be increased only by raising retirement benefits.

EARNINGS-BENEFIT COMPARISONS: It is important also to note that the spread between earnings and retirement benefits will grow even wider as long as growth raises the incomes of workers faster than we are willing to raise retirement benefits.

As an illustration, suppose we take a male clerical worker, high school graduate, who is 50 years old in 1969. He was 40 years old in 1959, when, according to census data, the average annual income for his occupation and educational level was $5,695. If we assume that his income changed in accordance with the age-related change for his occupation, and that he also enjoyed an annual growth-component increase of 3 percent, his income at age 50 would be $7,727. Extending the same assumptions for the remaining 15 years of work life, his annual pre-tax income would be $11,376 at retirement in 1983.

In contrast, his retirement benefits will probably be not more than one-third the estimated income at the time of retirement. A recent projection of incomes in old age estimates that in 1980 about half the couples and more than four-fifths of the unmarried retirees will receive $3,000 or less in annual pension income, both public and private. Three-fourths of the couples will be receiving pension incomes of $4,000 or less, with only about one-eighth having pensions of more than $5,000. When the 1980 estimates are corrected for price change (assuming that the 1955–65 price rise of 1.6 percent yearly continues till 1980), 81 percent of the retired couples are expected to have a real pension income plus asset income of $4,000 or less; the comparable proportion for 1962 was 84 percent. Continuation of past rates of growth in pension benefits, or even some slight acceleration in rate, will thus probably do little more than offset price rises.

Public pensions, which in this country are financed by payroll taxes on the incomes of persons still at work, transfer income claims against the nation's total output for workers to retirees. It is important to note that the transfer is from the workers in 1969 to the retirees in 1969, and not from a man who works in 1969 to the same man when he retires in 1989. The retiree of 1989 will have an income claim against the 1989 output, and his claim will be financed by a tax on the workers of that year. Transfers of income claims thus reallocate the annual output between workers and non-workers (including the young as well as the old), the measure of this redistribution being dictated largely by congressional decision.

Public policy in the United States has provided for a floor of income for retirees, but there has not yet been an attempt to use Social Security benefits as a means of smoothing the humps and valleys of income in any broad, life-range manner. The problem of poor fit between earnings and consumption needs persists, and is in fact accentuated by the rise in productivity and real earnings of persons at work. A shortening of work life relative to total life-span further complicates the problem of financial planning.

Reluctance to provide more generous public pensions for retirees reflects in part a failure to recognize the lengthening retirement period as a new life stage, and in part a belief that each family is in charge of its own financial destiny. Hence, private savings are expected to achieve whatever income-smoothing, beyond certain minimum pensions, is desired.

Yet Social Security benefits will obviously need to rise; debate hinges on the question of how fast this increase should be, and on the proper direction of tax policy. As to the extent of the increase in benefits, the wide gap between earnings and retirement incomes indicates the range within which income "smoothing" might advantageously occur. But even if benefits are raised to the point where this gap is minimized, the improvement will be temporary unless public policy also deals with the relationship of earnings and benefits through time. Until benefits are in some way tied to the growth in real income, the relative position of the retiree will lag behind earnings.

Further increases in payroll taxes will, of course, be necessary if benefits are to be financed exclusively from this source. Raising the taxable base will help to reduce the regressivity of the payroll tax, but significant increases in the rate may again raise the question of whether we are not taxing one low-income group heavily to raise the incomes of another. Discussion of general-revenue financing for some portion of retirement benefits is long overdue.

REFERENCES

BROTMAN, HERMAN B., "Income of Families and Unrelated Individuals, 1966," *Useful Fact No.* 29, Administration on Aging, Department of Health, Education, and Welfare, September, 1967.

KREPS, JUANITA M. AND DONALD E. PURSELL, "Lifetime Earnings and Income in Old Age," Joint Economic Committee, 1967.

SCHULZ, JAMES H., "The Future Economic Circumstances of the Aged: A Simulation Projection, 1980," *Yale Economic Essays,* 7 (Spring, 1967), pp. 145–212.

11

PROBLEMS OF THE AGING IN WORK AND RETIREMENT

Ida Harper Simpson

Retirement is becoming a new stage in the life cycle. By life cycle, I mean the stages of one's life: childhood, adolescence, adulthood, retirement, and possibly old age. Old age is usually used to refer to the age grouping of individuals who have retired. I prefer to call this stage of the life cycle retirement. When and if retired individuals become infirm and feel that they are old, they might then be classified with old age, but, as long as they feel that they are not old, to refer to them as old is to misrepresent their view of themselves. Retired individuals who are in fairly good health tend not to think of themselves as old, despite the fact that those younger than they think of them as old. That they do not is probably a reflection of the connotation of old age which suggests an image of a helpless, dependent individual. Such an image lends little ego support to the aging individual, who, given the problems he so often faces, needs to feel secure about himself. Therefore, to call this stage of life retirement is more appropriate to the situation of the aging individuals who are experiencing the situation. The limitation of this con-

Ida Harper Simpson is Research Associate, Department of Sociology and Anthropology, Duke University, Durham, North Carolina.
Preparation of this paper was supported in part by the Center for the Study of Aging and Human Development, Duke University, and research funds from the Public Health Service (HD-668) made available to the Department of Sociology and Anthropology through the Center.

ception is that it does not pertain directly to women who have not been in the labor force and who have not retired. Such women, however, are most likely to have a husband or to have had one, and they tend to be identified by the work status of their husbands.

Retirement is an emerging stage of the life cycle created by the technological advances of our society. During this century we have seen adolescence emerge as a stage of life. Before the turn of the century, when children were thought of as a financial asset, they tended to move directly from childhood to adulthood. But with industrialization and the emergence of age barriers in the employment of the young, adolescence came into being. We at this time see the emergent process of retirement as a stage of life, likely to be experienced by most employed individuals. We have known of retirement for some time, but the retirement of the past decades was a luxury which only the rich could afford. Today it is not an exclusive claim to leisure; it is for most mandatory without any recourse. The structure of the labor force suggests that retirement cannot be escaped by most workers; it is a fact of life, supported by much evidence.

Male participation in the labor force is related to age. The lowest rates of participation occur among the old and the young. In September of 1965 the participation rate for males between the ages of 14 and 19 was 41 percent. The rate increased rapidly to 86.9 percent for the age group 20 to 24, and reached its peak of 97.6 percent for men between the ages of 25 and 44. Thereafter, participation declined: for men between the ages 45 and 54, the rate dropped to 95.3 percent and for men 55 to 64, to 84.3 percent. At this age point of 65 and over the rate dropped sharply to only 28.3 percent. (The female pattern of participation differs from the male pattern. Age affects it, but not so much as does childbearing. For this reason, and also because men are most often heads of households, discussion will be restricted mainly to men.)

What does this curvilinear pattern of participation by different age groups reveal? It shows that our labor force does

FIGURE 1. Rates of Participation in the Labor Force by Different Age Groups, September, 1965.

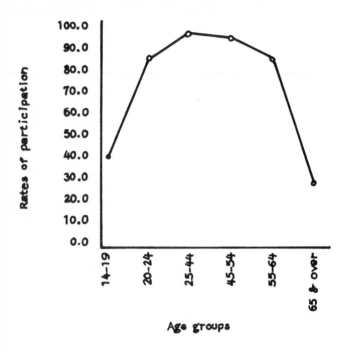

not need all the manpower available in our society. Almost 60 percent of the males between 14 and 19 and slightly over 70 percent of those 65 and over are outside the labor force. This underutilization of the young and the old by our labor force contrasts sharply with the labor force participation in nonindustrialized countries. Underdeveloped economies tend to use almost as high a percentage of their young and their old as of the in-between age groups. The average work life in nonindustrial societies is considerably longer than in ours. In 1965 the average expected work life in the United States was only 44 years.

Another characteristic of the curve of participation in the labor force (Fig. 1) is that it peaks at the age grouping 25–44; decline is evident thereafter. This pattern indicates that the age 45 is a significant one in the labor force. At age 45 men begin to experience difficulty securing employment. They enter the downward slope of participation in the labor force, characterized by age barriers. Some may withdraw voluntarily, but most who leave the labor force before age 65 undoubtedly are unable to find employment.

Still another characteristic evident in the curve of participation is an established cut-off age. The sudden dip in participation between the age groups 55 to 64 and 65 and over shows that a mass exodus from the labor force occurs between these age groupings. The extent of difference in the participation of the two oldest age groups (a difference of 56 percent) suggests widespread compulsory retirement at age 65. Many older individuals look forward to retirement, but, whatever their anticipation, alternatives to withdrawal appear limited. A minority, however, continue to work. Those who do tend to be self-employed or to work for smaller companies. Small companies more often than large ones employ older workers. Thus, this minority of the oldest workers who stay in the labor force tend to do so by being able to control their own destinies through self-employment or by having their desires for work taken into account by their employers. Opportunities for such control, however, are not widespread. Most employment is in large companies, which are less likely to adapt employment to the capacities and desires of their workers.

We have seen from the rates of participation in the labor force that older men are disadvantaged, and that the disadvantages appear around age 45. The extent of the difficulties older workers face in securing employment is partially indicated in the relation of their occupational representation to their total employment (Table 1). In 1960 approximately 37 percent of the employed labor force was 45 years of age and older. Their representation in the occupational structure, however, deviated from this percentage in all but three occupational groups. It was about equal to their total employment among the sales occupations, semiskilled operators, and skilled craft work. The old were overrepresented in farm-

TABLE 1. Representation of Males 45 Years Old and Over Among Occupational Groups in 1960.

Occupational Groups	Representation relative to total employment of older workers		
	Under-represented	Equally represented	Over-represented
Professional and technical	*		
Farmers and farm managers			*
Managers and proprietors			*
Clerical workers	*		
Salesmen		*	
Skilled workers		*	
Semiskilled workers		*	
Service workers			*
Laborers	*		

ing (about 16 old farmers to every 10 young ones), managerial and propriety occupations (about 13 older ones for every 10 younger ones), and service work (a 12 to 10 ratio); and underrepresented in the professional and technical occupations, clerical work, and laboring jobs. The older worker's best chance for being employed is in farming and in the proprietary occupations, where he is self-employed, and in low-paid service jobs such as janitorial work. His chances are about equal to those of the younger worker in sales, semiskilled work, and skilled craft work, and considerably less in professional, technical, clerical, and laboring occupations.

The disadvantages of older workers in these occupational groups are not truly represented by their employment ratio. The bulk of older workers in all occupational groups, with the probable exception of service work, are likely to have held their jobs for long periods of time. They tend not to leave a job voluntarily, because they fear they will be unable to find a new one and because of the fringe and pension benefits which they have invested in their jobs. Their equal representation in sales, semiskilled, and skilled work probably arises out of long tenure in their jobs. This tenure among semiskilled and skilled workers may have been protected by unions, to which large numbers of these workers belong. Even among farmers and proprietary workers, chances for securing work are overstated. Even if an older worker had the inclination and skills for entering these occupations, the capital needed for self-employment precludes trial by most older people.

Why are older people so handicapped in securing employment? Much of their difficulty may be indicated by juxtaposing their occupational representation to the changing occupational structure (Table 2). At the time these older workers entered the labor force, the occupational structure was quite different from what it is today. Skills of the older workers tend to be acquired before entering the labor force or during the early years of their work life.

TABLE 2. CHANGE IN PERCENTAGE OF TOTAL LABOR FORCE EMPLOYED IN DIFFERENT OCCUPATIONAL GROUPS DURING THE DECADES 1940–50 AND 1950–60.

| | *Percent change* | |
Occupational Groups	*1940–50*	*1950–60*
Professional and technical	+37.5	+47.0
Self-employed proprietors	n.i.a.*	−20.0
Clerical workers	+58.7	+33.8
Sales workers	+26.8	+18.7
Skilled workers	+51.2	+11.8
Semiskilled	+38.4	+ 6.4
Service workers	+ 7.9	+25.6
Farmers and farm managers	−16.3	−41.9
Laborers	+ 9.3	− 9.6

* n.i.a. means no information was available on self-employed proprietors.

The occupations of farming and self-employed proprietors, in which older workers are overrepresented, are declining occupations. Self-employed proprietors decreased by 20 percent between the years 1950 and 1960; farmers and farm managers decreased by 41.9 percent. Service work, in which they are also overrepresented, increased during the decade of the fifties; however, their chances for employment in service work stem from the limited skills which it requires and its low pay. The occupations of sales, semiskilled, and skilled work, in which the representation of older workers equals the percentage of employed older people, grew during the decade, but their rate of growth had slowed considerably from what it had been during the preceding decade. The growth of skilled occupations slowed to only one-seventh of its preceding growth and semiskilled to one-sixth. Occupations in which older workers are underrepresented, excluding laboring occupations, are the fastest growing. Laboring occupations decreased, but the underrepresentation of older workers is related *not* to the skills of these occupations, but to the relative lack of physical vigor of older people.

This growth and decline in occupations is referred to as structural transformation of the economy. Joseph J. Spengler feels that changes in economy occasioned by this transformation, more than mandatory retirement, account for the low participation of older people in the labor force. The structure of the economy has been transformed through the application of scientific and technological knowledge to the production, distribution, and consumption of goods and services. The result has been a continual upgrading in work skills and in educational attainment as job requisites. In 1950 it was estimated that 78 percent of all available jobs required 10 years or more of conventional schooling. This estimate is undoubtedly low for today. The occupations which have grown the fastest during the last 15 years require the highest education, and even ones with less growth have been affected by scientific and technological applications.

The unfavorable position of older works in the labor force arises, at least partially, out of their lower educational attainment. (Fig. 2) A curve of the average educational attainment of age groups in the labor force closely fits the curve of participation by age groups in the labor force. The young and the old whose rates of participation are the lowest have

FIGURE 2. MEDIAN EDUCATION OF AGE GROUPS OF EMPLOYED MALES IN 1960.

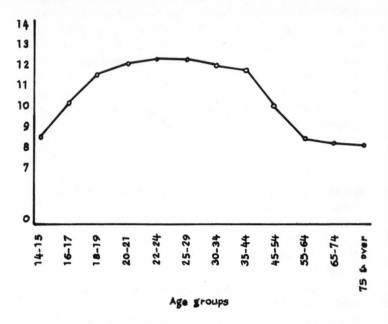

Age groups

received the least formal education. In 1960 the median education of employed male workers declined from 12 years for the 35 to 44 age group to 10.1 years for the 45 to 54 age group, and workers 55 and over averaged approximately 8.5 years of schooling. Thus, we see the nature of the difficulties which older workers face. Having less education, they are unable to apply for the many jobs which require considerable schooling. Their skills tend to be manual and are less needed. They have been bypassed by a changed economy.

The problem which they face is worse than their poor qualifications indicate. Population growth augments their difficulty by providing employers with a choice of younger workers. The average annual increase in the labor force, according to a study done in the late 1950's, was about 1 percent, or a little under one new worker for each 100 already in the labor force. Companies, when given a choice, prefer younger to older workers. This is especially the case among large companies. A study on age barriers to hiring conducted by the U.S. Bureau of Employment in seven large labor markets found that firms with seven or fewer employees specified a maximum age limit in 52 percent of their job orders filed with public employment offices, compared to 78 percent of the orders filed by firms employing 1,000 or more workers.

Reasons generally cited by firms for discriminating against older workers include increased costs of older workers arising from pension plans and pressures from unions. Non-union members are unable to apply if the company has a closed-shop policy, and, even when the worker is a union member, early retirement is often encouraged to give greater opportunity to younger union members. These seem legitimate reasons, but, in addition, companies are often prejudiced without foundation. They believe older workers are less productive, though studies have found lower performance only in laboring occupations requiring much physical strength; they believe older workers have higher absentee rates arising from poor health, but their rates are as low as, or lower than, those of younger workers. Those in poor health tend to leave the labor force. Because of these strong dislikes for older workers, companies tend to set a maximum age for jobs.

Age limitations, however, are not uniform among occupations. They are most likely among occupations with the lowest representation of older workers. According to the study conducted by the U.S. Bureau of Employment on hiring policies, the setting of an upper age limit from the most likely to the least likely were clerical, unskilled (heavy laboring occupations), professional and managerial, sales, service, semi-skilled, and skilled. This finding suggests that the tendency to set an upper age limit is partially a reflection of the lower probability of older persons possessing the skills and education needed for the jobs in these occupations. Remember, occupations with the lowest percentage of older workers, excluding laboring ones, have been upgraded in their skill requirements by technological and scientific changes.

What this brief analysis of the labor force tells us is that our labor market is highly selective in its hiring. Older people are disadvantaged by their lack of skills and educational attainment and by the pool of younger workers arising from the fact that the rate of growth of the economy is lower than that of the population. There seem to be few alternatives to withdrawal from the labor force by sizeable numbers of older workers. Retraining programs for older workers with sufficient education to participate might keep some in the labor force, but companies are reluctant to sponsor them because of their cost and the available supply of younger workers. Public efforts, apart from the employment opportunities, are likely to have little payoff; the labor market is discriminatory, and undoubtedly an older worker wonders whether he will get a job once he has completed a program. This comes down to the inescapable fact that older people will be eased out of the labor force and increasingly so. Thus, it seems that we should begin our planning for older people from this premise.

In planning for older workers, I would argue for compulsory retirement, *coupled with* safeguards for job security until the worker reaches mandatory retirement age, and increased pension planning. When the future is uncertain, people worry. By these provisions they would be assured of work for a period of time and of an income sufficient for their needs. Many workers will be disappointed by having to retire, but such disappointments lack the severity that worries over a livelihood have. Suggestions have also been made to phase out gradually workers who want to remain in the labor force rather than having them go from full employment to no employment. I do not think such a program is feasible; it would be very costly to ascertain individual preferences for reduced work or retirement and to structure employment to phase out workers gradually. Furthermore, society cannot forget its obligations to its young in its attempts to help older people.

Compulsory retirement will become more widespread, and, as it does, social action will be undertaken to help older people who have been removed from the labor force. What we are trying to do today in helping older people may be somewhat analogous to what happened in the passing of child labor laws. Some felt the passing of these laws denied children their rightful function. After children were removed from the labor force, the need to educate them became apparent. Although most workers are still productive at their retirement, we cannot expect them to remain so, especially as their life expectancy rises. Hence, a need exists to gain acceptance of retirement and to develop facilities for older people to lead meaningful lives. Leisure might become an established expectation for the later years just as work is an expectation of adulthood. Today the problem of community planning for older people is probably much greater than it will be a decade from now, since we are only beginning to take action relative to the needs which exist.

There is a general concern for successful planning. And success will largely be determined by the knowledge we bring to our efforts. I want to suggest some considerations for planning, founded on my research on the behavior of retired people. These suggestions are guided by the principle that *planning for older people should be based on the patterns of behavior that characterize their adaptation to life prior to their retirement.*

Older people do not change their basic patterns of living after they retire. Their interests, activities, associations, and relationships were formed during earlier years of their life. The setting in which these patterns are activated may change, but not the patterns themselves. We found that out of 306 retired workers, only 11 evolved any new interests or associations in retirement, and personal involvement in the new ones was much less than in long-established patterns. We are not saying that an individual's life is unchanged by his withdrawal from the labor force. The loss of work, whether experienced with favorable anticipation or dread, involves the loss of a significant status and a daily routine, coupled with the necessity of evolving new ones. Resources upon which a retiree may draw in adapting to this new uncertain situation of leisure are the patterns of behavior which characterized his life while working.

A man's characteristic mode of adapting to the world is

heavily conditioned by his work. Knowing his work, one may predict with a high degree of accuracy the kind of resources he will have to draw upon in retirement. Both in the labor force and in society at large, work is distinguished mainly by skill level. Associated with skills are educational attainment necessary for their acquisition and use and generality of responsibility ensuing from their exercise. While specific skills are many, variability in educational attainment and in generality of responsibility associated with them is much less. Using skills as a predictor of education and generality of responsibility, one may group workers with a high degree of reliability into three general strata: upper white-collar workers consisting of professionals and executives; a middle stratum composed of clerical workers, sales people, and skilled craftsmen and foremen; and lower blue-collar workers consisting of the semiskilled, service workers, and laborers. Ways of behavior differ by stratum; each tends to have its characteristic patterns of adaptation.

The patterns of life of upper white-collar workers facilitate the most satisfactory adaptation to retirement, despite the fact that these workers were the most identified with their work and received the greatest satisfaction from it. Their interests are varied and include favorable orientations toward activities involving things, people, and symbols. They are likely to belong to several voluntary organizations in the community and to be widely recognized and solicited for participation. The jobs which they have held involve freedom to organize their daily routines, and more than any other workers they plan their work and nonwork lives. Few of them favorably anticipate retirement, but when they are faced with it, their life patterns enable them to find meaningful substitutes for their work. These retirees do not need, and are not likely to want, community assistance, nor should community planners be concerned with them.

The middle stratum, often called the middle masses, include the retirees who most want help in their retirement. They, more than any other workers, look forward to retirement, but they lack the broadly based community roles and interests that effectively substitute for work. Their interests are less varied than those of upper white-collar workers and are influenced by the kind of object to which their work skills were applied. Objects of work situations include symbols, things, and people. Clerical workers deal mainly with symbols; salesmen and foremen work mainly with people; and skilled craftsmen work with things. Salesmen and foremen in their retirement engage mainly in activities oriented around people, and to a lesser extent in physical activities. Retired skilled workers have the most restricted interests; their activities are limited primarily to physical ones in which they deal with things. As their physical vigor lessens, they are left without meaningful activities. Retired clerical workers engage more often in physical activities than symbolic ones; but they, more than any other retirees from the middle masses, engage in symbolic activities. Symbolic activities are usually solitary, and ability to engage in them is least impaired by declining health and vigor. Associations of these middle stratum retirees are fewer and less extensive than those of retired upper white-collar workers; however, within their limited circles they enjoy recognition. Most of these retirees are financially secure, even though their incomes are lower than when they were working. Unlike upper white-collar workers, these retirees have been less accustomed to structuring their daily work routines. What they did and when they did it was largely determined by others to whom they were responsible. In retirement they are faced for the first time with ordering a routine. They found little intrinsic meaning in their work and looked forward to giving it up for a life of leisure, but they tend to be uncertain about what to do and how to do it. Their favorable anticipation of retirement, yet their uncertainty about their roles, prompts these workers more than any others to seek information and advice on retirement.

Lower blue-collar workers seem the most in need of help to cope with retirement; however, they are the least likely to know how to get it or, if it is available, how to use it. Their modes of behavior isolate them as much as they involve them with others. The low prestige of their work occasioned little recognition to support feelings of worthwhileness and self-confidence. Their associations are few and are limited primarily to kin and neighborhood. Lacking self-confidence, they feel insecure outside their limited world. Their interests are restricted to physical activities, and the decline of health and vigor takes a great toll on their few outlets for self-expression. They are not accustomed to planning for the future, because they have never been able to exercise much control over it. Their work was narrowly defined, providing little opportunity to order their day, and their financial and other resources are insufficient for predictable planning. Most of these retirees are severely handicapped by the loss of a pay check, which was their main motivation for work. Their enthusiasm for retirement is less than that among the middle stratum, not because they like their work more, but because of financial worries and their feeling of helplessness toward the events of their life. These are the people who need help, but how to give it is difficult. Their problem arises less from retirement than from their mode of adapting to the world, which has long been established.

How might these findings be applied in community action for older people? One course of action is volunteer work within the established religious, civic, and governmental organizations of a community. Such volunteer work might provide an avenue for self-expression and activity for older people who have been idled by loss of employment. Such programs should not be designed for or directed at upper white-collar retirees; they do not need them. Retirees from the middle stratum would seem the most likely candidates for volunteer work. This kind of activity appeals to them, but many are ignorant of the opportunities for involvement in it. In seeking volunteers, assignments patterned around their work skills should be suggested. For example, retired clerical workers might enjoy helping the County Board of Registrars update registration books. A retired electrician might enjoy an assignment of electrical maintenance within his church. Retired salesmen and foremen would seem good choices to solicit for charities.

Volunteer work should be centered in established community organizations. Organizations designed solely around the aged tend to segregate older people from vital community activities. Success of volunteer work depends heavily on the feeling of having contributed to others, and such motivation can best be furthered through linking older people to the essential functions of their community.

To aid in engaging retirees for volunteer work, a registry of retired workers in the community might be undertaken; volunteers could canvass neighborhoods for names. The registry might include the kind of work the retiree did, his memberships in community organizations, his interest in volunteer work and in paid employment. Organizations to which a retiree belongs might be contacted and invited to solicit volunteer work; an organization in which a retiree is most likely to be interested might be asked to invite him for volunteer work. To be invited to do things makes one feel good. And for the invitation to come from organizations suggests worthwhileness of the contribution and a meaningful social context for recognition of efforts.

Although most of the middle stratum are financially secure, some would like additional money for luxuries. The registry might be advertised; companies needing part-time workers on a limited basis could be put in contact with likely applicants. A full-time staff needed to manage a registry might be recruited from retired workers. And community chests could provide the needed financial support for its operation.

Lower blue-collar workers are not likely applicants for community volunteer work. Their skills are not appropriate for such programs, and they are also less interested in organizations and in their community. Action programs might best help these people by seeing that they are kept informed on governmental and other programs aimed at helping older people. Sending letters is not sufficient, for many are unable to comprehend the contents. Again, volunteers from the middle stratum might visit these people regularly to see what kinds of financial, health, and other personal problems they have and, in consultation with appropriate community officials, what help might be given. Many of these people who are physically able might be interested in paid employment. Companies are unlikely to employ them, but they might be hired by individuals as gardeners, by the city as substitutes for maintenance workers, and so forth. If those capable of handiwork are included in the registry referred to above, they could be contacted and hired for at least a few hours every couple of weeks.

SELECTED BIBLIOGRAPHY

BANCROFT, GERTRUDE. *The American Labor Force: Its Growth and Changing Composition.* New York: John Wiley and Sons, Inc., 1958.

LOETHER, HERMAN J. *Problems of Aging.* Belmont, California: Dickenson Publishing Company, Inc., 1967.

RUTZICK, MAX, AND SOL SWERDLOFF, "The Occupational Structure of U.S. Employment, 1940–60," *Monthly Labor Review,* 1968).

SIMPSON, IDA HARPER, AND JOHN C. McKINNEY (eds.). *Social Aspects of Aging.* Durham, North Carolina: Duke University Press, 1966.

PART V

SPECIAL PROGRAMS AND STRATEGIES

PART V

SPECIAL PROGRAMS AND STRATEGIES

The articles in this section are designed to help implement the theories presented in the preceding chapters. Frank Nicholson provides some principles basic to community organization which may be applied as groups in the community become aware of their need to set up services for the aging. He outlines steps in organizing local committees on aging,' warns against premature efforts without adequate knowledge of older persons and their needs, and clarifies some of the relationships between agencies on behalf of the aging on various. levels of government, emphasizing the significance of coordinating efforts at the local level. It is obvious that coordination of agencies and services is essential in alleviating or eliminating social problems, and those of the aged are no exception.

Nola Spain on recreation and James Ailor on the church, following the earlier remarks of E. Grant Youmans, indicate that the use of alert and healthy older persons as volunteers in local programs provides active roles for them and demonstrates to the community the potentials of these social participants.

The special area of recreation developed by Mrs. Spain is presented on the assumption that the elderly have more leisure time and unstructured activities than they previously enjoyed. In other words, recreation programs are a means of circumventing the increase of disengagement. However, involvement in such programs applies just as aptly to the "life course" theory, in which new choices of interest and activity are made at respective stages of the life cycle, an idea on which Mrs. Spain capitalizes in her emphasis of the "re-creation" property of recreation. She covers the qualifications for leadership and membership in groups of senior citizens interested in some phase of recreation. From her years of experience as a recreational leader, Mrs. Spain amplifies the "when, where, and what" of programs and comments in a most practical way on how to finance and publicize them.

In Ailor's consideration of the role of the church in the welfare of the aging, he is acutely aware that the prolongation of life has developed without a concomitant knowledge of how to live in these later years. American society is essentially without norms for how to act effectively in the later years. It is here, then, that the church can offer a helping hand. Its warmth, sincerity, and guidance can add meaning and zest to living, can overcome loneliness and fear of death, can stimulate opportunities for the "life review" discussed by Verwoerdt, and hold out the hope of immortality.

Ailor writes with great feeling about his rich experiences with the aged, and one wishes his enthusiasm could be generalized to all other areas and persons who work with the elderly.

The first chapter on housing, by John Chase, covers the housing needs of elderly citizens and what has been done through federal programs to meet these needs. He contends that housing is the appropriate nucleus around which the community plans improvements for its senior citizens. He describes the legislation basic to the provision of low-rent housing, rent supplements, and home rehabilitation loans and grants. These opportunities bring the comfort of home without the loss of neighborhood ties, something that was stressed by both Albrecht and Boyd.

In the closing chapter George F. Packard demonstrates the achievement of a dedicated minister supported by an equally dedicated board of churchmen confronted with the challenge of providing a functional apartment building near the church. Although he takes advantage of one of the federal programs mentioned by Chase, Packard's experience differs most with that of Chase in that the middle-income segment of the elderly population is served. This is particularly important in light of the fact that this is a group often forgotten in efforts to house the poor, and a group whose financial resources are most subject to the inconveniences of a vacillating economy.

12

MEETING THE CHALLENGE
Frank Nicholson

Careful consideration of the problems and needs in a particular community is necessary if effective services are to be devised in that community. In the field of social welfare, whenever we talk of people's problems and needs, we think of and respond in terms of services or assistance required for solutions. If the problems and needs are not taken into consideration, a service can be rendered, but no solution achieved.

There is a wide variety of services being rendered with and for older people in many communities across the country. There are certain basic services common to most communities, such as public assistance and social security insurance programs. Other services may or may not exist, depending upon the awareness of the need for the service by the community, the willingness to commit resources to the need, and the priorities which may have been established to meet a variety of needs which exist at a given time.

Ideas, services, and programs which may be accepted and are successful in some communities may not be successful in others. While various services and program ideas may be offered for consideration, to be successful there must be a felt need for, acceptance of, and responsiveness to the service in the community, and it must be properly organized and administered.

Frank Nicholson is regional representative, Administration on Aging, Region IV, Department of Health, Education, and Welfare, Atlanta, Georgia.

The reason that it is good to have some understanding of the real problems and basic needs of older people is to help you to be in a better position to evaluate the appropriateness of a given service for the older people with whom you are working. Creativity should be our goal in every situation, even though we may have a number of tried and tested plans. We should forever search for new and more effective services and for ways of providing them.

Services and resources may be provided for older people through a variety of agencies, organizations, and institutions. They may or may not be located in the community, such as state institutions located in another part of the state. The organization may be under the auspices of the city, county, state, or federal government, or any combination of these. Or it may be a private, voluntary organization which is supported through contributions, the community chest, foundations, fees, or selling services to a public agency. Churches and civic clubs may provide essential human services or support for them.

How will you as a member of an organization rendering a service for older people, or as a citizen of your community, go about meeting the challenge of encouraging the development of essential services for the senior citizens in your community? This is a challenge to you as an individual. It is a challenge to the agencies, organizations, and institutions with which you might be associated. It is a challenge to each and every community.

Sometimes challenges are made and not accepted. This may be due to a lack of conviction regarding the need to do something or to an attitude of indifference or apathy. There are others, however, who do respond. If you are one who is willing to accept the challenge and move forward, permit me to make several suggestions for your consideration as to how you might proceed in your community.

First, if you represent some organization, agency, or institution, think carefully of the group you represent in relationship to their services to older people. Do they have a policy to serve older people or permit older people to participate?

If so, how many are really being served? It is possible for the service to be available but not used because of agency practices or other circumstances which limit participation, i.e., dues, fees, and transportation. The absence of services may represent a repudiation of the aims of the organization. The extent to which services for older people are requested but not given is important. Perhaps expansion or extension of service for older persons would be in order, based on an analysis of current experiences. Ask these questions of your organization and accept it as a personal responsibility to encourage the expansion of the service or activity to include older people or to create a new service for older people where appropriate. Encourage and lead the organization in a self-appraisal of its programs as related to older citizens and toward the allocation of a portion of its resources for this purpose.

Second, we must recognize that no one organization or group can perform all the essential services which may be required in a community. A division of responsibility is necessary, with many diverse groups working together to provide a full range of services. In many communities, a community planning council endeavors to relate services to one another to avoid gaps in service and to prevent duplication of effort, thereby better insuring that needed programs are established and providing for more effective distribution of community resources. Many such councils have committees on aging which provide a sharp focus on problems and services related to older people. If there is no such council or committee on aging in your community, request an appropriate planning organization to establish one. Where there is no planning organization, assume the leadership yourself and start developing a committee. Talk with others. Identify those who share this interest in aging with you. Select from these a small group who know the community and who are considered "opinion-makers." Call a meeting and discuss the next steps in creating a council or committee on aging. If it is possible to obtain the sanction of county public officials to create the committees, do so. Place considerable emphasis on securing a chairman who is interested in assuming responsibility, and willing and able to do so. Establish a committee with broad community representation so as to provide channels of communication to a wide segment of the community. Include, but do not limit, the membership to older people. Representation should be countywide in scope or perhaps over a metropolitan area where it exists. Where funds and trained personnel are limited, perhaps two or more counties might join their efforts together. Professional salaried staff should be secured where possible to provide stability, continuity, and coordination to the effort.

Once established, the members of the committee on aging should proceed together to identify the problems and reach some consensus on those of primary concern. This should include a study and evaluation of the problem in the light of the situation, including an identification of existing services and gaps in services. Having selected the priorities, determine a course of action. Evaluate and consider various approaches and probable results. Decide whether or not there are existing agencies which should be approached, asked, and encouraged to include older people in their existing services or to expand services to avoid duplication of effort by building on the present agency structure. If existing agencies cannot or will not provide needed services, then consider moving toward establishing a new agency which could provide services for older people which other agencies do not provide. In many communities, new multifunction agencies have been established to serve older people, and in all probability many more will be created. To accomplish your objective, the employment of many methods may be necessary—education, promotion, legislation, fund-raising, etc.

The problem-solving process engaged in by a committee on aging is often referred to as community organization. Community involvement of people in strategic positions is essential to the success of the project. It is a mobilization of community resources—leadership, organization, knowledge, and funds. Relationships of organizations and individuals should be strengthened in the process.

Third, let us not assume that because we see and have a conviction of the necessity of developing services for older people, because we have secured some consensus in the community as to the needs of the aged, or because we have developed practical plans, results will come automatically. Unfortunately, there are those who do not see the need, those who prefer the status quo, those who object to the costs or another campaign or request for funds, and others who will want to do the job in a different way. To obtain results, constant and persistent leadership is necessary. Leaders who have the courage of their convictions must be involved. The local community and agencies may have to be prodded and stimulated. Persistent effort is required on the part of informed citizens.

Fourth, and last, remain flexible and sensitive to time. Incorporate the ideas of others where possible to win their support. Be ready to move when the situation is right.

I hope these brief suggestions will be of some benefit to you in meeting the challenge. It sounds like a big job, and it is. But do not be discouraged. You are not alone. There are others who will share the responsibility with you. And now let me tell you of other resources available to help you do the job.

"Meeting the Challenge of the Later Years" was the national theme designated by former President Johnson for Senior Citizens Month. A booklet by that same title was issued by the Administration on Aging as a guide to community action. Included are a number of program examples which may be of interest to you.

In 1961, the first White House Conference on Aging was held in Washington. At this conference, representatives from organizations, communities, and states across the country expressed a need for help in developing services for older people. In 1965, Congress responded to this challenge by enacting the Older Americans Act, which created the Administration on Aging. National objectives for older Americans were set forth in the act providing equal opportunity for the full and free enjoyment of the following:

An adequate income in retirement in accordance with the American standard of living; the best possible physical and mental health which science can make available without regard to economic status; suitable housing, independently selected, designed, and located with reference to special needs and available at costs which older citizens can afford; full restorative services for those who require institutional care; opportunity for employment with no discriminatory personnel practices because of age; retirement in health, honor, and dignity after years of contribution to the economy; pursuit of meaningful activity within the widest range of civic, cultural, and recreational opportunities; efficient community services which provide social assistance in a coordinated manner and which are readily available when needed; immediate benefit from proven research knowledge which can sustain and improve health and happiness; freedom, independence, and the free exercise of individual initiative in planning and managing their own lives.

To help accomplish the objectives in the act, three grant programs were established, as follows:

(1) Title V of the act authorizes the Administration on Aging to support, through grants or contracts to public and nonprofit private agencies and institutions for training, specialized training of persons employed, or preparing for employment, in programs in aging.

(2) Title IV of the act authorizes the Administration on Aging to make direct grants or to sign contracts for research and demonstration projects of national or regional significance with public and nonprofit private agencies and individuals. Projects must be related to the study of the current patterns and conditions of living of older people, identification of beneficial and detrimental factors, or development of new approaches and techniques.

(3) Title III is the grant program which is most significant to you. It authorizes federal allotments to the states to aid the state to establish or strengthen a state agency on aging. It also provides for project grant funds, as described below.

Some state agency is designated to receive and disburse federal funds, making them available to eligible local, public, and nonprofit private agencies. This may include county governments, local municipalities, local housing or city recreational authorities, community councils on aging, senior citizens clubs, educational institutions, and churches. A county welfare department would not be eligible, for example, because of its relationship to a state agency.

Project grant funds may be allocated for the following purposes: (a) community planning and coordination of programs; (b) demonstration of programs; (c) training of special personnel needed to carry out programs; (d) establishment of new or expansion of existing services for older people.

The project grants may be made for a maximum of 36 months. A matching contribution in the amount of 25 percent of the total project cost is required from the project applicant in the first year; 40 percent in the second year; and 50 percent in the third year. At the end of that time we would hope that the service would be sufficiently accepted by the local community that it would be supported from then on by local community resources. Thus, over a period of time, the local community assumes complete responsibility. The federal funds are used for seed money to help in getting the service established or expanded. The matching contribution may be in cash or in kind, or a combination of the two. Where an agency wishes to expand an existing service, it is possible to use existing resources as the matching contribution provided there is at least a 25 percent increase in the scope of operation.

The services to be performed under a Title III grant are determined by the project grantee and submitted on an application form to the state agency, which then processes it through a technical review committee, with the final decision made by the agency's board. Let me emphasize that the decision as to what projects will or will not be funded is made by *your* state agency.

There are agencies and communities which can establish or expand services for older people without Title III assistance.

Others will find it advantageous to seek and use Title III funds. An application kit may be requested from your state agency. Whether or not Title III funds are needed, consultation and information on the development of services for older people can be provided upon request by your state agency.

So much for the federal and state resources. These are of no consequence unless the local community accepts the challenge and responsibility. The chain is not complete until this is done. And informed people are the ones who can add the missing link to the chain. Let me urge all of you to make arrangements with others from your community to establish a date, time, and place for a meeting together. Then, at that meeting consider your local situation and decide the next steps to be taken, if you have not already organized for this purpose.

I should like to close with this appropriate poem:

> *Isn't it strange how princes and kings*
> *And clowns who caper in sawdust rings*
> *And common folks as you and me*
> *Are builders for eternity?*
>
> *To each is given a bag of tools,*
> *A mass of clay and the golden rule,*
> *And we must build 'ere life has flown,*
> *A stumbling block, or a stepping stone.*

I trust we shall work together to build many stepping stones.

SELECTED BIBLIOGRAPHY

Council on Social Work Education, *The Curriculum Study*, IV, (New York: CSWE, 1959).

Council on Social Work Education, *New Developments in Community Organization Practice and Their Significance for This Sequence in the Curriculum Area* (New York: CSWE, 1962).

DAHL, ROBERT A., "The Analysis of Influence in Local Communities," *Urban Planning and Social Policy*, ed. Bernard Frieden and Robert Morris (New York: Basic Books, Inc., 1968).

HARPER, ERNEST B., AND ARTHUR C. DUNHAM. *Community Organization in Action* (New York: Association Press, 1959).

KURTZ, RUSSELL. *Community Organization: A Social Work Method* (New York: NASW, 1958).

STROUP, HERBERT H. *Social Work* (New York: American Book Company, 1960).

WARREN, ROLAND L. *The Community in America* (Chicago: Rand-McNally and Company, 1963).

13

RECREATIONAL PROGRAMS
FOR THE ELDERLY
Nola Spain

The eighteen and a half million older Americans—men and women 65 years of age and over—account for one-tenth of the country's population, and this segment continues to increase faster than the population as a whole. While it can be said that our total population is growing younger, the older population is, in truth, growing older. In fact, more than 3,800 Americans reach their sixty-fifth birthday every day, and about half of our elderly are nearly 73 years old, not to mention the some 13,000 who have passed their one-hundredth birthday!

These developments in our population present great challenges now and for the years to come. Undoubtedly, the hours and years of free and unstructured time will continue to increase as automation becomes more universal and working time is shortened. Perhaps the greatest challenge of the future may be to find ways and to develop opportunities for the enjoyment of this leisure and the pursuit of meaningful living, both during the period of employment and after it has ended.

Here is how one program has met this challenge.

ONE COMMUNITY'S SOLUTION

We had become aware that some of our senior citizens were lonely, lacked recognition, and had time on their hands. When

Mrs. Nola Spain is program director, Parks and Recreation Department, Greenville, South Carolina.

we attended the National Recreation Conference in the fall of 1953, we found that the situation was the same all over the nation.

Upon returning home, we called together a group of retired persons and told them what we had learned and what we hoped to do with their help. Through a series of newspaper articles, we created community interest. Our original club, established late in 1953, consisted of 32 persons. The first meeting was held at the recreation center, and a Christmas program was presented by a group of children from the playgrounds division. Our only expenses then were for refreshments, but today it is different. There is much more awareness of the need in our community, and money comes from many sources.

I mention the type of program we had on the first meeting, because we have found that if activities can center around holiday themes, people somehow take more interest; they know something is going to happen, and attendance will be greater.

Your local recreation department can organize a club. It doesn't take too much help for a few oldsters to start things going, but to be permanent, a program requires several important assets.

QUALIFICATIONS FOR LEADERSHIP

Leadership, whether paid or volunteer, whether full- or part-time, must be qualified to do the job of working with elderly people. This takes thorough screening and preparation, and those members who are capable can be used on a volunteer basis.

Constant preservice and in-service courses should be conducted for all types of leadership. We begin this by allowing some whom we have screened to get really involved in the activities of the program, and then we casually observe how they act. It doesn't take long to "weed out" the ones who "just love old people" from those who are really interested in filling a need. But, for more concentrated training, we recommend enrollment in courses being added to the curricula at several colleges and universities, Multipurpose Senior Center Administration (to prepare persons to serve as administrators) and Recreation Leadership with Older Persons (designed for individuals who will work in the area of recreation and leisure services in such settings as nursing homes, extended care facilities, homes for the aged, and public recreation agencies).

Persons who have been trained as leaders in organizations devoted to the elderly have always ended up feeling refreshed, encouraged, and enthusiastic. This is due in part, we are sure, to the response senior citizens give to a good leader; it is remarkable in that it "re-creates" the leader as much as the persons for whom the program is designed.

Some of you who anticipate being leaders in such groups may be asking at this point: "What sort of things can you do with the oldsters? Aren't they hard to work with?" My answers are, first, that you can do almost anything with them, and I do mean *with* them. But, second, they are not a bit hard to work with if you will make a point to understand them. Understanding, you must realize, involves knowledge both of what they like and of what they do not like. Let me give you some examples from our experience.

Old persons know they are old. You don't have to emphasize that at all, and yet I have heard persons say when a group is assembling, "I am happy to be here with you older people today. I am glad to see an interest shown by our community in developing a program for senior citizens, because one of these days I am going to be old and be sitting out there where you are, and I hope the same interest will be shown in me."

This is the worst kind of welcome, particularly when it is followed by a verse or two of "Darling, I Am Growing Old."

Second, when elderly persons come to one of our programs, they know what we stand for. Ours is a recreation department. Therefore, we stick to recreation. Problems of employment, health, or other specialized services can better be cared for by others, and can only become controversial issues if introduced into our program.

One of the best ways to understand the elderly persons in your group is to ask them what they like and dislike, and the use of a simple and short survey questionnaire will provide some good insights. After you get to know them better, the group discussion will provide other insights. But, whatever you find out from your members, remember that their decisions have to be in the majority. Imposed programs are never successful and always lack tact. Recreation cannot be forced on a person and still be "re-creation."

QUALIFICATIONS FOR MEMBERSHIP

People vary greatly in how they define "being old," and we have found that it is wise to be very flexible when setting an age range for the acceptance of members. Women, for instance, tend to be shy about telling their age; some are about ten years shy! Not a few times we have heard women say something like this: "My husband has retired, but he is *much* older than I am, and I would like to come with him to the club." Some authorities suggest 55 as the starting point of being elderly for women. We go one step further and allow those who are 55 and have retired husbands to attend our clubs. There is a certain realism about this; although men outnumber women by 5 percent at birth, women outnumber men by 46 percent at 85 and over.

But having a retired husband is not the only criterion for allowing admission of a younger woman, say 50 years old, into your club. Since women live longer than men, marry younger than men, and remarry less frequently than men, there is a greater number of widows in the upper age levels. Two-thirds of the men and one-third of the women over 65 live with a spouse; consequently, the chances are that your club will have five women to every man.

Of course, a distribution such as this may create problems. We encourage both men and women to join our clubs. However, occasions have arisen when the women would say, "Don't let any more women join; there just aren't enough men to go around." In fact, one of our clubs began turning women away at the door when others called us the "lonely hearts club." The opposite may also prove true. Attitudes may arise which hinder men from joining, such as, "The club is essentially for women," or, "Nothing of interest here for men." We have responded to this by specifically planning for the men, and one of our groups of oldsters wants us to charter a bus trip to and from the ball games in Atlanta.

We would like to think that as few restrictions as possible could be imposed as to who should be admitted as members, but inevitably the unanticipated occurs, and this has led to the establishment of a few rules which are made clear to all new and prospective members. Examples of reasons for restriction include (1) a question of bad character, (2) continual drunkenness, (3) complete lack of interest and nonattendance, and, unfortunately, (4) resentment, especially by women, for a divorced woman. Barring problems such as these, it is far better to keep members on the roll and encourage in them a sense of belonging than to drop them because of illness, difficulty of transportation, and misunderstanding.

Good leadership and qualifications for membership come together when the regular members can be encouraged to adjust to new and different members. It is good to consider the writing of new rules to insure a smooth operation. This is the way to build up group loyalty.

PROGRAMS: WHEN, WHERE, WHAT

For the most part, our clubs meet on Tuesday and Thursday afternoons at a regular time—from two until five. We have set these hours since transportation problems seem to be minimal then, but, whatever your situation may be, it is important to study the endurance of your members, in terms of age and health, and strike a happy medium for the length of the sessions. However, two groups meet once a month on a Saturday evening, and this is but another example of trying to achieve the maximum flexibility in meeting the interests of elderly persons. In line with this idea of flexibility, birthdays, festivals and holiday celebrations, picnics, watermelon slicings, ice cream suppers, and trips away from home offer unlimited occasions for special meetings.

It is important not to equate flexibility of schedule with a tendency to change from one meeting place to another. This will create confusion, and there are too many factors to consider in selecting an appropriate setting which meets the physical needs and interests of the elderly person. Let me cite a few criteria important for this type of program:

(1) Many elderly persons, particularly in the larger communities, are moving to the central portions of the city. Your location is ideal, in such an instance, if it is within walking distance of the central part of town or if the local buses will stop at your door. (It is always desirable to have ample room for parking, but if this is not possible, a car pool may be arranged.)

(2) All members of your club will not be involved in the same activities at all times. Consideration must be given to rooms of different sizes, their location, etc. In all instances, the appointment of the rooms should be attractive.* If your physical plant is of high quality, the program will more likely follow in the same manner. The provisions of the physical plant, hopefully, will be dictated by the activities desired by your members, rather than the opposite. If they enjoy picnicking and shuffleboard, then the yard area should be large enough to accommodate these. If they like to prepare meals, a large enough kitchen should be available. If they just wish to sit and chat, an attractive lounge is indispensable.

(3) Many new senior citizens centers are constructed with one floor only, to allow easy access. The alternative to this is a multistoried building with an elevator. In each, however, the rest rooms should be accessible.

Several times I have referred to the development of a program based on the needs and interests of the group and adjusted to individual capacities; and I suggested the use of

---

*Editor's note: Miss Spain, in speaking of the decoration of the rooms, stressed the desirability of bright and friendly colors. Dr. Adriaan Verwoerdt, in this same regard, pointed out that with age the elderly person increasingly tends to see all colors the same if they are muted tones. Thus, a more vivid color scheme is recommended when considering the physically determined aesthetic limitations of the elderly person.

a questionnaire or involvement of the members in open discussion to determine these. The elderly person, generally, is a frank individual and will not hesitate to let you know what he likes or dislikes. But what may be a strong desire among your members at one time may not hold their interest at another; consequently, be flexible enough to meet these changing interests. We have defined a balanced program as one which takes into consideration the group as a whole, activities for a few, the season of the year, or a special occasion. We like to think that all our activities will be relaxing in one way or another, but this does not preclude having an occasional formal program, such as dress-up affairs, afternoon teas, an open house, or a banquet with a special speaker. These formal programs add dignity and frequently contribute to more widespread fellowship among all members than in those activities which are more individual- or small-group-oriented.

The range of activities that can be planned for and with the elderly is practically unlimited, and, as I mention a few, please notice how they frequently accomplish several things at once.

(1) Parties are always popular, and holidays, as I mentioned earlier, are ideal times to hold them. But don't overlook the virtue of celebrating the anniversaries of couples or birthdays. Here is the opportunity to emphasize the individual and his accomplishments.*

(2) Activities for individuals and for a few members at a time provide frequently desired "quiet times." Games, such as chess, checkers, dominoes, or cards, are particularly popular, as are guessing games and the universally enjoyed jigsaw puzzles. But the arts and crafts program, while enabling independent activity, frequently results in the group's recognition of a new budding "Grandma Moses." And here we have found various handicrafts, such as sewing, basket-weaving, painting, rug-weaving, and ceramic and shell crafts, of great interest to our members.

(3) Group activities include dancing, which is popular,

---

* Editor's note: Dr. Verwoerdt discussed this in his paper on psychological aspects of aging, under the heading of the "life review."

it seems, with all age groups; charades; singing the old but still popular songs; quartettes, bands, or orchestras.

(4) Motion pictures and travelogues are available from telephone and oil companies, education departments, or councils on aging. We have found that, unless these types of programs are short, our members become restless. The travelogues are shorter—about 30 minutes—and are excellent preludes to a trip that we might be planning. Our members like to make comparisons between a film and what they actually see on the trips.

(5) We plan a trip at least once a month if we can, and seldom do we have less than five or six a year. Whether we go to the mountains, the beach, historic places, or shopping in a nearby city, we find that we can charter a bus for a reasonable amount.

In conclusion, if there is one thing that can be said to be true about all these activities, it is that they are more of a success if "food" plays an integral part. Your members can do most of the planning and preparation for covered-dish luncheons, banquets, or picnics, and this brings up something about the degree to which the members actively participate in the program and govern themselves.

"Re-creation" means that something is happening within the individual, not to him. Therefore, to wait on him too much prevents a development or continuation of a sense of contributing to "his" club. The contribution he makes may involve a complaint, for instance, about some problem which is subsequently solved. We allow our members to complain, for this is also a benefit the club can provide the member—a place where he is free to speak up on a point of difference.

In the light of what I have said here, it would seem that some are correct when they comment that "ours seems to be the only nation on earth that asks its teen-agers what to do about world affairs, and tells its golden-agers to go out and play." But civic and community services are rendered by this age group, and for several years we have made caroling robes for the hospital auxiliary program, stuffed envelopes for the

Christmas Seal program, and made dolls for underprivileged children, thus proving that age does not prevent continued contribution to the welfare of the community.

Another activity in the area of community welfare was the leisure workshop conducted by a committee including several of our members, which taught others a number of skills such as cooking, painting, crocheting, knitting, etc.

Most of the groups similar to ours have adopted names which include the phrases "senior citizens" or "golden age." However, the creativeness or comic attitude of these older persons is frequently seen in such names as "DMA" (Don't Mention Age), "Young in Heart," "BXYZ" (Baptist Extra Years of Zest), and "YDS" (Youth Done Spent).

FINANCING THE RECREATION PROGRAM

With the exception of our volunteers, the salaries of the staff come from the general budget, but other funds are necessary, and the procurement of these, like almost everything else I have talked about, is carried out in a flexible manner. The individual clubs decide the amount that each member will contribute, whether this is in terms of a systematic contribution, a membership fee, providing refreshments, or whatever. Some clubs charge five cents per person per meeting, others as much as 75 cents, and one club adds to this kind of contribution an annual membership fee of three dollars.

A fee of some kind is good, for it contributes to each member's feeling of responsibility, and these funds do enrich the program, such as allowing purchase of special crafts materials. The members, on occasions, have sold these crafts and returned the profits to the purchase of new materials.

These comments should not be interpreted to mean, however, that we operate on a "begging-for-help" basis. This is not true. We feel that the members should contribute to "their" club, but never have we rejected participation in the program if an occasional individual or so is unable to give something.

THE IMPORTANCE OF PUBLICITY

We believe in publicity, and, when it comes to our clubs, we don't think too much can be said about the program. But there are factors other than mere public relations that enter here. Club members enjoy publicity, and a special article about the club and its members lends importance to what they are doing. Newspaper editors are very cooperative in providing publicity when they are notified sufficiently ahead of time of a special event—a birthday, a holiday celebration. Also, the club calendar can be published, and this increases the opportunity for all members to know about the programs.

If you have a lively publicity committee comprised of members working closely with the director, considerable enthusiasm can be generated. This same committee can be responsible for special bulletins, booklets, and monthly mimeographed newsletters.

CONCLUSION

I have related the results of almost 14 years of experience in working with elderly citizens in a recreation program. There have been many mistakes. We have corrected some of these and capitalized on our successes. But, after all these years, I feel that there has been a crucial element persisting in all our efforts, and it is simply stated: Expose yourself to enthusiasm!

An American philosopher, Sam Goldwyn, said: "No person who is enthusiastic about his work has anything to fear from life. All the opportunities in the world are waiting to be grasped by people who are in love with what they're doing." Ralph Waldo Emerson was of similar mind when he commented: "Nothing great was ever achieved without enthusiasm."

We have worked in an area which many persons not too long ago would have said was impossible, and we feel we have met the challenge in our community, but enthusiasm is the magical quality, overcoming inertia and banishing discouragement. If you possess it, it will pass on to those senior citizens with whom you work. If and when you find it in others, you can be sure that it will strike a spark in you.

SELECTED BIBLIOGRAPHY

Organization Clubs for Senior Citizens. North Carolina Recreation Commission, 1960 (Rev. ed.).

OWEN, MONICA BURRELL, "Group Work with Different Age Groups," *Group Work: Foundations and Frontiers,* ed. Harleigh B. Trecker. New York: Whiteside, Inc., and William Morrow and Co., 1955.

STOUGH, ADA BARNETT, "Brighter Vistas: The Story of Four Church Programs for Older Adults," *Patterns for Progress in Aging, Case Study No. 18.* Washington: Administration on Aging, U.S. Department of Health, Education, and Welfare, 1965.

WILLIAMS, ARTHUR. *Recreation in the Senior Years.* National Recreation Association, 1962.

14

THE CHURCH PROVIDES
FOR THE ELDERLY

James W. Ailor

While each generation is different from the one which preceded it, there have been fantastic happenings in this one that make the past 30 years different from any preceding period. These occurrences are at the same time the most confusing and, in many aspects, the most hopeful of all time.

We have, in the span of one generation, witnessed the birth of television, the atomic era, space travel, and medical advances that eclipse all discoveries of other centuries. Among the phenomena has been the evolution that has culminated in both wonderful and complex facts centering around an aging population that promises to increase daily.

But two scant generations ago, people who were 50 looked old, dressed old, talked old, acted old—were old. Today, most of us who are 50 feel that we are just getting into the prime of our lives, not the end of them. I have found myself over the past ten years working every day with people who are 85, 87, 90, 93, 96 years of age, and I am no longer surprised to discover their age or to note how youthful looking so many of them are, and to see how active and creative so many of them can be.

Increasingly, individuals and groups are studying many of the physical, sociological, psychological, and emotional aspects of aging. There are a number of fine teams across the

The Reverend James W. Ailor is associate minister, First Methodist Church, Lake Charles, Louisiana.

country, from many disciplines, actively engaged in researching the facts and problems, trying to point to some hopeful and positive good that can come out of people's living longer than many of them had planned on, or are prepared, at present, to live.

If the statement, "prepared to live," sounds strange, it is, in so many instances, nevertheless true. Our homes, as a rule, are not built for the three-generational family. The sudden discovery of "wonder" drugs and the use of new therapies have done much to prolong life beyond its original expectancy. In too many instances, the life of the individual has been prolonged without giving him any purpose to go on living.

Many medical doctors, psychiatrists, psychologists, sociologists, social workers, ministers—in fact, the populace in general—have become deeply disturbed. The fact that we have learned to prolong the physical processes of a person's life to the point that he so often exists in a noncreative state presents a real threat. Though body functions may go on and on and on, there are many who live in a vegetable state of mind and spirit.

Much thought is being given as to how long we have the *right* to prolong life without purpose, except in a medical sense, where we say we have kept a person from dying because "life is life." Our whole society is geared and trained to *fight* death, not to *meet* it. The long terminal illness, in which a person is kept alive by a combination of artificial means, without being given a stimulation to creativity or reason for living, has begun to haunt an ever-enlarging segment of society.

It is here, at this very tragic crossroad, that the church must not only stand, or speak, but must *act,* giving to people a renewed sense of self-hood, dignity, creativity, and, above all, purpose for living. While I do not resist the pattern of high worship at 11:00 on Sunday morning, nor do I fight the "structure" of the church, for it has its place, this is where the church *begins,* not ends, its service to children, youth, the middle-aged—and the elderly persons in our community.

Ten years ago, I was appointed by the Louisiana Conference of the Methodist Church to be one of the ministers on the staff of First Methodist Church, Baton Rouge. My title was "Minister of the Parish." During almost nine years on this staff, the task of "Minister of the Parish" took on many definitions, but never, in all the added tasks, did the pastor of our church lose sight of the first purpose for asking that I be appointed "Minister of the Parish" on his staff: to minister to the homebound (we called them shut-ins, then), to work with the chronically ill, to carry on an important hospital ministry, and to work in a very small beginning, at first, with the retired people of the community.

What none of us foresaw was the fact that, while my work with the homebound and chronically ill would triple while I was there, a very small group, about 35 in number, known as the XYZ Club (Xtra Years of Zest) would become the focal point of my work and one of the most important ministries of the church.

Out of this experience, in addition to the one I am now involved with, that of administering a home for the aged for the church, I see the role of the church in providing services for the welfare of the elderly person basically in these categories, apart from the normally prescribed services of the church: (1) a ministry to the homebound and chronically ill in the community; (2) a ministry to the sick and dying in their own homes, the hospital, and nursing homes, and to their families; (3) working with counseling services to three-generational families, and through the program of the church helping the family to find some answers or, at least, some relief; (4) provide Sunday and through the week—particularly through the week—a program that stimulates the creativity and imagination of people who feel that their day is past, and work toward bringing them back into the stream of life of church and community; and (5) provide, for those who need it, housing and supportive services that are not provided in quite the same way, or for the same motives, by other important organizations of the community.

I cannot do justice to all of these in a short presentation, though they inevitably will come out here and there in this paper. So, let me center on what the church can do in bringing new hope and life to people who feel that they have lived past their days of usefulness and creativity.

The XYZ Club was just a year old when I was appointed to direct it. It met once a month in the parlor of the church, and the women of the church served the group a meal once a quarter. We would start off with singing some of the old hymns and have a short devotional. Then we would have some kind of program. At first, it might be a magician, or, if it was near Easter, an Easter parade. Around Valentine's Day, our program often centered on music and talk about "How I met my mate."

Even with this rather meager beginning, I saw something happening. I began to see the group grow as our programs offered more and more, something that was interesting. Soon I began to see people who were on my "shut-in" list attending these monthly meetings of XYZ. We began to discover that so many people who all this time had thought that they were "shut in" had actually been, or allowed themselves to be, *shut out*. The fact that we had stimulating programs brought some of them out of their seclusion. The fact that we furnished transportation to those who needed it meant that many who before had had no way to get out—either because they had no transportation, or because their families were too busy or preoccupied to take them anywhere—could get out again. Many had been shut out, put on the shelf, more than they had been homebound by illness.

A foreshadowing of the *emotional* strength XYZ was to have in the lives of so many is best seen in a person about whom I am thinking now. The grandmother in the home was on my "shut-in" list, but I began to see her at XYZ monthly meetings. Strange—when I went to call on her, she was nearly always either in her bed, or, in "Whistler's Mother" style, sitting in a rocking chair. Then I got the story: Grandmother was in bed most of the time all month. She got out very little. But early on XYZ day she would call her daughter to help her dress. They would pick up a few friends on the way and go to XYZ. When the program was over, back home and to bed she went, for she was truly physically ill. This went on for a couple of years, and then one day she went home and did not get up again. She died before another XYZ program day came.

Our program began to grow and reach new people when the Official Board and the Commission on Education made it possible for us to have a luncheon each month when we met. There is something in eating together that is God-inspired. Not only was this the best meal many of them ate during the month, for a vast number it was about the only meal they really enjoyed, if they lived alone. For now, they did not have to eat alone! Older adults eat more than young people when they have a purpose for eating: fellowship.

As I became better acquainted with our people, we would make time for discussion in the meetings, trying to find out just what their interests were. Asking them to state their interests in writing did not work because of poor sight, poor hearing, poor handwriting, and a feeling of being put on the spot. But in an open, spontaneous discussion, ideas came out. What I was not prepared for was that, before these discussions ended, they often sounded more like an old-fashioned Methodist testimony meeting. Telling of the deeply personal things of his life, someone usually summed it all up by saying: "I just want to say that XYZ is my life-saver program." This puzzled me, for I was not sure what was meant by this statement. So one day I stopped the program and asked one person just what she *was* saying. She fixed her eyes on me and in the most serious tone said: "It is just what I said it was. It is my life-saver program. XYZ literally has saved my life!" And there were murmurs of agreement all over the room—and I did not know what to say.

But as I watched the program grow and develop, I came to believe that, though at first it sounded just a little extravagant, these people meant exactly what they said. The program grew from a meeting once a month to a luncheon meeting each month. Then a craft program of six people in a dark corner of the basement of the church on Thursday morning was begun, moving later to a little house which was available. Here a program of ceramics was added. Finally, there was built a beautiful ground floor adult center that would take care of 700 people. It was planned, however, with the ill, the retired, and the infirm in mind, with XYZ Club Day Center the heart and the purpose for the whole building. I had seen miracles happen, because the church had ceased to be a Sunday affair and was open throughout the week to minister to and work with people of all walks of life, of every faith, and some of no faith—just seeking.

It may be helpful to be a little more specific as to the cost of developing a center program for older adults. It is my experience that there *is* no format for such a program. Each community or particular group must develop its program around particular interests or needs. Each organization has to start where its people are and build its own program around the interests, the needs, and the general environment of the people working in the program. If an organization or club is not *needed,* don't start one! There is no need for more programs for programs' sake.

A club or a center can be as simple or as elaborate as the need. I have outlined how our program developed as we better understood the need and the interest. But, even when we went into arts and crafts, we started with six people in a basement. We started with what we could afford. When word got around, we did receive two gifts of 100 dollars each, but these were small gifts considering that the church had almost 5,000 members.

Though we did receive small memorial gifts from time to time, and one particular class eventually tried to do one important project for us each year, our money came from two sources. First we put out a "kitty." It was covered so that no one knew who gave and who did not. Older adults are proud, and it is our experience that they will do all they can to help themselves if given the opportunity. Unless the gift was by check, we had no idea who contributed. There was no charge for anything made at the center. They could take home anything they made. What surprised us was not how little money was always in the kitty—but how much!

The second thing we did was to hold an annual bazaar.

Anyone could still take home anything he made, without cost. But once the bazaar idea got across, we found our people making a few things for themselves, then something for the bazaar. As this program began to reach people of all denominations, however, and many of no denomination, and the Official Board found the church willing and able to shoulder the responsibility, a person *was* employed to direct the arts and crafts section of the program.

I think it has been proved that the place—either the building or the location, town or country—really makes no difference if the need is there. I am opposed to promoting programs for programs' sake. There is too much to do to badger people into participating in something they neither want nor need. But when the *need* is *there,* when imagination, hard work, and the enthusiasm of the people who feel the need for such a program are evident, it does not really matter *where* you meet. Our program was forced on us by people who felt a need for it. Basements are hard on older adults, but here is where our program started. While we were a big church which could afford to build a ground-floor building which doubled for church school space, we operated a *long* time without it!

Bethel Church is a little open country church, miles from just about everywhere. Yet they were able to start a program for older adults of the community because the need was there. Who said it was easy? There was little outlay of money—who had money? They turned to one of the best resources in the community for volunteer help: the Home Demonstration Department of the Agricultural Extension Service, and people trained in Home Demonstration clubs in the community where the church was. These people can teach you how to take almost anything you find around the house and make something of it—something beautiful. Our volunteer teacher of crafts at Biscayne Manor, where I was administrator, learned most of what she teaches our people through Home Demonstration.

It is not money, it is the need of people for people, and the knowledge that someone cares, that counts. Older adults, who have all that they need in other clubs, programs, gardening, hobbies, and family, may not need the company of people in such organizations as XYZ. We are concerned with the people who through their need find an answer in a special club for them. This does not necessarily demand expenditure of money—love, time, yes—but not necessarily a lot of money.

I have been seriously asked if I thought that to provide special ministry, including a day center for retired people, was setting them apart, isolating them, segregating them. But I have found that the very opposite was true. These people had already been isolated, set apart, and many of them forgotten. And now someone, the church, represented in the lives of a number of volunteer workers and drivers, and a skilled teacher, cared! People whose talents had been buried came alive! People who were so lonely they were losing their minds found that someone cared. People confused and bowed in grief over the loss of a loved one, uprooted and placed in a strange land, found the world had some people in it who were not strangers. Blind people, some of them literally forgotten by their friends, found new light and hope.

As the program grew, it took on many different facets: educational, musical, fun, and finally the day center with its art, ceramics, aluminum craft, wood burning, and many other crafts. The ancient arts of quilting and weaving were revived. More and more we came to see evidence that, while lives are perhaps neither lengthened nor shortened, through XYZ the creativity, the resourcefulness, and the selfhood of the people who take part in the programs are kept alive, or revived to the point that they stay alive as long as they live.

When we first went to Baton Rouge, we had many people with long, tedious, terminal illnesses. But after some years of experience we discovered that with increasing frequency a participant in the XYZ Club program would attend a club meeting on Monday, for example, and then die before he could get back to the center later in the week. Not long before I left, one man died in my arms of heart failure. But he died creative, in the place he loved to be, doing the thing he felt made life, in late years, worth the living.

Who can draw clinical conclusions from such an isolated situation? Yet, if mental and emotional attitudes have anything to do with the well-being of the individual, we *can* make some positive observations. While we had many terminal illnesses in which I was definitely involved as minister to the homebound, those who made the XYZ Center a part of their lives on a regular basis—though they had ulcers and were on strict diets, had diabetes, heart conditions, arthritis, and had had strokes—somehow, someway, seemed to find something at the center that kept them getting out and finding life interesting, where otherwise it would be so easy to stay in bed. More and more, our XYZ'ers having symptoms of the diseases common to the aging were told by their physicians that it was good to keep as active as possible. And they do, to almost the last moment of their lives! Over the past three or four years there have been few deaths that came at the end of a long, bedfast, terminal illness among the group active at the center.

Let us look at some illustrations which the people often described, would not recognize, or, if they did, would be pleased to have told in order to point out the role of the church among the aging. It is important to emphasize that the church worked in conjunction, many times, with other organizations and agencies in the community to bring positive, strengthened mental health, or at least a strong sense of selfhood, into the lives of retired people, many of whom had disease symptoms common to the aging.

It was not unusual for the state mental health center to refer one of its patients to our center. One day I received a call from the mental health center. The caller, one of the heads of the group, asked me if we would accept some of their referrals. Then he went on to say that families had often brought their aging members to the mental health center with a diagnosis of senile psychosis. After some work with the patient, however, they found that the patient was not psychotic, but was suffering from what they called "loneliness senility." These were people starved for companionship—someone to relate to. The amazing thing is that not only did the XYZ'ers never guess their story, we who worked with them often forgot which ones these people were.

A timid, sad, trembling voice on the other end of the phone asked: "Reverend, do you accept Catholics in your center?" I assured her that we did. Then she said, "I am embarrassed to ask you this"—and after a very long pause and nothing else, I said, "I don't embarrass easily, what do you wish to ask?" Then the story unfolded. Her physician said she must get outside herself. Grief had been heaped upon grief. He had suggested the center. But she was ashamed to come because it was the doctor's idea. However, she came, and after a few months she never let anyone forget that the center had "saved her sanity."

Forty miles from Baton Rouge is a state-operated colony for castaways—old people nobody wants. Some have been in the adjacent mental hospital but are not now classed as psychotic. We were asked to take a few of these residents on trial at the center. It was an obviously different, withdrawn group of eight people who entered the XYZ Center that first day. Perhaps only a group meeting in the church would have welcomed them. These people had been offered a craft program in the little village set apart for them where they lived. But they seemingly could not respond to it. It was decided to try an "outside" program.

After only a few months, our XYZ Center held "Family Night," in which the families of our members were invited to come see what "Mother" or "Father" or "Gran" was making. Few families were prepared to see the names of their own parents on the lovely works of art, ceramics, weaving, etc., which they saw that night. Least prepared of all for what he would see was the superintendent of the home dedicated to people nobody wanted. He had come, expressly at our invitation. However, he had expected to tell us that night that sending people 40 miles each way each week was a waste of money and must stop. Then he saw a basket here, a piece of ceramics there, done by "his" people. The capsheaf occurred when he came to a certain painting. Then he told me of the man who had done it—the man who, when he had first come to the village, would let no one see his face. He kept it covered with a cloth. He had to be hand fed with a table spoon. Gradually he came back to himself, but even the superintendent was not prepared to see this man express what he felt on canvas. He asked to be allowed to send a busload rather than withdraw his people.

A couple had lived together as man and wife for 54 years. Yet, while he was five years her senior, it did not dawn on her that he would go first. That morning they had talked about some things they would like to do to the house. He left the breakfast table, and two hours later, when he did not come back to the house for coffee, she found him lying dead in the field.

Things moved fast after that. She was numb! Her son, well educated and with a responsible position in his company, drove up to the old home place for the funeral with plans to take his mother back with him. There seemed nothing else to do. She was alone, and he could not leave his work for long.

In a matter of four or five days, the funeral was over. She had lost her husband, her friends, her home—modest though it was, she loved every nook and cranny of it. She had also lost her bank even though she had seen the banker grow up. Now she was just a magnetic number in a city. Her life and everything that was home vanished. What could be put into the car was taken with them, and her desk was shipped. She was set down in a bustling home of teen-agers: Boy Scouts, Girl Scouts, football, basketball, college—everybody going in all directions.

No one meant to neglect her—but she got lost in the hustle of a modern household. She could not even help her grandchildren with their arithmetic! She hardly knew them, anyway, for she had only seen them for two weeks or so each summer. Son had married the wrong girl. She had picked out a girl for him, but he went off to the big university and brought home another girl, and "Mother" never quite forgave him or accepted the mother of her grandchildren.

On the other hand, her son's family and her grandchildren, seemingly, made little effort to adjust their routines with her in mind—grandmother had to do the adjusting. She was alone long hours at a time. Son never quite had the time she needed for him to talk with her. She soon learned that two women could not work in the same kitchen. It was not long before she began to retaliate. When company came in, she *obviously* went to her room, slamming the door. Then, her son, through a neighbor, heard of the XYZ Center.

The first time I met "grandmother" she was so withdrawn by grief, confusion, and anger, that when, preacher-like, I extended my hand to her, she ignored it. For a long time she just sat at the center, doing nothing. It is amazing how you do not see what is happening before your eyes.

One day her son phoned me with tears in his voice saying that, if something was not done, his home would break up. I urged him to come to our supper and XYZ Bazaar that night. He came alone. The next morning he phoned me and said: "Jim, it is a miracle!" I asked what miracle, and he said, "Mother." I came alive! "What has happened to your mother?" I hastily asked. "Why, didn't you see her last night?" Then the story came out. His mother had been working at the Bazaar all that day. He had come by my office to make sure that I would not give away the fact that he had been behind his mother's finding the center. He did not want me to act as if I had ever seen him before. So, when I came back later to the gym, there was his mother, busy, waiting on people. She took time out to introduce me to her son, whom she reminded me she had told me so much about. Then she was busy again, showing him around and working in the Bazaar. It had come about so gradually, I had not seen it myself, or been aware of its being unusual. But the son said: "I have never seen *this* mother before!" Then he told me of a mother who, when his father was alive, cried and got her way, and still was trying this trick in *his* home. Eventually, we were able to call a family conference in my office: son, daughter-in-law, and grandmother. We helped grandmother find a new place to live, on her own. She was never a happy person, but she did work with us, and a home that seemed unable to adjust to three generations was probably saved.

So, we could go on and on. There was the scientist, whom I had always thought lived "in another world," working in ceramics and wood-burning. The veteran of World War I whom I found in a veterans' hospital came to the center to continue the hand therapy he had started in the hospital. He brought veteran after veteran with him. He often made me go with him to see someone who had had a stroke whom he felt could find creativity, usefulness, and selfhood through the XYZ Center.

One day my phone rang, and the voice on the line was that of the head of a department in the university. His mother, who also had her doctorate, had just retired and moved into his home and was like a fish out of water. She could not accept the fact that she could no longer as a tutor even hold the interest of a student. The children in his home were suffering. Would we let her come to the center? He had been referred by the School of Social Welfare of the university. His mother came. She was of foreign background, and had so lived in the foreign language she had taught that she had the characteristics of the people, and actually had a language barrier. We found a young woman who had grown up speaking the Americanized dialect of that language who would sit and help the older woman with ceramics. They would talk: the girl in Cajun, the teacher in pure French. You could hear them laughing all over the very large general crafts room, as the girl, speaking vernacular French, made what were, fortunately to them both, funny errors. This story is of particular importance to me because it so ties in with my work now. Here was a woman who could not accept the thought of retirement, much less the idea of going to a retirement home. The XYZ Center at the church became the bridge. After several months at the center, the lady was able to accept going to a retirement home.

Woven throughout my work as the minister of the parish were the threads of my work as director of the XYZ Center. It became impossible at points to distinguish between the center and my homebound people. Often they were the same. More and more, however, this weekday program became identified with what the church was all about, and what my ministry was about, in the minds of the people.

Frequently I was asked to call on someone who "needed" the center, just as I was asked to call on someone who was physically ill, or "needed" the church in any other capacity— or its ministry. It became an integral part of my ministry. More than this, I saw the people become the church—the church in action—and the ministers.

We finally employed one of our excellent volunteers as Arts and Crafts Coordinator for the center, and she now heads the XYZ program. None of us could have seen the miracles that happened without the large group of lay volunteers, recruited both by the minister of the parish and the Arts and Crafts Coordinator, but *trained* by her, to work *with* older adults (not for them) and to love them and to recognize them as sacred personalities—people.

Though only one worship service was held a month, and attendance at this was, of course, optional, we saw people of all faiths, who some way found "the church" and *became* the church in action. Many of our XYZ'ers belonged to other organizations for older adults in the community, but they professed to find something at the center that they did not find in the other programs. Some could define it, others would not have found it possible to say just *what* it was—but it was different, and this difference was of utmost importance to them. We call it the church, and often, without their knowing it, they too had become the church and the ministers.

Grief and age were the two basic things they all had in common. One would come to the center, bowed in grief, direct from all the breakups of home and life that the death of a mate denotes. Sometimes they were withdrawn. At the center, with the XYZ'ers, they found understanding ears— understanding in *many* ways. At first, each person was accepted without question. If he was withdrawn, no one pushed him. If at first the individual could do nothing but talk about his grief, this was accepted, too. And then, in a way only one older adult can do for another, someone would help the grief-stricken one to realize that grief is universal—it had happened to them all. There was no harshness that I ever saw or heard, but gradually, and sometimes firmly, they *handled* each other's griefs and found reconciliation and fortitude. Nothing an ordained minister had said, or would say, could do it. The people, however, being the church, the people ministering to each other's needs, led another along the path to hope and peace and life again.

I spent hour upon hour working with counseling problems in grief, three-generational families, emotional crises. I found the resources of the whole community behind me. It was amazing to me for people highly skilled and trained in their professions to turn to a ministry of the church as a means of undergirding their own work with people. Doctors, mental health centers, family counseling service, social workers, psychiatrists—and these usually turned out to be people of faith —working hand in hand with the church—no, I think they became the church, as we teamed up to work, each with his own training and discipline, with people who needed more than we ourselves alone could give or do.

A social worker, who was physically blind himself, brought four blind people to the center. One of these blind men (and each of these people had an unusual story in connection with the center) had not been out of his home for six years except to go to the doctor, or occasionally to the welfare office. When his neighbors saw a car pull up each Tuesday morning and take him away, they became curious and asked him where he went. "To the center down at the Methodist Church." "Are you a Methodist?" they asked. He was not and told them the church to which he belonged but which he had not been in for many years. It turned out that a neighbor down the block belonged to that same church. The neighbor began to come each Sunday and take him to church—and somehow this blind man reflected in his own glory and enthusiasm what the church *really* is. He learned to make baskets; he learned to weave. But most of all he became significant, important, creative, a "self"—but more, he became the church in action, reflecting the church in all his enthusiasm—for indeed he was lost and was found, was blind, but saw as he had never been able to see before!

The role of the church in providing services for the welfare of the elderly person in the community is not just perfunctorily to get him involved in "busy work," but to help him to find himself—to help people dangerously withdrawn, grief-stricken, lonely, sick and afraid, back into the stream of life —life with a purpose for living, creative, with a new sense of selfhood that is God-given. This is not "busy work," but the church in *action* calling the elderly to action as the church redemptive—the redemptive fellowship!

SELECTED BIBLIOGRAPHY

EMMONS, HELEN B. *The Mature Heart*. New York: Abingdon Press, 1953.

GRAY, ROBERT M., AND DAVID O. MOBERT. *The Church and the Older Person*. Grand Rapids, Mich.: Erdmans, 1962.

KUBIE, SUSAN H., AND GERTRUDE LANDAU. *Group Work with the Aged*. New York: International Universities Press, 1953.

MAVES, PAUL B., AND J. LENNART CEADERLEAF. *Older People and the Church*. New York: Abingdon Press, 1949.

NARRAMORE, C. M. *The Mature Years*. Grand Rapids, Mich.: Zondervan Press, 1961 (paper).

OATES, WAYNE E. *The Revelation of God in Human Suffering*. Philadelphia: Westminster Press, 1959.

STAFFORD, VIRGINIA, AND LARRY EISENBERG. *Fun for Older Adults*. New York: Pantheon Press, 1956.

STERN, EDITH, AND MABEL ROSS, M.D. *You and Your Aging Parents*. New York: Harper, rev. ed., 1965.

15

BETTER HOUSING FOR SENIOR CITIZENS
John A. Chase

What do we really seek as a nation, as a society, as a state, and as a community for our American citizens of *distinguished* age? It is my belief that we seek to develop a normal and natural place in society for this three-score-and-ten segment of our population. The physical environment for the elderly *must* provide a normal and natural setting in our communities, embracing many types of living arrangements to permit personal preferences and responsive to the varying demands of age, health, and the pocketbook.

Thoughtfully developed housing should be the *nucleus* from which should proceed all other efforts of the community to provide independent, active living during the senior years. Programs in health and income maintenance, retraining for employment, continuing education, recreation and social activities may become futile if the basic security of the "right" home, in terms of size, safety, design, and location, is not available at rates reasonably consistent with ability to pay.

Consider the dimensions of the need for senior citizens' housing. How many of the elderly do not have adequate housing, and to what extent are their choices limited by income?

In 1960, the U.S. Census of the Population disclosed that 30 percent of all families headed by persons 65 and over occupied housing that was dilapidated, deteriorating, or lack-

John A. Chase is the administrator of the Columbia Housing Authority, Columbia, South Carolina.

ing in some facilities. This represents about 2.8 million deficient housing units, and in nearly 2 million of these the household income in 1959 was below $2,000. Also reported were another 2 million units in which senior citizens lived with their children or other relatives, and of these more than 400,000 units were deficient. In addition, a substantial number of the 6.5 million standard housing units occupied by families headed by elderly persons are probably quite unsatisfactory for their needs; they may be unsafe, difficult to maintain, too large for efficient living, or lacking in services needed by older people. Even among these it is significant that more than 35 percent had 1959 incomes below $2,000.

Narrowing the focus to any state, and in turn to any one town, the above figures doubtless apply proportionately.

With this profile in mind, consider the programs administered by the Department of Housing and Urban Development that respond to senior citizen housing needs throughout the nation. By far the largest federal program for housing the elderly is the low-rent public housing program, with two-thirds of all federally assisted housing for senior citizens in this category, providing standard housing for some 325,000. In June, 1967, for example, there were about 60,000 low-rent dwellings specifically designed for the elderly in some 1,800 communities. Contracts had been executed for another 74,000 units for the elderly, and 23,000 more were in applications in process. However, this does not represent the total effort in low-rent public housing for the elderly. Older people, also live in public housing which is not specially designed for them. There were nearly 197,000 units, including specially designed units, occupied by the elderly, or about 32 percent of the total number of low-rent public housing units available.

What other kinds of low-rent housing programs are available? Mortgage insurance, rent supplements, and direct loans are available to create adequate homes for the aged. A brief description of these follows.

The mortgage insurance programs are operated by the Federal Housing Administration and include the housing program for the elderly (Section 231) and the nursing home program (Section 232). Section 231 provides for up to 100 percent of replacement cost for nonprofit sponsors and up to 90 percent for profit-motivated sponsors, thus making services available to older people of varying incomes. The nursing home program provides up to 90 percent of the FHA-estimated value of construction to nonprofit and profit-motivated groups.

Long-term, low-interest loans to private nonprofit sponsors, to consumer cooperatives, and to certain public sponsors to develop specially designed housing are provided under the "202" Program. Income limits have been established under this program, varying from community to community within national limits of $4,000 for single persons and $4,800 for couples.

The rent supplement program is a natural partnership of public and private enterprise to aid the poor. Generally, rent supplement housing is developed under FHA 221(d)(3)— market rate mortgage insurance. Those who are eligible for rent supplements are required to pay 25 percent of their income for rent. The difference between this amount and the full market rent for their dwelling generally will be the amount of "rent supplement."

The "leased housing" program is still another innovation for the benefit of low-income groups and the elderly. It authorizes local housing authorities to purchase and, if necessary, to rehabilitate private homes or even to lease existing private housing, thus making suitable housing available more quickly than through new construction.

Finally, there are two other programs that can be helpful to the elderly living in urban renewal or code enforcement areas. These are the direct-low-interest home rehabilitation *loans* and home rehabilitation *grants* for low-income owners. Not only will they provide better places in which to live, they will also reduce the need for dislocation from friends and familiar environments.

The new Neighborhood Facilities Program helps to provide neighborhoods with much-needed services in centers that give older and younger people a common meeting place. These centers can be important factors in helping the elderly retain their independence, with meaningful opportunities to contribute to their communities and continue useful and socially productive lives.

Experience indicates that if any housing program for senior citizens is to be successful, under whatever sponsorship, it must mobilize local, state, and federal resources. Every interested group—housing sponsors, local government, voluntary associations, private industry, future residents, and individual citizens—should somehow become committed to the program once there is understanding of its purpose and objectives.

SELECTED REFERENCES

BACK, KURT W. *Projets and People: Social Psychological Problems of Relocation in Puerto Rico.* Durham: Duke University Press, 1962.

SCHORR, ALVIN L., "Housing the Poor," *Power, Poverty, and Urban Policy,* ed. WARNER BLOOMBERG AND HENRY SCHMANDT. Beverly Hills, Calif.: Sage Publications, Inc., 1968.

SCHORR, ALVIN L., "National Community and Housing Policy," *Urban Planning and Social Policy,* ed. BERNARD FRIEDEN AND ROBERT MORRIS. New York: Basic Books, Inc., 1968.

WEAVER, ROBERT C. *The Urban Complex.* Garden City, N.Y.: Doubleday and Company, Inc., 1964.

WHEATON, WILLIAM L. C., "The Two Cultures and the Urban Revolution," *The City Church,* September–October, 1962.

16

A CHURCH HOUSES THE ELDERLY

George F. Packard

With the improved facilities for health, retirement plans in industry, and longer life, there are more active people among the 18 million over 65 years of age than ever before. And their number will increase appreciably over the years.

The elderly comprise a segment of the population to which the church has or should have a ministry and responsibility. What *is* the church's role in respect to the senior citizen? Should it be content to sit by and expect the usual organizations within it to absorb this group, or should the church be on the leading and creative edge of the missionary thrust to reach and serve these people?

Very little has been done, although some parishes have tried with varying success and frequency the Golden Age type of meetings in the parish house. Others have senior groups within the framework of the Episcopal Churchwomen, while the majority of parishes do little or nothing.

I repeat, the church *does have* a responsibility to the aging and aged! And this will be particularly true in the downtown or semisuburban congregations.

The areas of greatest concern to the elderly include family relationships, health, activities, and housing. Because it is a family itself, the church can assist families to understand their elderly members and thereby cement intergenerational relationships. But we have to realize that many elderly members

The Reverend George F. Packard is the Rector of St. Mary's Episcopal Church, Baltimore, Maryland.

do not fit into the family scheme today as in the past, if for no other reason than their past involvement in an agricultural society which had both a need and room for the elderly in the economic life of the farming family. But with the passing of the farm and the emergence of an urban way of life, the senior members of the family tend to be just so much surplus humanity. Since he doesn't "fit" as readily, and since his interests differ radically from those of his children, the church should be concerned with both the elderly person's housing and his more personal needs.

How, then, shall they be housed, in what kind of housing are they to be placed, and who is going to provide this special type of housing? I have already answered the last question, and examples of what has been done in the past include the following: *Nursing home care* is the area in which the church has played its most significant role in the area of housing in the past, but the demand for more of these remains. Some churches, secondly, have built nursing-type homes, but without the inclusion of bed-care facilities. In these the residents come to a common dining room for meals, and the bedrooms are generally little more than just that. This arrangement is referred to as *complete care housing,* and, depending on the special needs of the individual, there is a basis for having more units of this type.

The third type of accommodation, a recent development, is the *apartment house* designed specifically for the elderly and allowing for independence and a security not available in ordinary apartments. Under the Housing and Home Finance Agency of the Community Facilities Administration, funds are available from the federal government to nonprofit charitable groups at a low rate of interest payable over 50 years. Under this agency churches can sponsor and construct housing which will fill a growing need in our society. The church will serve the aged better if housing is constructed near the church, so that full use of its facilities can be made. Also, the greater the proximity of apartment house to church, the better will be the communication between each apartment and the church office.

St. Mary's Church in the Hampden section of Baltimore was among the first of our parishes to plan such a facility, St. Mary's Roland View Towers, completed in December, 1964. To fit the individual needs of the residents, there are 13 two-bedroom, 13 alcove-efficiency, 67 one-bedroom, and 56 efficiency apartments in the Towers, which rise 14 stories and are located beside the church on one of the highest spots in Baltimore. In addition to a garden area on the roof, from which the view is breathtaking, is the dining room, which is glassed on two sides and affords a splendid panorama of the Chesapeake Bay and harbor and the downtown area. In pleasant weather the doors of the dining room can be opened and the residents can dine on the terrace if they wish. The apartments, centrally air-conditioned with individual controls in each, contain full kitchens, wall-to-wall carpets, drapes, and bathrooms. Cost for utilities is included in the rentals, which range from 75 to 140 dollars a month.

The building has meeting rooms, areas for arts and crafts, a library, and recreation areas. Laundry and incinerator facilities are located on each floor, and accommodations exist for a drug store, a beauty shop, and dry cleaning.

The program for the residents is under the direction of the manager, who is a priest of the church. The motto of the Towers, "Not merely living but a way of life," is given expression in the variety of activities—films, concerts, arts and crafts, clubs, lectures, and church services—available to those who wish them. St. Mary's itself offers the usual activities of a parish and encourages participation in parish life for persons of all ages. We *care* for our elderly citizens who live with us, and we daily inquire on each resident and provide the services of a nurse at any hour.

St. Mary's program was the answer of the church's vestry to a question which I presented to them several years ago: How should we serve the community? A small committee appointed by the vestry voted to tear down the old rectory, and a nearby home was purchased to make room for the Towers. The vestry also planned for a second similar apartment unit, which will be located across the street from the

Towers, and, in addition, four homes to the rear of the church were purchased to make way for a nursing home to be built in the near future.

The fulfillment of our dream has not been without struggle. A few members of the parish felt that this was beyond the scope of the parish church. There were delays, many problems of construction and planning had to be considered and solved daily, but the flood of applicants proved the great need which we eventually filled. Over 320 applications were received by January, almost twelve months prior to the completion of the Towers, and new applications continue to arrive to this day.

Those over 62 years of age and within the middle-income group can reside in the Towers. There are no restrictions on the basis of race, creed, or color, although the great majority of applicants are members of the Episcopal Church. Each applicant is given a preliminary interview, and a committee of the Board of Trustees reviews each application, approval of which is followed by two months of trial residence in the apartments. Within this time a resident may withdraw or be asked to leave should the need arise, an indication of our conviction that the program is more a *home* than merely an apartment building, and members must be congenial and *enjoy* the type of environment we wish to develop and maintain.

Another chapter could be written on what has taken place in the lives of those who have chosen the Towers as their home. Briefly, with its opening, the residents of Roland View Towers were given the opportunity to use and develop skills and be of service beyond the usual number of years. Equally important has been the discovery by the church of a new era of service to the elderly, who have become enfolded into the life of the church.

SELECTED REFERENCES

GLAZER, NATHAN, "Housing and the Consumer," *Metropolis: Values in Conflict*, ed. C. E. ELIAS, J., and others. Belmont, Calif.: Wadsworth Publishing Company, 1964.

SHERRARD, THOMAS D., AND RICHARD C. MURRAY, "The Church and the Neighborhood Community Organization," *Urban Planning and Social Policy*, ed. BERNARD FRIEDEN AND ROBERT MORRIS. New York: Basic Books, 1968.

WINTER, GIBSON, "The Suburban Captivity of the Churches," *Metropolis: Values in Conflict*, ed. C. E. ELIAS, JR., and others. Belmont, Calif.: Wadsworth Publishing Company, 1964.

WURSTER, CATHERINE BAUER, "Housing: A Wider Range of Choice," *Metropolis: Values in Conflict*, ed. C. E. ELIAS, JR. and others. Belmont, Calif.: Wadsworth Publishing Company, 1964.

CONCLUSION: AGING IN PERSPECTIVE
Charles G. Oakes

"It is pleasant to be transferred from an office where one is afraid of a sergeant-major into an office where one can intimidate generals, and perhaps this is why History is so attractive to the more timid amongst us," wrote E. M. Forster. "We can recover self-confidence by snubbing the dead. . . . The schoolmaster in each of us awakes, examines the facts. of History, and marks them on the results of the examination."

In this summary and concluding remarks I regretfully lack the consolation of commenting on the past. My colleagues too readily will answer back, and my readers—you who work with the elderly, live with them, study them, and are among them—will answer back. My task is to be honest and just with that which has preceded. A few liberties will be reserved, however, in attempting to indicate some of the implications of these readings, and others, for the immediate and distant future.

Briefly, what has been said in the foregoing pages? Our sociologists have pigeonholed the elderly into categories and in some instances into special groups. Their brethren the psychologists in typical fashion have subjected the aged to personality tests and psychoanalyzed them. The biologists titrate their parts and study the residue as to the degree of blueness or redness, a parody on how the elderly must fre-

Charles G. Oakes is on the faculty of the Duke University Medical Center and also Director of the Division of Planning and Evaluation, North Carolina Regional Medical Program.

quently feel as a result of our attempts to understand them! Physicians diagnose, treat, and, alas, lose the elderly to other physicians, and charlatans, and admit frequent frustration. The economists recommend retirement *and* subsequent re-employment. We plan recreation for the elderly, provide housing, invite them to church, and still wonder why they don't take advantage of the array of counseling services we have so carefully made available.

How do the elderly feel about all this going on?

In rereading the above remarks, I am reminded of Ferdinand Tönnies' critique on empirical science and shudder at his disquieting intimation that when we analyze we fragment, and fragmentation is destruction; all analysis leads to fission of the whole. Without the help of all the king's horses and all the king's men, then, I truly wonder if our distinguished senior citizens can possibly be put back together again.

Running like a connecting thread through all the chapters of this book is a vocabulary that includes the following: stereotypes; the evitable and inevitable; needs, interests, and problems; and challenge and dutiful and obligatory individual, group, and community response. Clearly, men of intelligence and good will differ over the interpretation of these ideas. Some of you will have found your own views reinforced and will defend them with renewed confidence. Others will have been swayed by new and persuasive knowledge and arguments. Still others who have had no position on certain critical aspects of the aging may now find themselves with strong convictions. And cutting across these three categories will be those who have read *only* the chapters in which they had some prior interest. For this group, the fallacy of analysis persists.

A realistic appraisal of the world recognizes others who, despite all that has been discovered and forwarded by gerontologists, will retain their prejudices and stereotypes, much evidence to the contrary. They too constitute a challenge.

However, some readers—the most thoughtful—will feel compelled by the chapters seen in perspective to move beyond them, to raise other fundamental questions, and to seek avenues for the implementation of their answers.

The subjects to which we have been drawn, and about which misconceptions abound, are family and peer relations; health, illness, and medical care; retirement and capabilities for post-retirement employment; housing; and involvement in recreational and religious activities. The following elaborations of these do not appear in any special order; perspective dictates inextricable weavings in and out.

Not too many years ago commentators held a polarized view of the family. A prototypical form found in nonindustrial, largely rural farming areas was characterized by cohabitation of several generations under the same roof, or under separate roofs in close proximity to each other. Contrastingly, in modern highly urbanized societies, so the opinion went, the family is isolated, each generation of a once extended arrangement disinterested in the other. But this view is inaccurate. The research of latter-day pioneers such as Eugene Litwak, Marvin Sussman, and William Knox leads George Maddox and Rosamonde Boyd to state firmly that apparent separation of the generations is vitiated by frequent contacts among family members and by the regular contributions each generation makes to the other. A type of symbiotic relationship has developed, the young adults being helped by their parents to establish their own families, and the children helping their parents when they are in need.

Wives regularly outlive their husbands, and recognition of this led many to assume that "living alone" invariably brought about loneliness. Studies comparing single with married women, however, show that the former are more likely to make a better adjustment on retirement. It does not follow that single women are precisely comparable to widows, but aloneness per se is insufficient to explain desperate loneliness. In questioning the idea that the old were isolated, Ethel Shanas found that 80 percent of the older people are living with a spouse or with others. Of those who live alone, three-fourths are women, but Miss Shanas estimated that less than

6 percent of all old people in this country are socially isolated. If community leaders have established senior citizens'
centers to combat loneliness, we can understand, in the light
of Miss Shanas' study, why fewer elderly than expected have
gravitated to the centers. Not only have we overestimated the
degree of loneliness or isolation, but few of the elderly, as is
the case in all other age categories, join voluntary organizations.

Other reasons may exist for the aged's noninvolvement in
voluntary organizations; these provide some clues for future
planning. In Chapter 11, for instance, Ida Simpson advocates
compulsory retirement, but quickly acknowledges the benefits
of some kind of continuing activity for retirees. Studies show
that most occupational groups tend to view retirement nega-
tively. Continued productivity seems to be built into the
physiology of *Homo americanus,* regardless of socio-economic status. Is it not possible that in our attempts to provide
"busy time" for the elderly we are saying: "Poor soul; nothing to do; come play and pray with us." And in so doing we
dramatize and institutionalize the very condition abhorred by
the elderly, the condition of idleness and/or nonproductivity.

Some will point to the successful foster grandparent programs and say that certainly these are contrived efforts to
keep the oldster busy. Yes, but look carefully at the type of
busyness: the elderly are *paid to work* in association with
children, and in so doing play a definite social role in the
community; they are paid for doing an important, humane
public service in providing love, warmth, and attention to
youngsters. In Chapter 7 a similar type of program is proposed for hospitals wherein elderly persons could minister
to their ill counterparts.

The current problem of unemployment among the elderly
has grave implications for the future, when the retirement
age is expected to drop appreciably, when we can expect not
only more persons of retirement age but more years of retirement. Juanita Kreps in Chapter 10 anticipates one dimension
of the problem in her comments on the diminishing purchasing power of the retirement dollar over 20 or so years of

retirement. No matter how the economic stability of the elderly is achieved, the problem of idleness will loom larger, particularly for the middle and lower classes. If the problem of idleness is solved, it may be possible to eliminate or at least decrease in importance the problem of ever-increasing subsidization of the elderly. Let me explain.

It has been suggested that younger persons be trained in more than one occupation, and with modern techniques of programmed learning this is already quite possible. One occupation would be reserved for the younger years, the other for the later ones. In the Foreword, James Wiggins mentions the ubiquitousness of age-grading; "age-specific job grading" can become a reasonable requisite for living in a highly technological society.

For those who advocate putting the learning of a second skill off to the years immediately preceding or following retirement, it is necessary to look at the literature on adult socialization, in which several factors favoring training in the earlier years are mentioned. In the several years prior to retirement these skills could be reviewed and upgraded relative to current standards. This would be consistent with those studies that show that *sudden* retirement is more disconcerting to the retiree than *gradual* desocialization from the job through longer vacations and the like. During vacation layoffs, the skill learned earlier could be revitalized. Additional support for earlier socialization in multiple skills comes from Raymond Payne, who says that for oldsters to accept the *young* as agents of their own socialization represents a direct and complete (and, I add, intimidating) role reversal. For society to have age-graded structures, preparation for admission to which is accomplished early in life, would facilitate for the elderly retention of the personal integrity valued by all of us.

Adriaan Verwoerdt and Frances Carp, in Chapters 5 and 8, see the possibility of continuing productivity in the later years in their discussions of the biological and psychological characteristics of the aging. In terms of changes in sensation and perception, vision and hearing, and the mechanisms of response and locomotion, Miss Carp cites various occupations in which elderly persons continue to function well to the satisfaction of profit-oriented employers. Verwoerdt alludes to the fact that the major biological problems of the elderly revolve around the chronic diseases, and, while these presently pose major problems in medical research, their eventual solution will reduce disabilities to a minimum. A brief review of the progress made in medicine in recent years will give some indication of what we can expect in the years ahead.

Death has been regarded as the inevitable end result of living, but some medical scientists protest instead that the only factor which prevents our living forever is death. In 1900, for instance, one could expect on the average to live 40 years; today three score and ten is a common reality—a 30-year gain in just over half a century. These figures, set in more dramatic terms, show that for each additional year of medical research we can anticipate living about seven additional months. The evidence, though still not yet overwhelming, suggests that modern man can look forward to living 150 years.

Medical research and practice have succeeded in almost completely changing the cause of death in the medically advanced countries of the world, so that instead of the majority of deaths resulting from infectious diseases, four out of five deaths in 1958 were due to chronic or degenerative ones, such as cancers and tumors, cardiovascular and renal diseases, and imbalances of the endocrine glands. René Dubos adds that along with the chronic diseases of old age mental illness is a major crippler in our society. In poignant style typical of Dubos, a picture of the etiology of mental disorders is drawn, bringing into clearer relief through comparative ethnographic descriptions the fact that the "idle" societies are the sick ones, not those in which the people are "preoccupied," in his words, by the "ancient need for being a real participant in the act of creation," or entrenched in the "long saga of difficulties overcome, or emergencies that had to be met . . . ."

In our society, then, we have progressed admirably in two spheres of activity: medicine and industrial technology, the first guaranteeing greater longevity, the second promising ever fewer years of employment. The two counterposed creates the sociological monster with which we are here concerned. True, we have bowed at the altar of longevity. And to achieve longevity we have willingly deprived ourselves of many undelayed gratifications through our private and legislated contributions to the coffers of medical research. But now we find ourselves defining those who achieve longevity as not being "our kind of people." They are our kind of people if they keep active, but whether manufactured activity is what *they* want is another matter, and whether our institutions change to make continued use of them or whether the elderly create their own institutions which may or may not "mesh" with the larger social structure is yet to be seen. Leonard Cain has suggested that the aged segment of the population is "ripe" for forming a massive social movement. As this segment increases in number and, because of better health, in capability, the probability increases for a retirees march on Washington!

Continuing with matters of health, we are concerned with the extent of illness, the amount spent on medicines and physicians, and the impact that research in these areas has had on public policy. Several of the contributors to this book state that only between 3 and 5 percent of the elderly are in institutions, and for this reason Miss Shanas' study of the noninstitutionalized part of the aged population is important for its clarification of obscurities and misconceptions. She reported that only about 14 percent of the aged outside institutions can be classified as "very sick," but these data are derived from what the elderly say about themselves. And George Maddox's research cited in Chapter 7 indicates that those who are socially isolated cannot be relied upon to give accurate appraisals of their health status. Since the isolated are also more prone to exaggerate the severity of health problems, therefore, Shanas' figures probably overestimate the actual number who are very sick.

In their discussion of the economic status and problems of

the elderly, Juanita Kreps and Ida Simpson make only incidental reference to the costs of medical care. Miss Shanas reported that only 8 percent of those she studied stated that they were not using medical or dental care because of lack of money, and a 1966 federal government publication reports that middle-range income retired couples spend only about 8 percent of their income on medicine, physicians, and other medical needs. Miss Shanas also found that about 70 percent of noninstitutionalized older people who incurred costs for physician services paid these costs themselves; and at least 60 percent who incurred hospitalization costs met them from their own resources: income, savings, or health and hospital insurance.

Pyramiding research data may be having results on images of the aging held by public agencies; Gordon Streib and Harold Orbach remark that "after the findings of the Shanas . . . survey appeared . . . the division of Program Research in the Social Security Administration no longer stated that *all* the aged are poverty stricken or *all* the aged are sick."

Turning to some of the strategies of medical practice discussed by Carl Eisdorfer in Chapter 8, we find that one criticism in particular is applicable to persons of all ages, not merely the aged. He correctly states that the elderly represent a generation accustomed to close personal doctor-patient relationships; the absence of these in modern medicine creates a treatment environment alien and repugnant to the elderly person. However, hospital studies of alienation among patients of all ages indicate that the greater the social distance between the patient and the staff member, the slower the response of the patient to treatment.

Eisdorfer's recommendation for the elderly, then, is a need of all patients. Social scientists working in conjunction with medical educators and practitioners are increasingly recognized for their contributions to the social and psychological dimensions of medical practice.

Let us assume for the moment that the problems of medical care for the elderly envisaged by Eisdorfer were solved. Even if this were the case, I have grave reservations that we would be home free, if for no other reason than the problem associated with the continuously renewed differences between the generations.

Karl Mannheim observed that the succession of generations regularly involves a "fresh contact" with the accumulated heritage, "a novel approach in assimilating, using and developing the proffered material." However, in periods of rapid social change, typical of the United States for over half a century now, a new generation is likely to develop a more distinctive outlook and aims, and to come into more acute conflict with the older generations. Our present concern with the generation gap and its focus on youth overlooks the gap between pre- and post-retirement generations which these readings have all too lucidly emphasized. The conflict between generations, say some observers, has become more intense, "and many of the protest movements in all countries express the resentments and aspirations of a younger generation . . . ." There is evidence to suggest that the old, in terms of this analysis, are resentful and have aspirations of their own, and this can be seen in the area of medical care.

In a penetrating dissection of the "health food movement," Hans Toch centralizes on the "exploitation of predispositions." "The consumer of health foods is given *authoritative sanction for his hopes*. He derives confirmation for his unhappiness with the pessimistic prognoses of conventional medicine, while he simultaneously gets the benefit of professional backing for a more congenial view." Not only can the elderly person "dismiss his family physician's cautious appraisals as proof of medicine's susceptibility to the profit-inspired propaganda of chemical firms, but he can bask in his own familiarity with tradition-oriented quotations on bottle labels and the literature circulated by manufacturers." For the elderly person, therefore, health foods, whether harmful, beneficial, or of no consequence whatsoever, constitute a syncretistic bridge between modern science and tradition implicit in the emphasis on "natural" products. Toch continues: "Beyond immediate gains, there are the benefits of membership in the health food *movement*. Among these benefits are the partnership with nature, the support of others in the battle against infirmity, the feeling of increased sophistication, the joy of evading physicians, the adventure of the scientific chase, the satisfaction of preserving tradition, and—most importantly—the profit gained from the belief that preventive action can be taken."

The above premise, contrary to the image Eisdorfer says represents the views of many doctors about the elderly, transforms the maturing and aged person from a helpless instrument of the aging process into a controlling party. And, corroborating Eisdorfer, Toch concludes, "the attractiveness of health foods for the aging person might diminish if and only if he received concrete assurance *from his physician* that they could jointly take every possible measure to furnish him with a happier and a more productive existence" (emphasis added).

It is quite possible, then, that, regardless of efforts to solve present specific problems of the elderly, there will be renewed with each generation the timeless phenomenon of the desire and perceived right of the incumbents of *all* generations to strive for and maintain an identity uniquely of their own making.

The foregoing refers to earlier comments bearing on some type of continued self-sufficiency or autonomy among the aged, a theme which persists in a majority of the readings. Autonomy suggests that one is, in some way or another, in control of an environment of which he is a crucial element. The "life review" described by Adriaan Verwoerdt is a maneuver by which the elderly person, in summarizing the meaningful events of the past, symbolically controls an environment void of temporal barriers. Certain structures facilitate this control. Rosamonde Boyd offers the important role of the grandparent as "family historian," and with James Ailor adds that the church is a place in which the life review can be institutionalized. Caution is recommended in assuming that the church is a principle locus for this, since the findings on participation in religious activities, contrary to what most people think regarding the elderly, is not as significant as we have imagined.

The hypothesis that the aged turn toward religion or that religiosity increases with age is not supported, says Harold Orbach; M. L. Barron concludes that rather than turning to religion, "most older people simply persist in the religious patterns of their earlier age-statuses," a theme indorsed by Maddox, Verwoerdt, and Simpson in their respective discussions. Lois Dean and D. S. Newell, however, specify one condition under which piety does seem to increase; they find more piety in the years immediately adjacent to retirement than after the crisis of retirement is reconciled with a new style of life.

In line with Miss Dean and Newell, Ailor in Chapter 14 correctly perceives one of the responsibilities of the church as that of providing counsel concerning death and holding out the hope of immortality; but to assume, even if one is in agreement with Ailor, that attempts at such programs will result in great success is unwarranted. For, as Wendell M. Swenson reports, elderly persons differ significantly in how they view death. "Persons engaged in frequent religious activity or demonstrating a fundamentalist type of religion evidenced a very positive or forward-looking death attitude, whereas those with little religious activity or interest either evaded reference to death or feared it."

A comparison of religious activities and beliefs of earlier generations with those of today will recommend implementation of *more* counseling in or by the church in the future, inasmuch as fundamentalism is on the decline; and, although membership in the church has not appreciably decreased, the role of the church in commanding the member's time and influencing his life view has.

There is little doubt about the church's assumption of a significant role in the "handling of impending death," but, if earlier religious beliefs and activities determine who attends in the later years, then the very persons who would need the most counseling are least likely to be found in churches today or in the future. This raises the often stated proposition that, unless the church's ministry demonstrably extends beyond its physical boundaries, its efforts will be minimized, if not totally lost, and current trends indicate that its problems in this area will increase. Take, for instance, the conditions under which people die. More and more, death is institution-alized outside of the family, occurring mainly in specialized "dying institutions"—hospitals, old people's homes, and nursing homes. This situation issues in a view of death rationalized in modern scientific terms which are in contrast to the message of immortality.

In contrast to pre-industrial societies, in which symbolic contacts with the spirits and ghosts of the dead were fre-quent, intimate, and often long-lasting, there has been a sig-nificant decline in the authority of the dead. This coincides with the youthful orientation, receptivity to innovation, and dynamic social change that characterize modern societies. Observing Catholics in this society are almost the only major exception to this. For others, contact with the dead is limited to specific spacial boundaries such as cemeteries, and then only for brief, socially specified periods following death. Robert Blauner proposes that "perhaps it is the irrelevance of the dead that is *the clue to the status of old people in modern industrial societies.* In a low-mortality society, most deaths occur in old age, and since the aged predominate among those who die, the association between old age and death is intensified" (emphasis added). Elsewhere, Herman Feifel remarks that American society's rejection of (and even revulsion for) the old may be because they remind us un-consciously of death. If the church, then, finds difficulty in making death honorable for a significant portion of the popu-lation, it may be the lot of the physician to do so; but medical gerontology is not that popular yet, and so far the arguments favoring an honorable death through euthanasia are met with sufficient consternation as to forbid any but the most aca-demic discussions of it.

None of the special areas alone or in combination will enjoy meaningful expression apart from a consideration of the community or county for which they are planned. To local community leaders and other interested laymen and professionals, Frank Nicholson in Chapter 12 issues the warn-ing that no action should be taken without adequate knowledge of older persons and their needs. The greatest service that these readings can render is to sensitize people to the great heterogeneity among the elderly, and, whereas the contributions to this book can serve as springboards for your own efforts, considerable care is required in generalizing from them to local situations. Not only will the needs and interests of the elderly vary from one community to another, but even within the same community the priority of issues will fluctuate.

Consider the following as an example of differences in priorities. In the various chapters of this book, housing, religious, and recreational programs, and economic, medical, social, and psychological aspects of aging are viewed. In their study of older people in Thurston County, Washington, however, Carol Stone and Walter Slocum state that very few respondents had difficulty in using their free time, only 10 percent indicated any interest in special types of housing, and many reported that they were getting along reasonably well on limited incomes. *But,* the need for transportation was mentioned frequently by older people living in all areas of the county. A description then follows on how transportation could be provided in accordance with Thurston County's specific needs and resources.

In rural counties where traditional religion remains predominant, ministers may benefit greatly from institutes which upgrade their counseling skills. In urban communities having large migrant populations, housing and income maintenance may be warranted. Consider briefly the caution to be followed in planning housing units for the elderly.

John Chase and George Packard support from their own experiences the contention that the success of housing programs requires the cooperation of many groups in the community and not infrequently of groups outside it. They do not, however, discuss at length the composition of residents in these housing programs. Irving Rosow reports that the density of the aged population in a given area may have significant consequences for the residents of a housing program. In contrast to proponents of heterogeneous areas and housing units, which are thought to contribute to the social and psychological functioning of the aged, Rosow's data indicate that the personal and group needs of the elderly person can better be met when the proportion of the aged in a given area reaches 50 percent or more. A higher density of older people is, further, more beneficial to those who have experienced role losses, such as widows and retirees.

Meeting the economic needs of the elderly likewise will vary from place to place, and estimates of need should take into account not only the cost of living but the availability of part-time jobs or privately owned gardens or livestock. Reliance on statistics reporting national median incomes and costs of living, in other words, may be misleading to the extent of committing a community to programs that, if not needed, are at least inappropriately geared to local conditions. A dramatic, perhaps exaggerated, example of the localistic nature of defining economic need is found in the elderly midwestern gentleman who, when asked by a survey interviewer what kind of community service he was engaged in, replied, "I give to the poor." *He* had an annual income of five hundred dollars! Exceptions such as this do not prove any point except that there are exceptions, but it is important to remember that the requirements of the aged have changed from those of their earlier years. Payments on home and automobile mortgages and insurance premiums have generally stopped by the time of retirement. Expenditures for children's education, entertainment, and new clothes are greatly reduced, either because of their nonrelevance or their unimportance. Therefore, when local community leaders inquire of the needs of the elderly, to develop programs for them, it is strongly recommended that the elderly themselves be asked for *their* views.

The value of carefully surveying community needs should not be overlooked for another reason, which is the utilization of local residents who have been trained by researchers in the gathering of information. Community residents frequently sense accurately what local needs may be. Commenting on the use of such persons in collecting information, Leonard

Breen says: "In many cases, the findings themselves at least *support* actions and decisions taken by persons in the community and are used to justify that behavior. Where tentative steps are taken in response to community behavior shown as appropriate for re-examination, the findings themselves constitute a kind of encouragement to those who would seek to make changes."

Apart from what is needed to understand and, where necessary, assist elderly persons, little attention has been given to the direct and indirect contributions *they* have made to society. This book is ironic evidence of some of the direct contributions—senior citizens produce issues! The issues result in investigations by academicians who give lectures and write books, which are thrown into the general market as commodities. Politicians run on the issues, win elections, and write laws; others interpret them, and institutes are held to enlighten the general public as to the impact of new legislation. There are few academic disciplines which have not produced within their ranks a breed of gerontologists, and so professional societies are augmented by increasing variety.

Gerontology, says Leonard Cain, "regularly associates itself with scientific endeavors, the gerontological literature, gerontological organizations and conferences, and the proclaimed commitments of many gerontologists display the characteristics typically associated with a social movement." However, and here is the catch, membership in the movement is recruited primarily from among those who want to understand and help the aged, but *not* from among the aged themselves. A. Holtzman comments that gerontology as a social movement has taken over the age-graded Townsend Movement of the 1930's and the more recent California Institute of Social Welfare, apart from which there are few organizations of major proportions, although Robert Wray cites a number of budding groups in Appendix 3.

Why do people become gerontologists either in the investigative or applied sense? And who among laymen appropriate the gerontological perspective? On the history of the movement, the reader is referred to Streib and Orbach's article in *The Uses of Sociology* cited at the end of this section. As to the "why"—the motivations—I take full responsibility and offer as my only evidence some personal observations. You may, however, recognize from your own acquaintance some people who fit the descriptions.

Two (very) broad categories are offered. The first employs as a frame of reference earlier statements pertaining to the fallacy of analysis, and these persons I will call the "anti-historians." In a rapidly changing society a sense of history tends to be of little importance, so that the essence of all yesterday's experiences are dismissed in the perceived relevance of the moment. The icons of the antihistorian are encompassed in the behavioral trappings of David Riesman's "other directed man," in W. H. Whyte's "Organization Man," in brief, in the short-lived ethos of nihilism. The elderly remind them of a day gone by, but the antihistorians' past was a mere 24 hours ago, and the old are, after all, much more ancient than that! As he dissects the past, a historiographical paradox, the antihistorian revels in the illusion that he has destroyed it, made it irrelevant to the present, or, if not irrelevant, at least ignored. Only the present and the future are important. Some nations, by official decree, rewrite history periodically to make it compatible with five-year plans. The youth of some movements have never read history and scorn those who are not young for never having "experienced" whatever it is they say they are unprecedentedly experiencing. Some of us even know antihistorical historians, academicians, who have ceased to teach their subject and instead, behind their pulpits, not lecterns, turn to a poor grade of prophecy.

If Herman Feifel is correct, then the activities of antihistorical gerontologists are means of dismembering their research *subjects,* of placing them in controllable panacean cubbyholes and hoping, as Carl Eisdorfer says, that they will "purr for us." And the louder the purring the better, as long as the social, psychological, economic, and political tranquilizers fed to the old ones keep them from *speaking* back from within their brave new world.

Admittedly, the antihistorian is too civilized to adopt the parricidal values of the Arctic Eskimo; for the Eskimo, nevertheless, even death is honorable and publicly recognized as a lasting contribution to his group. The antihistorian does not commit all octogenarians to institutions; his perceptiveness refuses the economic consequences of this. Remember now, spend just enough to keep them quiet. He has, nonetheless, in Erving Goffman's term, turned the aged into "non-persons," living and seen yet unseen, breathing and heard yet unheard. But there are rumblings. And in response to these rumblings the "historians" are beginning to take notice and answer.

In small but significant ways some people are beginning to realize that (despite pestilence and wars and the threat of wars, regardless of economic and psychological depressions and bare subsistence levels of living) the secrets of a long and successful life are to be found in those who have survived and possibly have the answers to the problems which we face today. A recent national leader implored each of us to learn to live with anxiety and uncertainty in this anxious and uncertain world. His father could have recommended the same thing and *given ways to accomplish it*. So many of us have forgotten that we ever had fathers who knew days of trouble far in excess of those we are experiencing.

Today the geneticist has as one of his most provocative inquiries those who, perhaps by virtue of natural endowment, have lived to four score or four score and ten or twenty years. Even in the deaths of their elderly patients, physicians can still learn, by respectful observation, the secrets of a peaceful death. The group dynamics experts have yet to learn as much about enduring and successful interpersonal relationships as is evidenced in the lives of couples who have long passed their golden wedding anniversaries. And if the home economists want to tell us how to balance a budget, let them look to the mountain on which stand those who have endured unpredictable financial setbacks and still saved enough to send their children to college to become gerontologists.

Some observers say that it is not the incidence of mental

illness that has increased, only our methods of detection and our intolerance of those who are different. Detection be damned if instead we could recapture tolerance and long-suffering as authentic human attributes.

Other historians will add to the list.

As we look with deference to our parents and grand-parents, we may in truth find the answers to many of the problems which are of our own creation. Close scrutiny will reveal that they were, and still are, worthy of full involvement in a society which depends upon them for their as well as our own welfare.

SELECTED REFERENCES

BLAUNER, ROBERT, "Death and Social Structure," in Marcello Truzzi (ed.), *Sociology of Everyday Life* (Englewood Cliffs, New Jersey: Prentice-Hall, Inc., 1968.)

BRIM, ORVILLE G., AND STANTON WHEELER. *Socialization after Childhood: Two Essays* (New York: John Wiley and Sons, Inc., 1966.)

CAIN, LEONARD D., JR., "Life Course and Social Structure," in Robert E. L. Faris (ed.), *Handbook of Modern Sociology* (Chicago: Rand McNally and Co., 1964.)

DUBOS, RENÉ, "Modern Horsemen of the Apocalypse," in John G. Burke (ed.), *The New Technology and Human Values* (Belmont, Calif.: Wadsworth Publishing Co., 1966.)

FEIFEL, HERMAN, "Death," in Norman L. Farberrow (ed.), *Taboo Topics* (New York: Atherton Press, 1963.)

FELDMAN, JACOB J. *The Dissemination of Health Information* (Chicago: Aldine Publishing Co., 1966.)

FORSTER, E. M., "The Consolations of History," *Abinger Harvest* (London: Edward Arnold, 1953.)

MANNHEIM, KARL, "The Problem of Generations," *Essays on the Sociology of Knowledge* (New York: Oxford University Press, 1952.)

SCHOECK, HELMUT, AND JAMES W. WIGGINS (eds.). *Scientism and Values* (Princeton, New Jersey: D. Van Nostrand Co., Inc., 1960.)

STILL, JOSEPH W., "Why Can't We Live Forever?" in John G. Burke (ed.), *The New Technology and Human Values* (Belmont, Calif.: Wadsworth Publishing Co., 1966.)

STREIB, GORDON F., AND HAROLD L. ORBACH, "Aging," in Paul W. Gouldner and S. M. Miller (eds.), *Applied Sociology: Opportunities and Problems* (New York: The Free Press, 1965.)

STREIB, GORDON F., AND HAROLD L. ORBACH, "Aging," in PAUL F. Lazerfeld and others, *The Uses of Sociology* (New York: Basic Books, Inc., 1967.)

SWENSON, WENDELL M., "Attitudes toward Death Among the Aged," in Robert Fulton (ed.), *Death and Identity* (New York: John Wiley and Sons, Inc., 1965.)

TOCH, HANS. *The Psychology of Social Movements* (New York: The Bobbs-Merrill Co., Inc., 1965.)

WYNNE-EDWARDS, V. C., "Population Control and Social Selection in Animals," in D. C. Glass (ed.), *Genetics* (New York: Rockefeller University Press and Russell Sage Foundation, 1968.)

APPENDIXES
INDEX

APPENDIX 1

RECENT LEGISLATION FOR THE AGING
Virginia M. Smyth

CURRENT LAWS AFFECTING THE AGING

The Administration on Aging, an agency established by the Older Americans Act in 1965, has the following functions:

(1) to serve as a clearinghouse for information related to problems of the aged and aging;

(2) to assist the secretary in all matters pertaining to problems of the aged and aging;

(3) to administer the grants provided by this act;

(4) to develop plans, conduct and arrange for research and demonstration programs in the field of aging;

(5) to provide technical assistance and consultation to states and political subdivisions thereof with respect to programs for the aged and aging;

(6) to prepare, publish, and disseminate educational materials dealing with the welfare of older persons;

(7) to gather statistics in the field of aging which other federal agencies are not collecting; and

(8) to stimulate more effective use of existing resources and available services for the aged and aging.

In looking at governmental programs for older people it is important to recognize that governmental activities are organized today along functional lines. Many special programs for aging are parts of much larger programs having the same

---

Virginia M. Smyth is regional director, Social and Rehabilitation Service, Department of Health, Education, and Welfare, Atlanta, Georgia.

or similar objectives for others in the population. When such is the case, the programs affecting older people along with other age groups are usually administered by the agencies having responsibilities for the broader program.

In addition, in creating domestic programs Congress has followed a definite and progressive trend with reference to placing responsibility for administering, financing, and operating federal programs under a broad and diverse system involving state and local governments and nonprofit, nongovernmental agencies and institutions.

I want now to turn to the broad picture of federal programs for older people. In these you will recognize both functional responsibilities of the programs and the joint federal-state and local administrative arrangements which exist in some of the programs.

FEDERAL PROGRAMS FOR OLDER PEOPLE— SCOPE AND ORGANIZATION

In 1965, in a report prepared for the Committee on Appropriations of the House of Representatives, it was estimated that programs and services for the population age 65 and over administered by the federal government totaled some $18.7 billion. For 1966, this amount rose to an estimated $21.6 billion, or an increase of about 13.6 percent. It is significant to note that about 98 percent of this amount goes either for direct cash payments in the form of social security, other public retirement benefits, or public assistance payments, or for payment for various health and medical care expenses.

Listed below is a general outline of the present major federal programs of importance to older people:

I. INCOME MAINTENANCE

(1) The Department of Health, Education, and Welfare, through its Social Security and Welfare Administration, administers the major public income maintenance program for older people—Old-Age, Survivors, and Disability Insurance—and makes grants to the states for old-age assistance,

aid to the blind, and aid to the disabled, three public assistance programs the major recipients of which are exclusively or largely persons age 65 and over.

(2) The Railroad Retirement Board administers a somewhat similar social insurance program to that of OASDI for railroad employees and their families.

(3) The Civil Service Commission administers a public retirement, disability, and health benefits system for federal retirees. With the growth in public employment by all levels of government in recent years, the impact and importance of public retirement programs and benefits is also increasing in importance.

(4) The Veterans Administration administers a large and growing program of significance to retired veterans, their families, and dependents through cash payments for eligible veterans with service-connected disabilities, survivors of such veterans, permanently and totally disabled veterans, and their survivors. For the fiscal year 1966, an estimated $2.316 billion in such benefits were paid to veterans. With an estimated 22 million veterans in our population at the end of 1966, this program will increase in importance in the future.

(5) The Department of Labor supervises the administration of the Federal-State Unemployment Insurance program, which in fiscal year 1966 paid $252.3 million in unemployment compensation benefits to persons 65 and over.

(6) Other income support programs include the Food Stamp and Surplus Commodities program administered federally by the Department of Agriculture and the special tax provisions for aged taxpayers administered by the Department of the Treasury.

II. HEALTH AND MEDICAL CARE: In the important field of health and medical care, as we are all aware, the federal effort has grown extensively and dramatically during the past few years with the passage of such legislation as Medicare, Medicaid, the Cancer, Heart Disease and Stroke Act of 1965, and the Comprehensive Health Planning and Facilities Act of 1966. To summarize quickly, the major federal efforts in health and medical programs for the aging are lodged in these agencies:

(1) The Department of Health, Education, and Welfare, whose constituent agencies either solely or jointly administer an extremely wide variety of programs of prime importance to older people including Medicare: Title XIX; the Hill Burton construction program for hospitals and related facilities; research on the physiological, biological, and psychological aspects of aging through the National Institutes of Health, Public Health Service, and other parts of the Public Health Service and of the department; food and drug protection; the rehabilitation services for the chronically ill and aging; and direct technical assistance and consultation in all of these functions to state and local government agencies, nongovernmental organizations, colleges and universities, and various professional and occupational groups.

(2) The Office of Economic Opportunity, as part of its concern for stimulating action to improve the availability of health services for the poor (including the elderly poor), have made grants for the training of home health aides, for support of demonstrations in home care services to elderly persons in low income areas, for food service programs in senior citizen centers, and for consumer education programs for older people living in poverty.

(3) The Department of Housing and Urban Development and the Small Business Administration make available, respectively, mortgage insurance for construction of both proprietary and nonprofit nursing homes and loans to privately owned health facilities, including hospitals and nursing homes.

(4) The Veterans Administration directly operates many medical care facilities for the older veteran and is particularly concerned with long-term care programs for the older and chronically ill veteran. Also, the VA has been active in medical and related research on aging. This interest has been spurred by the rising average age from 56 years to 61 years of the veteran receiving medical care for degenerative diseases in VA hospitals and facilities.

(5) Not to be overlooked are the programs of the Department of Defense and Civil Service Commission in the health area. The former administers a health program for retired military personnel and the latter's responsibility for the Federal Employees Health Benefits Act also encompasses virtually all retired federal civil service employees.

242

(6) Finally, the Department of Agriculture has been giving particular attention to nutritional research affecting older people, often in conjunction with efforts being undertaken by various agencies within HEW and the Office of Economic Opportunity.

III. HOUSING

(1) Under legislation enacted or strengthened in recent years, the Department of Housing and Urban Development administers a variety of housing programs which include special provisions to help meet the housing needs of older people living on reduced incomes in public housing or on moderate retirement incomes. In the past few years, the department has also acquired several new programs encouraging a broader choice of housing for senior citizens, such as the rent supplement program. The current effort in the implementation of the so-called "Model Cities" program will also give particular attention to the present and future housing needs of older people in urban areas.

(2) Although on a much smaller scale, the Department of Agriculture administers generally comparable housing programs for older people living in rural areas. In some states very imaginative housing for older people has been built. Despite the decline of farm population in the United States, it is known that older people are more likely to remain on farms and in rural communities than younger people. If this trend continues, housing and the development of other facilities and services for the rural elderly will continue to grow in importance for this segment of the older population.

IV. EMPLOYMENT

(1) The Department of Labor, through arrangements with state employment offices and joint efforts with other departments such as OEO and HEW, provides counseling, training, or retraining programs, and placement services for older workers. Most of these efforts are directed to helping workers 45 to 64 stay in the labor force, although many state employment offices are also giving special attention to the employment interests of persons 65 and over.

(2) Recent legislation enacted by Congress has also directed the Office of Economic Opportunity to develop additional employment opportunities for the elderly poor under the Economic Opportunity Act, following the lead of such employment-community service programs as Operation Medicare Alert, Project Green Thumb, and the Foster Grandparent Program.

(3) The Department of Health, Education, and Welfare also has several programs which can contribute to providing new or expanded employment programs for older people. The Vocational Rehabilitation Administration has consistently increased both the number and the proportion of older handicapped workers receiving rehabilitation services and sponsors various research and demonstration projects on helping the older disabled worker return to employment, the use of sheltered workshops for older people, and geriatric rehabilitation programs. The Administration on Aging, in several of its demonstration projects under Title IV of the Older Americans Act, is supporting new employment and service roles for older people. In the field of health manpower, the resources of the Office of Education for vocational education programs represent another major avenue for creating both full- and part-time employment for older people.

V. COMMUNITY SERVICES AND PLANNING

(1) The maintenance of community involvement by older people and related services and planning efforts are largely, but not exclusively, lodged in the Department of Health, Education, and Welfare. The Older Americans Act, the new "partnership in health" legislation, the 1965 Public Welfare Amendments, the Community Mental Health Centers Act, and similar legislation have a direct or indirect impact and influence on activities in this area.

(2) The Office of Economic Opportunity can and does make grants to support various service programs for the elderly poor either through community action programs or on a national demonstration basis.

(3) The new Model Cities program also places the Department of Housing and Urban Development in a key role

of coordinating facilities and services to older people, especially with respect to community centers in specialized housing for older people.

VI. EDUCATION AND TRAINING: As in the areas noted above, a multiplicity of resources is being developed under federal auspices to support various educational and training programs for and about aging and to meet manpower needs emerging in this field. These resources include:

(1) Grants for the training of various professional, semi-professional, and technical personnel administered by the Administration on Aging, the National Institute of Mental Health, the National Institute of Child Health and Human Development, and other agencies of the Department of Health, Education, and Welfare.

(2) Grants for vocational education administered by the Office of Education.

(3) Grants, under the Higher Education Act and Library Services Act, which can increase educational opportunities for and participation by retired people, including pre-retirement education programs.

(4) Efforts conducted by the Civil Service Commission to promote pre-retirement planning programs for federal employees and a very major resource represented by the Extension Service of the Department of Agriculture for organizing and holding various classes of interest to older people.

(5) Finally, though by no means last in importance, the Department of Labor through its manpower and training programs is a major resource for general training efforts of technical and subprofessional careers, many of which are particularly suited for older people with previous work experience and skills.

The outline of federal programs available to meet needs of older people is probably more extensive than many people realize. At its worst some call it chaos, and at its best some may call it a "smorgasbord" of resources from which can be selected the particular elements which will meet particular problems and needs of older people.

Commissioner Bechill of the Administration on Aging has said that one of the central issues confronting us in aging is that of "dispersion," which he defines as the present distribution of federal programs in such basic areas of importance to older people as income maintenance, health, housing, employment, education and recreation, social services, research, and community planning, and the multiplicity of relationships involved within the federal government on the one hand and with the state, community, and nongovernmental agencies on the other.

One of the basic purposes of the Older Americans Act of 1965 was to establish at all levels—federal, state, and community—effective organizations that could improve coordination and planning, and thus minimize some of the more unfavorable aspects of this dispersion. In fact, much of the appeal of the act rested upon the fact that a central focus would be provided which could prevent overlapping and confusion.

This is a difficult task. It is the foundation of what President Johnson called "Creative Federalism." It requires that we effectively pursue a partnership between federal, state, and local entities, that state and local governments be strengthened in leadership so that they may carry a greater share of the responsibility for effectively utilizing available federal programs to meet needs of older people, and of all people in our society.

In the Administration on Aging we have made a beginning in the area of coordination and planning and are attempting to deal with the problem of dispersion.

On a regular basis, both in Washington and at the regional level, our staff is in constant communication with a host of federal, state, and local agencies whose programs reach older people. Our job is not only to know what is going on in various programs and fields, but also to support and stimulate the joint planning and action that is needed.

We are the first to concede that the Administration on Aging has not been able to do all it would like to do in the areas of coordination, program stimulation, and cooperative planning, three things that are at least partial answers to the issue of dispersion. Besides being new, the Administration on Aging is a small agency as federal agencies go, and we are still building the competence and capacity we need to meet our broad legal mandate. Even with our limitations, a considerable amount has been done. The Foster Grandparent Program, while funded by the OEO, is administered by the Administration on Aging. The program has been extended to 47 projects. Working agreements have been concluded with the Food and Drug Administration for consumer education and with the Welfare Administration for protective services. Arrangements have been established for regular interchange of information on research, demonstration, and training grant proposals with many other federal agencies. Planning is underway with the Department of Agriculture on nutritional services and with the Department of Housing and Urban Development on the relationship of services to older people in programs such as Neighborhood Facilities and Model Cities. In our regional office we are engaged in carrying out similar efforts.

Some of the steps being taken by the Department of Health, Education, and Welfare represent the second mechanism for dealing with dispersion in the field of aging, and in other fields with which the department is deeply involved. These steps reflect a determination to deal constructively with the problem of fragmentation of services and programs. Among the steps is the recent establishment of a Center for Community Planning in the department to provide a focal point for coordination of HEW programs having to do with the Model Cities Program. Another is the establishment of the many task forces that cut across organizational boundaries to find answers to common problems. There is also greater emphasis on decentralization and delegation of authority to the regional offices.

The third mechanism is the President's Council on Aging. Created in 1962 by executive order of President Kennedy, the council is composed of the secretaries of Health, Education, and Welfare, Agriculture, Commerce, Housing and

Urban Development, Labor, and the Treasury; the administrator of Veterans' Affairs; and the chairman of the Civil Service Commission. The executive order directs the council to make a continuing study of the problems of aging, to recommend to the President policies and programs to meet federal responsibilities, particularly on matters which do not fall within the jurisdiction of a single agency, and to identify and take appropriate action on matters which require coordinated action by two or more agencies.

The functions of the council complement the legal responsibilities of the Administration on Aging. There have been several meetings of the executive committee of the council, and agreement has been reached on certain projects which the council believes should be given immediate and long-range attention. Also, several member departments of the council were active in the development of the proposals President Johnson sent to Congress in his message on older Americans.

The fourth mechanism is the Advisory Committee on Older Americans. Although the committee has no formal role for coordination, it can and does consider and recommend approaches to coordination. Many of its ideas and recommendations in various fields bear significantly on the jurisdiction of another agency or department. As a result, the committee has stimulated staff action and planning in several major program areas which have been helpful to the Secretary of Health, Education, and Welfare.

The problems of dispersion at the federal level have implications for state agencies on aging.

Many parallels can be drawn between the situation faced by the Administration on Aging and the state agency on aging. Both have basic authority and responsibility to promote coordination and comprehensive planning. Both are governmental agencies created to give a central approach to the needs of older people. Both are comparatively new governmental institutions with broad mandates which are still building the staff, fiscal, and other resources needed to do the best and most thoughtful kind of job. Both have extensive relationships with the other public and voluntary organizations concerned with the major needs of older people. And both are under pressure from the public they serve to produce, stimulate, and initiate more meaningful programs, opportunities, and services.

In communities where local councils on aging have been established, the parallel just drawn can be extended to the local situation.

If those of us interested in meeting needs of older people are to do our work well at any level—whether as paid staff or as lay leaders—it is necessary to keep in mind that:

(1) Resources for programs and services for older people are available through many channels and arrive at the state level through nearly as many doors as they leave the federal level.

(2) Federal, state, and local agencies on aging must acquire an intimate and comprehensive knowledge of what the resources are, where they lie in the different levels of government, and how they can be made available to meet the needs of people at the community level. It is also important for persons in leadership at all levels to acquaint themselves with knowledge of the key individuals and agencies administering the resources in order to be able to deal with them constructively.

(3) Armed with this knowledge, leadership at the various levels must then help create the formal and informal mechanisms which are required to assure the success of the overridingly important tasks of joint planning, program coordination, and finally joint action.

HEALTH INSURANCE FOR THE AGED
UNDER SOCIAL SECURITY
Ralph D. Derrick

Based on data in the *Social Security Bulletin—Annual Statistical Supplement,* 1964, there is a distinct clustering of retirement claims at age 62 and again at age 65.

TABLE 1. AGE OF WORKERS AT TIME CLAIM AWARDED, BASED ON SOCIAL SECURITY CLAIMS FILED IN 1964

Age	Men	Women	Total
62	119,861	144,867	264,728
63	70,650	51,776	122,426
64	50,637	28,097	78,734
65	189,924	69,595	259,519
66	85,395	33,439	118,834
67 and Up	135,685	61,881	197,566
Total	652,152	389,655	1,041,807

These figures show that in 1964 two-thirds of the men and three-fourths of the women who were awarded retirement benefits by social security were in the 62–65 age group. It is significant that 70 percent of the social security retirement awards fall in the age group of early eligibility. The heavy preponderance of women being awarded benefits at 62 should

Ralph D. Derrick is district manager, Social Security Administration, Spartanburg, South Carolina.

not be interpreted as a different retirement pattern, but as an indication that many women workers are already out of the labor market before reaching retirement age and are just waiting until 62 to get retirement payments.

Some of the basic considerations and principles that were employed in the establishment of the health insurance for the aged program will be discussed. Following that, I will summarize the benefits provided and give a report on the accomplishments in the first year of medicare.

Congress in its medicare legislation offered (1) a hospital insurance program to provide basic protection against hospital and post-hospital costs, financed through a separate earnings tax; (2) a supplementary medical insurance plan in which individuals may elect to enroll and pay premiums, matched by the federal government, providing payment for physicians' services and other medical expenses; and (3) an expanded medical assistance program.

The legislation included certain safeguards against federal control. The statute says that there is no authority to exercise supervision or control over the practice of medicine or over operation or administration of medical facilities. Advisory groups advise the government with respect to the administration and operation of the program. State agencies designated by governors certify participating organizations and are available for consultation and coordination. Intermediaries administer the benefits, enabling the government to profit by their long experience in dealing with and reimbursing providers of service and physicians.

Financing the health insurance program was quite a balancing act. For the hospitalization insurance program, a tax on earnings similar to the social security tax already being collected for retirement, survivors, and disability insurance was designated. The employer, the employee, and the self-employed pay at the same rate. A separate trust fund is maintained. The general funds of the government are drawn on for the cost of care of those who receive no cash payments and for the matching premiums under supplementary medical insurance. The beneficiaries pay a premium for supplementary medical insurance and also share in the cost of the system through meeting a deductible and a co-insurance.

All persons 65 or over who were entitled to social security or railroad benefits were automatically entitled to hospital insurance but had to enroll in supplementary medical insurance. Most persons 65 and over who were not eligible for social security or railroad cash benefits could become entitled to hospital insurance under the transitional insured status provisions. However, individuals reaching 65 in 1968 and thereafter must have six or more quarters of coverage under social security and must meet the regular insured status requirements if they will not reach 65 until the early 1970's. In other words, eventually only beneficiaries of cash social security benefits will be eligible for medicare benefits.

A health insurance card showing name, claim number, sex, coverages, and effective dates has been issued to each beneficiary. When he needs medical care, he shows the card to the provider of services. If he loses his card or shows up without his card, the social security district office is called on for help.

There are three primary benefit periods used in the insurance industry: (1) the calendar year; (2) the benefit year (365 days after first admission); and (3) the spell of illness (a period beginning with admission and ending after a fixed period of consecutive days without institutional care). The great defect of the first two is the long period without protection for those who use all of their coverage in the early part of the year. The spell of illness is more quickly renewable. A spell of illness ends when the beneficiary has been out of any hospital or extended care facility for 60 days, and a new spell of illness can then begin.

Another concept introduced by medicare is the extended care facility (ECF). A patient who has been hospitalized at least three days may be moved to a skilled nursing home for continued treatment by a physician. This frees the hospital bed for acute care cases and permits the patient to recuperate in less expensive surroundings. Custodial care in a nursing home is not covered.

There is a provision for a utilization review plan. Its purpose is to prevent patients being kept in expensive institutions longer than is medically necessary. The utilization review committee has at least two physicians plus other personnel. They review all cases that have remained in the hospital or extended care facility longer than a specified period. Admissions, length of stay, and medical necessity of services are the areas subject to review. There is no appeal from the decision of the utilization review committee.

Services not covered by medicare are hearing aids, dental care, routine physical checkups, eye glasses, orthopedic shoes, custodial care, cosmetic surgery, and prescription drugs that can be self-administered.

Payments to providers of services under the hospital insurance part of the program is made on the basis of reasonable costs. Reimbursement on the basis of reasonable costs assures payment of our fair share of the patient's care costs so that costs of services to beneficiaries are not borne by others and costs of services to those who are not beneficiaries are not borne by the program.

The medical insurance plan pays 80 percent of reasonable charges for medical and other health services after the first 50 dollars of medical expenses in a year has been incurred. The beneficiary and physician may agree on assignment, in which case the physician submits the claim. Or the beneficiary may pay his bill and submit the receipted statement for reimbursement. Physician's services must be based on reasonable charges. This determination is made by the intermediary that has the contract to handle medicare claims.

The specific benefits provided by the medicare legislation are shown in detail in the *Your Medicare Handbook*. Nineteen million copies of this booklet have been distributed.

Summarizing the first year of medicare, Commissioner of Social Security Robert M. Ball has listed these accomplishments:

. . . . *Older people have received from 15 to 20 percent more inpatient hospital services during this period.*

. . . . *Many who would have had some hospital care anyway have during this past year because of medicare received treatment as a private patient rather than as a ward patient, and they have received the care on the orders of their own private physician.*

. . . . *Medicare has made available insured alternatives to hospital care; that is, hospital outpatient services when appropriate for diagnosis or treatment; posthospital extended care when further hospitalization is not the most appropriate level of care; home health care when that is the most appropriate medical response; and the coverage of physicians' services for home and office visits as well as in the hospital.*

. . . . *Medicare has meant that older people had the security that comes from knowing that serious illness is much less likely to be a major financial problem for them or require them to seek financial help from their children.*

. . . . *Upgrading of health care is taking place as the result of the quality standards established under medicare.*

APPENDIX 3

PROJECTS IN GERONTOLOGY: TRAINING, TEACHING, RESEARCH, AND COMMUNITY ACTION

Robert P. Wray

Retirement brings with it the need for activities to fill the time periods previously devoted to gainful employment. Persons who have served in professional and executive positions find opportunities for service with organizations such as the International Executive Service Corps, Experience, Inc., the Service Corps of Retired Executives, and Programs for Retired Professionals. In these organizations many persons with accumulated "know-how" offer consultation in return for expenses to struggling domestic and foreign businesses that are unable to afford such help.

There are other organizations, such as Retirement Advisors and the Bureau of Business Practice, that help employees to prepare for retirement by furnishing booklets on such subjects as finances, housing, health, recreation, and community resources. Other institutions offer instruction that ranges from refresher courses to academic study of complex scientific knowledge.

In some instances persons need training in order to acquire new skills and knowledge on how to work with older adults in the many community service centers that are being developed. There are training courses for managers of retire-

Robert P. Wray is Chairman of the Council on Gerontology, Center for Continuing Education, University of Georgia, Athens, Georgia.

ment housing, recreation leaders, and teacher aides in the public schools.

To help those who are handicapped by the infirmities of old age, there are numerous service programs, many of which are operated in whole or in part by those retired people who still have an abundance of ability and energy. These services include: ICR centers (Information, Counseling, and Referral); visitation services, homemaker services, home health care services, nursing home services, hospital services, residential housing, income maintenance, protective health services, dietary services, transportation services, legal services, pre-retirement programs, activity programs, educational services, foster care services, and home repair services.

SELECTED PROJECTS IN GERONTOLOGY

ACTIVITY PROGRAMS PRIMARILY FOR RETIRED PROFESSIONALS AND EXECUTIVES

(a) IESC (International Executive Service Corps), *545 Madison Ave., New York, N.Y. 10019, is a private organization with partial public support. It was organized in 1965. Through IESC American businessmen, primarily retired executives, volunteer their personal services free to struggling foreign business in return for travel and living expenses. There were 45 participants in 1965; 140 in 1966; and about 350 in 1967. The average length of stay is three months. Long stays are discouraged, but returns are permitted after a six-month interval for evaluation.*

(b) Institute of Lifetime Learning *of the American Association of Retired Persons, Washington, D.C. Attendance limited to retired persons. Study ranges from refresher courses, such as typing, to academic study of scientific knowledge.*

(c) Institute for Retired Professionals *of The New School for Social Research, 66 W. 12th St., New York, N.Y. 10011, is open to both young and old. Courses include international relations, languages, literature, arts, and sciences.*

(d) Forum for Professionals and Executives *of the Washington School of Psychiatry, Washington, D.C., aims "to make possible the utilization of the accumulated knowledge*

and experience of the members—and to create an environment of continuing intellectual stimulus."

(e) Experience, Inc., *Minneapolis, Minnesota, gives retired executives and professors a chance to serve as consultants to industry.*

(f) SCORE (Service Corps of Retired Executives) *is operated by the Small Business Administration, Washington,
D.C.; Regional Office, 52 Fairlie Street, N.W., Atlanta,
Georgia 30303. Retired executives offer consultation to
small businesses with fewer than 25 employees who could
not otherwise afford consultants. There is no fee, but they
are reimbursed for travel and meals.*

(g) VISTA (Volunteer in Service to America) *is operated
by the Office of Economic Opportunity. It is open to older
as well as younger persons.*

(h) Retirement Planning Workshop, *Bureau of Business
Practice, 1701 Pennsylvania Ave., N.W., Washington, D.C.,
offers 12 monthly portfolios on emotional, financial, social,
and health problems that face employees as retirement nears.*

(i) Pre-Retirement Counseling Booklets, *Retirement Advisors, Inc., 3 East 54th Street, New York, N.Y. 10022,
issues quarterly booklets on subjects related to retirement:
housing, health, taxes, community resources, etc. The series
provide a five-year pre-retirement program. Monthly newsletters are also sent to retired employees.*

(j) SERVE (Serve and Enrich Retirement by Volunteer
Experience), *Staten Island Volunteer Project, 56 Bay Street,
Staten Island, N.Y. 10301, recruits retirement-age persons
as volunteers, finds opportunities for their service, and provides transportation for groups of volunteers on a regular
basis.*

(k) Planning for Retirement: A University–Labor Union
Program, *developed jointly by the Labor Division of Roosevelt University, Chicago, and Local 1859 of the International Brotherhood of Electrical Workers, offers light sessions, weekly, two hours each, emphasizing the positive
aspects of retirement.*

(l) Retirement—A Second Career, *Bulletin No. 8, Teaching Units on Preparation for Retirement, has been prepared
by the Bureau of Adult Education, State Education Department, Albany, N.Y.*

(m) Senior Musicians Association. *Local 802, Associated*

Musicians of Greater New York. 261 W. 52nd St., New York, N.Y. 10019.

(n) PRP (Programs for Retired Professionals) *is composed of a number of men and women who have retired, or are preparing for retirement, from professional life, including executives in business and industry. They meet together to assess their needs as retired persons and formulate activity programs. This leads to the organization of local groups, such as the White County (Georgia) Achievement Council, Council on Gerontology, University of Georgia, Athens, Georgia.*

(o) Forty Plus *brings together men 40 years of age or older who, in spite of excellent experience, have difficulty in finding jobs. There are chartered clubs in New York, Philadelphia, Washington, Chicago, Denver, Phoenix, and Los Angeles. The organization has a very high placement record. Members must have earned at least $10,000 a year when employed.*

(p) Over-60 Employment Counseling Service of Maryland, Inc., *maintains a staff of 30, chiefly volunteers, and an active list of about 1,800 job-seekers and 450 open jobs; it makes about 55 placements per month. The address is 309 N. Charles St., Baltimore, Maryland 21201.*

Training Projects

(a) A Graduate Program in recreation for directors of multipurpose senior centers and recreation leaders who work with older people is offered by the University of North Carolina. Dr. Thomas A. Stein, 209 Alumni Bldg., Chapel Hill, North Carolina 27514, may be consulted for information and applications.

(b) Short-term Educational Programs in Gerontology for managers and other personnel of retirement housing are directed by Dr. Howard R. Smith, University of Georgia, College of Business Administration, Athens, Georgia 30601.

(c) A Retirement Opportunity Planning Center to aid 500 people, aged 57 to 62 to prepare for retirement is directed annually by Eugene J. Paul, Drake University, 2500 University Ave., Des Moines, Iowa 50311.

(d) A demonstration project to recruit, train, and employ 30 people over 55 as teacher-aides in language and indus-

trial arts classes in six secondary schools was administered by Marshall Hurst, Dade County Public Schools, 1410 Second Avenue, N.E., Miami, Florida 33132.

(e) A Seminar in Aging for 40 Unitarian-Universalist Ministers, Pennsylvania State University, was conducted by Dr. Charles Taylor, University Park, Pennsylvania.

(f) Development of a model for a comprehensive coordinated social, health, rehabilitation, and community service program for the elderly has been undertaken at the Galena Park Home, Peoria Heights, Illinois.

SERVICE PROGRAMS, PRIMARILY LOCAL

(a) Crafts-on-Wheels teaches arts and crafts and a variety of recreational program techniques. It uses trained volunteers. The operational costs are shared by the community or agency sponsoring the program and the facility in which the activity is given. Alfred M. Volpe, Senior Citizens' Activities Recreation Commission, City Hall, New Rochelle, N.Y. 10801, may furnish additional information.

(b) Day Camp for Senior Citizens of the Second Presbyterian Church, Providence, R.I., has received favorable comments.

(c) Transportation Services, organized by the Oklahoma City Methodist Churches, uses a fleet of buses to transport persons to Sunday School and church on Sunday and to educational classes—literature, art, science, etc.—the other six days of the week.

(d) Fon-a-Friend is a reassurance service. Calls are made at a specified hour with follow-up personal visits if necessary. Mrs. Jerome Biederinann, 1125 N.W. 15 Court, Fort Lauderdale, Florida, is in charge.

(e) COP (Community Organization Project) by Comeback, Inc., is an Urban Demonstration Project at the University of Scranton (Pa.). Graduates of the therapeutic recreation training program conduct activity programs in nursing homes.

(f) Green Thumb, a pilot project, employs retired and low-income farmers on highway beautification work. National Farmers Union is the sponsor.

(g) VAVS (Veterans Administration Voluntary Service) has completed twenty years of service in VA Hospitals, re-

gional offices, and outpatient clinics. Voluntary Service Staff, Department of Medicine and Surgery, VA, Washington, D.C. 20420, is responsible for this service.

(*h*) Project FIND (Friendless, Isolated, Needy, Disabled) *uses older people to locate other indigent older people who need public services such as housing, health, care, and employment and directs them to such services. National Council on Aging, 49 West 45 St., New York, N.Y. 10036, is responsible.*

(*i*) Project for Academic Motivation *uses older volunteers with skill and experience to motivate school children and counteract loneliness and inaction of retired persons. Board of Education, Winnetka, Illinois, directs the project.*

(*j*) Free Bank Services to Depositors over 65 *holds informal afternoon and evening sessions. William J. Allen, Marquette National Bank of Minneapolis, Minnesota 55440, leads this program.*

(*k*) Free Tuition to Regular University Courses *by the University of Kentucky and University of Massachusetts is an innovation of benefit to senior citizens.*

(*l*) Protective Services for Older People *locates and coordinates local community resources to provide home health care, legal services, and assistance with living arrangements for older people who are unable to take action in their own behalf. Community Welfare Council, San Diego, California, has promoted this service.*

(*m*) Service Programs *employs retired men and women to provide services for senior citizens in six rural counties in Arkansas under Arkansas Farmers Union, Little Rock, Arkansas.*

(*n*) Foster Grandparents *has been funded by OEO and operates as community projects.*

RESEARCH PROJECTS FUNCTION IN THE FOLLOWING AREAS AND SUBJECT FIELDS:

(*a*) *To develop new knowledge about the needs of women who are widowed during later periods of their lives and to determine possible solutions of their problems. Roosevelt University, Chicago, Illinois.*

(*b*) Planned Change in Social Provisions for the Aging.

A study of the social provisions for older people in Champaign County, Illinois, to define goals and construct a model program and begin implementation and evaluation. The United Community Council of Champaign County, Illinois.

(c) A study of retirement hotels in Florida *to determine needed services and their availability, and the characteristics of older people residing in such hotels. Florida State University.*

(d) A study of a group of older White and a group of older Negro residents of Philadelphia, *to determine their needs and examine the extent to which community services are available and used by each group. Chairman, Department of Sociology, Pennsylvania State University.*

INDEX

Administration on Aging, functions of, 239; programs and achievements of, 246–47; mentioned, 175
Advisory Committee on Older Americans, 248
Aged, stereotypes of, 2, 73; definitions of, 7–8, 27, 100; multiple problems of, 56; increased numbers of, in future, 57, 72, 77, 180, 192, 222; medical needs of, 60–65; realistic medical expectations for, 72–74; physical and emotional illnesses of, 75–76, 87–88; need for continuing edution of, 90–91; greater reliance on physicians among, 91–92; psychological patterns among, 98–99; and learning, 99; "life review" of, 99; changes in psychological functions of, 103–15; ego function in, 118; employment problems of, 152–61; living patterns of, after retirement, 161–62; housing needs of, 207–8; housing programs for, 208–10; divergent needs of, 228–29, 230; contributions of, 231
Age-related changes, in bodily functions, 60–66; distinguished from environmental adjustments, 102, 115; in psychological functions, 103–15

"Age-specific job grading," 221
Alcoholism, 60–65
Ambivalence, complicates grief reaction, 124
American Academy of General Practice, 76
American Association of University Women, 36–37
Anger, in response to loss, 125
"Antihistorians," vs. historians, 232–34
Anxiety, and aging, 22; and illness, 88; about learning, among aged, 111; and loss, 119, 123; and neuroses, 130–31; physical manifestations of, 132–33
Anxiety reaction, 130
Apathy, and depression, among aged, 124–25, 126
Appendix 1—Recent Legislation for the Aging, 230–49
Appendix 2—Health Insurance for the Aged under Social Security, 250–54. See also Medicare
Appendix 3—Projects in Gerontology: Training, Teaching, Research, and Community Action, 255–61
Arteriosclerosis, 62, 63; cerebral, 132
Arthritis, 57
Automobile accidents, among aged, 110